THE QUAKER AND THE GAMECOCK

THE QUAKER AND THE GAMECOCK

Nathanael Greene, Thomas Sumter, and the
Revolutionary War for the Soul of the South

ANDREW WATERS

CASEMATE

Philadelphia & Oxford

Published in the United States of America and Great Britain in 2019 by
CASEMATE PUBLISHERS
1950 Lawrence Road, Havertown, PA 19083, USA
and
The Old Music Hall, 106–108 Cowley Road, Oxford OX4 1JE, UK

Copyright 2019 © Andrew Waters

Hardcover Edition: ISBN 978-1-61200-781-6
Digital Edition: ISBN 978-1-61200-782-3

A CIP record for this book is available from the British Library

Printed and bound in the United States of America

Typeset in India for Casemate Publishing Services. www.casematepublishingservices.com

For a complete list of Casemate titles, please contact:

CASEMATE PUBLISHERS (US)
Telephone (610) 853-9131
Fax (610) 853-9146
Email: casemate@casematepublishers.com
www.casematepublishers.com

CASEMATE PUBLISHERS (UK)
Telephone (01865) 241249
Email: casemate-uk@casematepublishers.co.uk
www.casematepublishers.co.uk

Contents

Introduction

Although the American Revolutionary War general Nathanael Greene was born to a devout Quaker household in Warwick, Rhode Island, and his legacy as one of America's great military commanders has been juxtaposed against the faith's well-known pacifist principles numerous times, some would dispute his characterization as "The Quaker General." No less a modern-day expert than Dennis M. Conrad, editor of the superlative, 13-volume series *The Papers of Nathanael Greene*, notes Greene officially severed his connection to the Society of Friends in 1777, and by then his religious convictions would have been most accurately described as "deist," like those of Washington, Jefferson, Benjamin Franklin, and many of his Colonial-era contemporaries.[1]

In my apologies to Conrad and others who minimize Greene's Quaker heritage, I would argue *Deist and the Gamecock*—or perhaps more accurate still, *Christian Humanist and the Gamecock*—just don't have the same zing as *The Quaker and the Gamecock*, even if such titles might be more historically accurate.

And this apology is a qualified one, for two reasons. First, I think their point ignores the lingering influence of a devout religious upbringing on the adult psyche. A child of the South, I know many friends and contemporaries who have renounced their childhood affiliation to fundamentalist Christian doctrine yet still experience its influence in their opinions toward social issues ranging from abortion to gay marriage to the death penalty. "Everything depends on upbringing," wrote Leo Tolstoy, and though I left the Presbyterian church of my childhood long ago, I still feel its Puritan influence in my daily practices and beliefs. To characterize myself as a "Presbyterian" today might be an unfairly broad generalization, though still accurate at some fundamental level of my soul.

Other contemporary Greene scholars echo my argument. The writers John M. Moseley and Robert M. Calhoun believe Greene's Quaker upbringing profoundly shaped his military leadership, pointing specifically to the influence of the Quaker principle called *discernment*: a centered search for truth that enabled listening and speaking with discipline and circumspection. The influence of discernment, they argue, was one of the founding principles of Greene's Republican ethics, along with his Whig ideology and his later embrace of rational Universalism, what Conrad might call "deism." And to this Republican ethic they attribute the pragmatic moderation that has become a defining characteristic of both Greene's overall leadership style and also his penchant for unconventional tactics. "Greene was not just a moderate," they argue, "he was a historic moderate. His Quaker background, his Universalist religious convictions, his self-education in Enlightenment writings, and his difficult apprenticeship in command under Washington from 1776 to 1779 all made him conscious of his political heritage."[2]

★　★　★

Greene's moderate instincts would serve him well in the "Southern Campaign," what historians call Greene's leadership of the Southern Army during the period from 1780 to 1782, where his challenge was cultural as much as it was administrative. For the Revolutionary War in the South was very different from the one in the North. In the South, Greene observed, "there is no such thing as national character or national sentiment."[3] In the North, as Greene well knew, after a successful but mostly unhappy stint as the Continental Army's quartermaster general, it was the Continental Congress that provided provision, reinforcement, and supply for the Continental Army. The Southern Army operated on a provincial basis, with the individual colonies taking responsibility, or not, for provisioning the troops from their own state.

The primary burden for this fell on South Carolina, where the Southern Army was headquartered for much of the Revolutionary War. Major General Benjamin Lincoln, who commanded the Southern Army from 1778 until after the fall of Charleston in 1780, became so frustrated with the army's "abject dependency" on South Carolina's government that, he complained, he could not even march his troops "without the consent of the President of this State, however urgent the necessity."[4]

But Greene was a different type of leader than Lincoln, with keener political instincts and a preternatural flair for administrative operations. "Greene was a leader who was attuned to public opinion and morale," writes Conrad. "A hallmark of Greene's generalship was his recognition of the importance of public perception and opinion when the contest was for the loyalty of the citizenry."[5]

Nowhere was this more important than in South Carolina, which, following his brief but memorable foray into North Carolina, culminating with the Battle of Guilford Courthouse on March 15, 1781, would become Greene's primary theater of operations. And upon his arrival in Charlotte in December 1780, Greene quickly realized the important political and military influence of Thomas Sumter, South Carolina's famed "Gamecock."

Brash, charismatic, and impulsive, Sumter was easily the most prominent and powerful military commander in the American South at this time. As brigadier general of the South Carolina militia, commissioned by South Carolina governor John Rutledge back in October 1780, he was the undisputed commander-in-chief of South Carolina's irregular militia forces. With Rutledge in exile after the British Army's successful siege of Charleston in May 1780, and the Continental Army disgraced at the Battle of Camden on August 16, 1780, Sumter was arguably the colony's military dictator at the time of Greene's arrival.

Ever the pragmatist, Greene attempted to woo Sumter with his characteristic deference and a charm that could be hit or miss, visiting Sumter almost immediately after taking command. At first the strategy seemed to work, due in part to the fact Sumter was convalescing at the time from a serious wound he received at the Battle of the Blackstock's Farm on November 20, 1780. After this visit, Greene initiated a cordial correspondence with Sumter and claimed, at least, to give due consideration to the Gamecock's suggestions on strategy.

But things quickly turned sour when Greene gave authority to General Daniel Morgan over the South Carolina militia as part of his "Flying Army," the mobile body of Continental troops and local volunteers who famously defeated Banastre Tarleton at the Battle of Cowpens on January 17. Sumter viewed Morgan's command as an affront to his authority, and instructed his subordinates not

Brigadier General Daniel Morgan. The great Daniel Morgan, hero of the American Revolution. During the lead-up to Cowpens, Morgan would find Sumter uncooperative, the first stirrings of Sumter's discontent. (Library of Congress)

to cooperate with him. Greene tried to make amends, writing to Sumter, "In what respect General Morgans command embarrassed you I am at a loss to Imagine; but I dare say I cou'd explain it to your perfect satisfaction in a few minutes, could I have the happiness to see you."[6]

What followed was a long correspondence that serves as the basis for this book—the troubled and sometimes contemptuous relationship between Nathanael Greene and Thomas Sumter. And this is the other reason I think *Quaker and the Gamecock* works as the title for this book: it speaks to the conflicted yet symbiotic relationship between these two military leaders of wildly divergent backgrounds, temperaments, and styles. It is through the lens of this relationship that I chronicle the decisive though often underappreciated "Southern Campaign" of the American Revolution.

★   ★   ★

On many levels the relationship between Greene and Sumter is analogous to one of the United States's most important political discourses—the divide between the ecstatic populism ruling the nation's rural areas versus the egalitarian federalism prevalent in urban ones. Thomas Sumter understood his rural militia had little interest in the Enlightenment principles of self-governance that so enamored Greene, Washington, and many of the founding fathers. What mattered to South Carolina's backcountry settlers in the winter of 1780 and spring of 1781 was their own personal safety and protection of their property, both of which were fundamentally threatened by civil war, with the Loyalist cause predominate thanks to the British occupation of the state. To those who remained loyal Patriots, Sumter was the right leader at the right time. True to his nickname, Sumter was proud, resourceful, and courageous. He had an innate understanding of his constituents' character and motivations. If his military tactics were primitive, often putting his men's lives at unnecessary risk, at least he would never back down from a fight.

The esteemed South Carolina historian Walter Edgar notes that, by the 1770s, issues of class and status now plagued the South Carolina backcountry, exacerbated by ever-present sectarian and ethnic divides.[7] If the backcountry's first few waves of Scots-Irish settlers, mixed in with a few Germans and English, all started at the same subsistence level, clearing land and living in crude cabins until establishing their homesteads, some of those settlers were starting to accumulate substantial property and wealth by the time of the American Revolution, creating class divisions. That the backcountry's crude judicial system still failed to provide adequate resolution over legal and property disputes between neighbors only added to the tinder soon to be lit by the Revolutionary flame.

Much like the US's 45th president, Donald Trump, Sumter understood instinctively it was action, not prudence or sound policy, motivating the backcountry character. And if that action resulted in the plunder of a Loyalist neighbor's property and stock, such were the fortunes of war. His backcountry followers responded both to his magnetic enthusiasm and his conditional morals, even if his impulsivity sometimes led them into dire straits. In their biographical note on Sumter in *The Papers of Nathanael Greene*, the editors write, "As a partisan leader, he was bold, imaginative, and pugnacious, although a poor tactician and careless battle commander."[8]

But to dismiss Thomas Sumter as a rube or a pugnacious fool is to discredit his obvious intellect and the important role he served during the Southern Campaign. He clearly possessed natural charisma and was a keen psychological motivator. As we shall soon read, he lived a remarkable life before, during, and after the American Revolution. Though the Gamecock could be pugnacious, insubordinate, and deceitful, he was a force to be reckoned with, as Greene intelligently recognized.

★   ★   ★

As might be inevitable between two leaders of strong will and intellect, if opposing leadership styles, Greene and Sumter's relationship soon devolved into backbiting and criticism, though these were more civil times, and they mostly kept their complaints to themselves … or shared them only with close associates. "General Greene was deeply disgusted with the conduct of General Sumter," wrote Greene's officer William R. Davie in his memoir, recalling the dark days following Greene's defeat at the Battle of Hobkirk's Hill.[9]

It was Greene's indiscrete comment on Sumter in a letter to his friend Joseph Reed, published in a popular history of the war, that so angered U.S. Congressman Sumter several years later, he tried to prevent Congress from authorizing compensation for Greene's wartime debts. Surely Sumter must have uttered similar oaths against Greene, but if so, he had the good sense not to put them in writing. No correspondence of Sumter denigrating Greene to a third party has been uncovered by historians.

More than one historian has claimed Greene's expectations of Sumter were unrealistic. At Hobkirk's Hill, Ninety-Six, and Eutaw Springs, Greene expected Sumter and his militia to support Greene's Continental Army in traditional battlefield tactics. This stands in opposition to the basic nature of irregular troops, these historians argue, who are best suited for guerilla, hit-and-run operations. If there is some truth in this argument, it is also true that irregular militia fought with distinction at Cowpens and King's Mountain. And as Sumter's battlefield victories at Hanging Rock and Blackstocks illustrate, it wasn't that Sumter and his troops couldn't fight in formal battle against the British and Loyalist forces; it was that they didn't want to, at least not under Greene's command.

But if Sumter's disobedience contributed to Greene's defeat at Hobkirk's Hill, and arguably to the unsuccessful siege of Ninety-Six, if it has sullied his reputation as a Revolutionary War commander, it was precisely the kind of provocative effrontery that endeared him to his backcountry constituents, propelling him into a long political career after the war, and serving as a model for many populist libertarians that came after him.

By the end of this narrative, with Sumter's political opponents persecuting him for his unfortunate scheme to pay troops in captured slaves, his status as South Carolina's de facto military dictator long since diminished by the enmity of his militia colleagues, and his legendary industry sapped by what amounted to little more than garrison duty far behind the front lines, one almost feels sorry for the Gamecock. Greene's legendary diligence, moderation, and pragmatism, coupled with his occasional brilliance, had carried the day, taking the Quaker General to the gates of Charleston, the Southern Campaign now effectively won.

But to say the Gamecock was defeated is to denigrate his defiant character, as it is to belittle the emotive resilience of his backcountry constituency. Sumter's supporters represent an important characteristic of the American spirit, and to belittle or mock it is to convey a profound misunderstanding of the country. Relying on his instincts for moderation, Greene did neither, and in his patient cultivation of Sumter, his sympathetic pragmatism when dealing with South Carolina's partisan politics, he won the Southern Campaign and preserved a delicate harmony between North and South, between libertarian populism and egalitarian Federalism, that still defines the United States's political landscape.

Prologue

On Hobkirk's Hill

Nathanael Greene was livid. "I want to know very much your situation, and how you have disposed of yourself, so as to cooperate with our Army on any particular emergency," Greene fumed to Thomas Sumter.[1] The date was April 19, 1781, the day Greene's weary army of 1,500 arrived at Hobkirk's Hill, a sandy ridge about 2 miles north of Camden, South Carolina. With plans for the Continental Army's assault on the British outpost there hinging on Sumter's cooperation, Greene was desperate to hear from the famed Carolina "Gamecock." Yet Sumter would not respond.

Greene wrote the Gamecock again on April 23: "I wrote you a day or two ago of our arrival in the neighborhood of Camden, and desired to know your strength and situation, to which I have received no answer … I long to hear from you that I may know how to take my measures respecting Provisions and other matters."[2]

Though Sumter was camped not far away on the Broad River, his response would not arrive for two more days. But Nathanael Greene was no fool; he received Sumter's message loud and clear. "Sumter refuses to obey my orders, and carries off with him all the active force of this unhappy State on rambli[ng] predatory expeditions unconnected with the operations of the Army," Greene complained a few weeks later to his trusted lieutenant, Colonel William R. Davie, in a conversation Davie recalled long afterwards in a published memoir.[3] Greene and Sumter's relationship would be damaged for the remainder of the war. Later, after Greene's unexpected death from heat stroke on June 19, 1786, it would turn toxic, when Greene's brutal, private assessments of Sumter would be made public, igniting the Gamecock's wrath from the floor of the United States Congress.

But as Nathanael Greene weighed his situation on Hobkirk's Hill in April 1781, that future conflict was years away. For now, Greene's lot required Sumter's cooperation, if not his loyal support. Greene's plans to defeat the British occupying force in South Carolina relied on its Patriot militia, and for better or worse, Thomas Sumter was their acknowledged leader, the state's de facto military dictator. As frustrated as Greene was in private, he could not afford to reveal it in his correspondence, which strove toward deference to the Gamecock, even as his desperation grew.

To be fair, Sumter was not the only Patriot commander disappointing Greene in his failure to support the Continental Army. His pleas for help had been sent as far north as Philadelphia. But it seems Sumter's recalcitrance angered Greene most, one he associated with a general state of civil war and partisan carnage afflicting the South Carolina countryside.

Finally arriving at Camden after a desolate march from North Carolina following the bloody stalemate at Guilford's Courthouse on March 15, 1781, Greene was disappointed to find the town better defended than he had been led to believe, increasing his need for militia support. "I have critically examined the fortifications of this place [Camden] and find them much superior to what I expected," Greene admitted to Sumter in his letter of April 23.[4]

Commanding Camden was Francis, Lord Rawdon, the 26-year-old British officer Cornwallis had left in charge of the British occupation force in South Carolina and Georgia, a body totaling approximately eight thousand troops, though Rawdon now had only nine hundred with him at Camden. Born to Irish nobility, Rawdon performed brilliantly as a combat officer in several campaigns of the American Revolution, one of the few British officers whose reputations were enhanced, not damaged, in the conflict.

The town Rawdon defended was a simple 6 by 15 grid, according to the surveyor James Cook's 1773 map titled "A Map of the Province of South Carolina." But since occupying Camden in June 1780, the British had enhanced its defenses formidably. Four redoubts, or earthwork fortifications, guarded the four corners of the town. In the town center was a large stockade surrounded by high walls.[5]

With no reinforcements in sight, his provisions growing more depleted by the day, and Camden's defenses seemingly impenetrable, Greene desperately sought some strategic advantage against Rawdon. But after a series of maneuvers around the town failed to provoke Rawdon into attack, Greene returned to Hobkirk's Hill, setting up his camp in battle formation. "A position to induce the Enemy to sally," Greene wrote to Samuel Huntington in his later report on the battle. "It [Hobkirk's Hill] was covered with Timber and flanked on the left by an impassable Morass. The Country between that and the Town is covered by heavy Wood and under Brush. In this situation we lay constantly upon our Arms ready for action at a moments warning."[6]

Greene arranged his defenses in three lines, with his trusted Continentals in the forward line and the militia in the second. This was a reverse of the famous "Cowpens formation" Daniel Morgan had employed at Cowpens, placing his militia in front to act as skirmishers. To the rear of Greene's formation was William Washington's Continental Light Dragoons with a detachment of North Carolina militia. In reserve was a hand-picked force from the 1st and 2nd Maryland Regiments, Greene's most experienced and trusted men, nicknamed by history as the "Irish Light Infantry" for the Irish heritage of most of its soldiers.[7]

To maintain discipline and battle readiness, Greene ordered, "Roll is to be taken at least three times a day, and absentees reported and punished." The desertions that had plagued Greene's march from North Carolina continued; it is likely his army was now a few hundred men smaller than the 1,500 or so who arrived at Camden on April 19. "Every part of the army must be ready to stand to arms at a Moments warning," he commanded.[8]

Despite these admirable intentions, the morning of April 25 found Greene's Continental Army enjoying a moment of repose. Around 10 a.m.

the Continentals were cleaning up from breakfast. Greene himself had just settled down for a cup of tea when shots sounded from the picket line.[9] Within a few minutes, Greene realized Rawdon was offering exactly what he wanted—a fight.

It was time for Greene to put his frustrations with Thomas Sumter aside. He would deal with the South Carolina partisan later, or perhaps not at all. Such were the fortunes of war. Now the objective for which he had traveled to South Carolina was before him: battle with the British Army and the opportunity to liberate one of their most formidable outposts in the South Carolina interior. General Nathanael Greene called his troops to order and stormed once more into war.

CHAPTER I

Gamecock

As a young man Thomas Sumter stood before King George III and fled crowds of thousands in London, like some latter-day rock 'n roll god. In the American frontier, he faced down mobs of hungry bears and noble Cherokee chiefs. In a wrestling match that would best any cable television main event, he captured a French provocateur in hand-to-hand combat, helping to preserve a fragile peace. He escaped from prison, only to return decades later to settle the debt that put him there. Before he became the famed Carolina "Gamecock," leading a partisan resistance in the latter stages of the American Revolution, he was a prosperous merchant and local politician in the South Carolina frontier, then a respected Continental Army officer. Afterwards he became a United States congressman, a United States senator, and a man of substantial wealth. He speculated badly and lost it all. He died in 1832 at age 98, the last surviving American general of the Revolutionary War. If the Gamecock has taken on the stature of American myth, Thomas Sumter was also indisputably human, as we shall soon see.

Before exploring this uniquely American life, let us dispense first with the origin of his spectacular nickname. According to Sumter biographer Anne King Gregorie, the name was bestowed during a recruiting visit in the South Carolina backcountry, probably during the summer of 1780. The Gillespie brothers were noted cockfighters, known for a particularly successful and resilient blue hen cock named "Tuck," who never refused or lost a battle. Cockfighting was a popular entertainment of the day, one Sumter himself enjoyed during his younger days. Arriving at the

Gillespie settlement, and finding them engaged around the cockpit, Sumter challenged them to fight the British with him. He'd show them a battle of men, he told them. Captivated by Sumter's vigorous speech, the Gillespies hailed him as "Tuck," with the fighting spirit of their prized blue hen chicken. From this alleged encounter, the "Gamecock" nickname began.[1]

This mythic Gamecock was born of the most humble circumstances in 1734. According to family lore, his mother, Patience, eloped with a man below her social class, escaping a comfortable upbringing in London for the New World. Shortly after their arrival, this first husband died. Soon Patience was married again to William Sumter,[2] whose family originated in Wales, then moved to England before emigrating to Virginia.[3]

The couple settled on Preddy's Creek, near present-day Charlottesville, Virginia. There William and Patience bore a son, Thomas, but William died prematurely after establishing a farm and a mill. Patience was once more a widow, eventually becoming a respected midwife in the community. Though Thomas Sumter rarely talked about his youth, seemingly embarrassed by its humble circumstances, he is said to have spoken affectionately of his mother's self-sufficiency.[4]

He worked hard in the family mill and neighborhood farms, gaining a reputation for frivolity and gambling. Gregorie reports his education was "only such as could be obtained in his day," though he possessed a keen intellect and an outgoing, gregarious spirit, to go along with a commanding physical presence.[5] Sumter biographer Robert Bass describes this physicality as "slender, muscular, and wonderfully quick and powerful," though only "of medium height."[6]

In 1756, he enlisted with the British to fight in what is known in America as the "French and Indian War," elsewhere the "Seven Years' War." Sumter seemed to find contentment in the military lifestyle. Perhaps like others before and since, the military provided for Sumter structure and focus to the rambunctious energy that otherwise could lead him toward mischief. It was as a soldier fighting for the British that he undertook the great adventure of his young life, when in 1761 he was sent with the Virginia troops under Colonel Adam Stephen to invade the Cherokee territory. Stephen's troops marched along the Holston River, then the "highway" between Virginia and the Cherokee towns, pausing at a place called Long Island to build a fort. Earlier that summer the Cherokees had endured the bloody "Grant Expedition," led by Colonel James Grant. Grant's army of 1,200, including Sumter's future comrade and sometime-rival, Francis Marion, burned 16 Cherokee towns and most of the tribe's summer crops.[7] Facing a long, hungry winter, the Cherokees had no appetite for fighting Stephen, and that November, the Cherokee chief Kanagatucko arrived at Stephen's camp to sue for peace. A peace agreement was signed on November 19, but as part of the negotiations, Kanagatucko demanded a white officer travel home with him as a sign of good faith. Lieutenant Henry Timberlake volunteered for the assignment, and with him went his sergeant, Thomas Sumter.

Sensing the opportunity to make a few dollars on the assignment, Timberlake declined Kanagatucko's invitation to travel overland with his war party to the Cherokee Upper Towns, instead deciding to make the journey on the Holston River in a canoe loaded with trade goods. Never one to miss an investment opportunity himself, Sumter borrowed 60 pounds from Alexander McDonald to purchase trade goods on his own account. Traveling with Timberlake and Sumter was the Cherokee interpreter John McCormack.

The Holston River journey was an ill-fated one, featuring freezing weather, low water, and lost cargo. One night, their camp was attacked by a gang of black bears, dispersed only when McCormack somehow managed to get his wet rifle to fire. Finally, in late December, the starving and dejected trio reached the Cherokee town Tomotley, where they were greeted warmly by the town's somewhat astounded chief, Ostenaco.

The Virginians wintered among the Cherokee, where Sumter picked up bits of their language. In March, Ostenaco volunteered to escort the party back to the Virginia settlements along with about a hundred Cherokee warriors. Eager to re-establish trading with the Cherokees, the Virginia authorities greeted Ostenaco and his party warmly, eventually ushering him to Williamsburg for a meeting with Virginia Lieutenant-Governor Francis Fauquier, acting governor at the time, with Timberlake and Sumter still closely attending their Cherokee friend.

After much feting in the Virginia capital, Ostenaco happened upon a portrait of King George III. "Long have I wished to see the king my father," Ostenaco supposedly pronounced. "This is his resemblance, but I am determined to see him myself; I am now near the sea, and never will depart from it till I have obtained my desires."[8]

Fauquier addressed this diplomatic conundrum by arranging passage to England for Ostenaco and two of his fellow Cherokee chiefs, Wooe Pigeon and Conne Shote. Timberlake and Sumter were again commissioned to accompany the Cherokee delegation, along with Cherokee interpreter William Shorey. But Shorey died during the journey, leaving Sumter and his rudimentary Cherokee the delegation's primary interpreter when it arrived in England on June 16, 1762. They were given a house on Suffolk Street and squired around London like celebrities, visiting Westminster Abbey, the Tower of London, and all the popular sites of the day. Timberlake and Sumter bought sumptuous uniforms and passed themselves off as British officers. On a visit to Vauxhall Gardens, they were mobbed by ten thousand spectators. When they were finally received by King George III later that summer, Sumter struggled to interpret Ostenaco's heartfelt, lengthy speech.[9]

The delegation returned to America by way of Charleston, South Carolina, not their departure port of Hampton Roads, Virginia, allowing Sumter to negotiate an extra service fee. When they arrived there, South Carolina Governor Thomas Boone ordered Sumter to accompany Ostenaco back to Tomotley at the Cherokee chief's request. Along the way Sumter first saw Eutaw Springs, a picturesque spring on the Congaree River in the South Carolina midlands.

Sumter enjoyed a pleasant respite with the Cherokees that fall and winter, but as he was preparing to leave, he learned a French provocateur named Baron des Jonnes was attempting to once more instigate the Cherokee against the British. Sumter's request to apprehend des Jonnes was granted by his Cherokee hosts on the condition he did it singlehandedly, without weapons. Sumter tracked his quarry to the Cherokee town of Tokowee and wrestled des Jonnes into submission. According to family lore, he tied des Jonnes on his horse and delivered him to English authorities.[10]

Sumter's exploits earned him renown in Charleston, but little acclaim back in Virginia, where he still owed Alexander McDonald money for the trade goods he had purchased on credit. Upon his return to Virginia in November 1763, he was imprisoned for his debts but escaped and returned to South Carolina, where he believed he was still owed money for his service in the Cherokee delegation. Henceforth, Sumter was a South Carolinian, though many years later, as he was traveling through Virginia to begin his first term in Congress, he finally repaid McDonald for his debt.[11]

Using the money owed to him by the British government for collateral, Sumter bought land at a fork on the road just below Eutaw Springs, the place on South Carolina's Santee River that had previously captivated him. At this strategic location, on the border between the South Carolina low country, its established plantation region, and its wild and ungoverned "backcountry," Thomas Sumter established a store.

Was it this experience as a merchant that gave Thomas Sumter such keen insight into the soul of the backcountry settler? Was it his service as a soldier? Both, undoubtedly, but also an understanding of the human condition, and the cunning to appeal to its basic tenets, good and bad. A natural charisma and imposing physical presence didn't hurt either.

His constituents were the residents of the South Carolina backcountry, defined by South Carolina historian Walter Edgar as the colony's interior region "about fifty miles from the coast. In the low-country parish of St. George Dorchester was a crossroads called Parish end. The name said it all, except that it might have been more appropriately called World's End. The rest of the colony was dismissively referred to as the 'backcountry.'"[12]

If the South Carolina low country was the domain of the planter and Charleston merchant, along with a robust slave population upon whose industry the Charleston region's economy ran, the backcountry was the domain of the Scots-Irish and German immigrant, though Germans were not more than five percent of the colony's population at this time.[13] These settlers arrived primarily on the "Great Wagon Road," the settler highway running from Harrisburg, Pennsylvania, down through the Appalachian mountains of Virginia and into the North Carolina

Piedmont, then to the South Carolina town of Pine Tree Hill (later to be renamed Camden) before continuing on to Georgia.[14] Charleston may have been South Carolina's cultural, political, and economic capital during the Colonial era, but its society and conventions had little influence on the backcountry settler.

Descended from the lowland Scot Protestants, and often persecuted in Scotland for their religious beliefs, they were encouraged by the British government to settle in the Ulster lands of northern Ireland, where the English hoped they would mitigate opposition by the Irish Celts. With these Celts, whom they called the "wild Irish," the Scot Protestants fought bitterly, a conflict that still influences Irish politics. Many prospered in their new Irish home as farmers, weavers, and traders in linen and wool, but by the late 17th century, religious persecution and a series of severe economic depressions led to massive migrations to the North American colonies.[15] Fervently religious, typically Presbyterian, the Scots-Irish were proud and bellicose people. In America, they tended to settle in family clans, though some immigrated in religious communities.

A generous land policy allowing 100 acres for each male head of household and an additional 50 acres for each family member and servant, along with a more laissez faire attitude toward their religious preferences, attracted the Scots-Irish to South Carolina's interior. The land they found there was rich and fertile, mostly rolling piedmont, with plentiful forests and an abundance of rivers and streams.

These Scots-Irish settlers intermingled and proliferated—by the beginning of the American Revolution, nearly one-half of South Carolina's total population, and 80 percent of its white population, lived in the backcountry.[16] But for the most part, at least until the beginning of the 1770s, they kept to themselves in small, clannish settlements. True, Charleston was an important trading destination, but there was little to connect the settlers socially to Charleston. Nor did they place much value in building towns, though a few important trading centers did eventually form in the backcountry interior—Camden, on the Wateree River, and Ninety-Six near present-day Greenwood, South Carolina, where Cherokee trade was centered.

South Carolina's colonial administration offered no legal system or law enforcement to these people. Backcountry disputes, including feuds with the Cherokee, were settled among themselves, often violently. From their wars with the Cherokee, the backcountry settlers had been organized into militia units for almost 30 years prior to the American Revolution, a culture of volunteer military service the British always underestimated. These militia companies were complex social organisms, built on decades of intermarriage and family connections among isolated folks. Militia leaders were typically elected by their members and operated on consensus, a democratic system that would later frustrate Nathanael Greene and other officers of the Continental Army. Sometimes political tensions in militia units flared into violence, and they fought among themselves.

By the 1760s, looting and lawlessness plagued the backcountry, along with growing class divisions between established settlers and those recently arrived. Gangs of itinerant settlers and outright bandits terrorized established backcountry residents in an era of looting, lawlessness, and thievery. Meanwhile, the colonial administration in Charleston refused to provide any protection. In reaction, the backcountry settlers formed vigilante gangs to confront the outlaws, a movement forcibly thwarted by the colonial administration, which feared a threat to its own authority. Known as the "Regulator Movement," this class conflict culminated in 1767, when the House of Commons formed two Ranger companies, comprised mostly of the Regulators themselves, to restore order to the backcountry. But when the Regulators passed their own "Plan of Regulation" in 1768, governing almost every aspect of individuals' lives, they went too far. Eventually another group rose up called the "Moderators," squaring off against armed Regulators on the banks of the Saluda River in March 1769. Conflict appeared inevitable until Richard Richardson, a prominent backcountry politician, convinced both sides to stand down. Shortly thereafter, the House of Commons passed a circuit court act establishing seven district courts, four of which served the frontier, restoring some sense of law and order to the South Carolina wilderness.[17]

Thanks in part to his innate talents, Sumter prospered as a merchant and caught the eye of Mary Jameson, a recent widow 11 years his senior. Permanently disabled by infantile paralysis, Mary was a member of the locally prominent Cantey family, whose deceased husband left her affluent in land and resources. Sumter's biographers describe her as a gentle and amiable woman. That the marriage in 1767 vastly improved Sumter's financial stock they agree, yet there was also genuine affection between the two, leading to the birth of Thomas, Jr., their sole surviving child, in Mary's 45th year.[18]

The years leading up to the Revolutionary War found Sumter ever more engaged in his business, farming, and real estate ventures. Though Sumter is not associated with the leaders of the Regulator Movement, a warrant for his arrest was issued in 1768, suggesting he was a known agitator. Certainly, the Regulator Movement awakened in Sumter a political awareness that would eventually align with the Patriot cause. And when the colonial administration established district courts and law enforcement in South Carolina's interior, Sumter was appointed a Justice of the Peace, probably around 1773 or 1774, a position of prominent local leadership.[19]

In 1774, he was elected to the First Provincial Congress, essentially the beginning of South Carolina's Revolutionary government, and the first South Carolina election to include backcountry districts. In 1775, he was appointed an officer in a new body of state rangers in support of the Patriot, or Whig, cause. On February 29, 1776, he was elected lieutenant colonel of yet another new regiment of State Troops, which he recruited from the Waxhaws area, a region of South Carolina near the Catawba Native American nation. Many Catawbas served in Sumter's new regiment.[20]

★   ★   ★

In June 1776, Sumter and his regiment served in Charleston when the British launched their first assault on the city. Accounts of the battle suggest Sumter manned a palmetto redoubt at Bolton's Landing on Breach Inlet, successfully repelling part of the British naval attack during the main assault on June 28.[21] Later that summer, when South Carolina's state regiments became part of the Continental Army, Sumter's state commission transferred into the newly formed national army. He was now Colonel Sumter of the Continental Army, commanding the 6th Regiment of the South Carolina Continental Line.

Sumter's Continental regiment fought against the Cherokee during the fall of 1776 and winter of 1777, the campaign known as the Second

Cherokee War. Then Sumter campaigned against Loyalists around Savannah, Georgia, and northern Florida. But these efforts were frustrating and ineffectual: in the final two years of Sumter's Continental Army service, his 6th Regiment never fired their rifles in action, despite marching hundreds and hundreds of miles through difficult coastal terrain.[22]

The activity took a physical toll on the now middle-aged Sumter. And while Thomas Sumter struggled to overcome a bout of malaria, Mary Sumter became permanently disabled, probably the victim of a stroke. The couple also lost a young daughter named Mary to some unknown infirmity during this time.[23]

In September 1778, with the Revolutionary War effort now centered around the Philadelphia and New York City areas, Sumter resigned his Continental Army commission. Though his service as a Continental officer was not particularly notable, it would pay future dividends. Through it Sumter forged strong relationships with both the leading military commanders and politicians of the day. More importantly, his recruiting efforts during the early years of the war created a strong personal network along the Santee and Catawba river basins. From this network, he would soon recruit his militia forces and garner his political influence.

He was elected to the 1779 session of the South Carolina General Assembly and expanded his business ventures, establishing a new ferry on the Santee River. He seemed to ignore growing concern over a renewed British invasion of the South, preferring to live the life of a country squire. When the British attacked Charleston again in May 1780, Thomas Sumter stayed home, keeping a watch on his fragile family and business interests. It was a peace destined to be spoiled by a man who would become one of his greatest rivals, the British lieutenant colonel who will go down in history as "Bloody Ban."

★   ★   ★

Banastre Tarleton's infamous "British Legion" was comprised not of British citizens at all, but of Americans loyal to the British cause. It was composed of both infantry and light troops and functioned as a "flying," or mobile, force. Though only 25 at the fall of Charleston in 1780, Tarleton would become one of Cornwallis's most trusted officers, despite a reputation that already included accusations of brutality. Born in 1754 to a wealthy merchant family in Liverpool, England, Tarleton joined the British Army in 1775 when his father purchased a cornet's commission for him in the King's Dragoons Guards. He volunteered to serve in America, arriving there in 1776 to take part in General Henry Clinton's first, unsuccessful, attempt to capture Charleston in June of that year. Though he went on to serve with enough distinction in the Philadelphia and Monmouth campaigns to attain a field commission of lieutenant colonel and assume command of the Legion in 1778, it was not until the British Army returned to the South in 1780 for another attempt on Charleston that Tarleton's reputation as a legendary light cavalry leader emerged. During the second Charleston campaign, he won important victories at Monck's Corner on April 14 and Lenud's Ferry on May 6 as the British noose tightened around Charleston. The city finally surrendered after a month-long siege on May 12, 1780.[24]

Tarleton's infamy was secured at the Waxhaws on May 29, 1780, when his Legion overtook a vanguard of about five hundred Continental troops and South Carolina militia guarding South Carolina Governor John Rutledge as he escaped into North Carolina following Charleston's surrender. The Waxhaws was a small settlement on the main road between Charlotte and Camden, the same road corridor where Greene would later set up his defenses on Hobkirk's Hill. Though Rutledge escaped during the fighting at the Waxhaws, the American forces were routed, then slaughtered by Tarleton's Legion after they surrendered. According to one account, "The demand for quarters … was at once found to be in vain; … for fifteen minutes after every man was prostrate they [Tarleton's troops] went over the ground plunging their bayonets into every one that exhibited any signs of life." American casualties were reported at 113 killed and 203 captured, almost all seriously wounded.[25] Thereafter, "Tarleton's Quarter" became slang for British atrocities and a rallying cry for Patriot partisans; for his oversight of the slaughter, Tarleton became known as "Bloody Ban."[26]

Two days prior to the Waxhaws, Tarleton's vanguard passed through Eutaw Springs, and paused to burn the house of Thomas Sumter, one of its most prominent citizens. According to family legend, Sumter was away when the British arrived, but Mary was in the house, and possibly harassed by British soldiers. Sumter was furious, leaving his family the next day to begin recruiting a retaliatory force. With his trusted slave attendant, Soldier Tom, he rode north to American headquarters in Salisbury, where he proposed to raise militia and fight a guerilla war against the British. His proposal was approved, and on June 1, 1780, 19 United States Loan Office certificates of $1,000 were issued to him to fund and outfit a new fighting force.[27]

It's tempting to align political interests with national identity during the Revolutionary War. The Scots-Irish had good reason to be angry with the English monarchy, and it's true many Scots-Irish settlers came down on the side of the Patriot cause. But these alliances were not transparent in South Carolina, where the colony's wealthy low country planters and merchant class resented British trade policy like the Stamp Act, which restricted their growing wealth born of international trade. Despite their mostly British heritage, many of these low country elite became vehemently pro Patriot.

Some backcountry settlers sided with the British during the Revolutionary War because they resented the patriarchal attitudes of the low country gentility. Others feared losing their land grants if the British lost. Some remembered the overreach of the Regulators and wanted no part of their petty tyrannies. In his book, *King's Mountain and Its Heroes*, the 19th-century historian Lyman Draper suggests those "who really knew nothing of the issue. This class followed their cunning and intriguing leaders" may have been the most prevalent proponent on either side of the conflict.[28]

Sumter qualified as both cunning and intriguing, the foundation of his success as a military and political leader. In contrast stood men like Thomas Fletchall, a wealthy landowner, coroner, and magistrate who lived near the Fairforest settlement in modern-day Union County, South Carolina, and commanded a Tory militia unit of approximately two thousand men during the war. Both men were followed as much for their charisma and social status as for their political beliefs.[29]

Sumter set up his Rebel base in what was then known as the New Acquisition district east of the Catawba River, in the area of South Carolina near present-day Fort Mill. Not coincidentally, this was near the Catawba

Native American settlements, where Sumter successfully raised troops for his Continental Army regiment four years before. Soon he recruited several veterans from his old 6th Regiment along with approximately two hundred Catawbas. Several prominent militia leaders from the region—Colonel William Bratton, Colonel William Hill, Colonel Richard Winn, and others—along with their men also flocked to Sumter's camp.[30] Despite Sumter's financial endorsement from the Continental Army, he was not exempt from the democratic conventions governing militia organization. On June 15, 1780, the militia assembled at the New Acquisition camp elected Sumter as their general.[31]

Thomas Sumter, the great Carolina "Gamecock." In the aftermath of Charleston's defeat, Sumter led the South Carolina militia army, making him de facto military governor of the state. (Library of Congress)

During this time, in June and early July 1780, Sumter's volunteer army was the only organized Patriot resistance in South Carolina; all remaining remnants of the Continental Army had either been slaughtered, captured at Charleston, or escaped into North Carolina. It is a status that bears noting. Although other Patriot militia leaders would soon rise to the cause, in Sumter's mind it gave him primacy over them, a conviction that would motivate his actions later in the war.

Following the capture of Charleston, the British Army moved quickly into the backcountry, establishing a string of interior outposts ranging from Augusta and Ninety-Six in the west to Camden and Georgetown in the east. The British strategy was to galvanize their Loyalist supporters, subdue the Patriot resistance, and establish a beachhead for an invasion into North Carolina and Virginia. But the move also set in motion a wave of violent civil war. After five long years of abuse and repression from their Patriot neighbors, South Carolina's Loyalists were eager for retribution, and the British invasion provided its impetus. At places like

Fishing Creek Church and Stallions Plantation, partisan anger flared into murder and destruction, with atrocities committed by both sides. The British Army's laissez-faire policies exacerbated partisan tensions. Its officers allowed Tory militia to loot and burn Patriot homes, and looked the other way when Patriot women, children, and religious clergy were terrorized by their Tory neighbors.[32]

Sumter and his militia were soon moving against the British occupiers and their Loyalist supporters. Sumter was in command at Rocky Mount on August 1, 1780, where after eight hours and three unsuccessful attempts to charge a Loyalist garrison, Sumter called off the attack.[33] After uniting with the North Carolina militia of Major William Richardson Davie, Sumter was back in action on August 6, 1780, when his combined militia successfully attacked the British garrison at Hanging Rock, located near present-day Lancaster, South Carolina. The victory over a combination of Loyalists and some British regulars was one of his greatest battlefield successes, killing or wounding two hundred and capturing 73, while only losing 20 killed and 40 wounded.[34]

The victory at Hanging Rock galvanized Sumter's volunteer army, drawing to it additional troops and supply. But with news of General Horatio Gates and the Continental Army approaching Camden, Sumter's confidence perhaps exceeded his capacity. To the Continental command he suggested a grand strategy for cutting off the British supply lines to Camden.[35]

Gates adopted Sumter's strategy, sending a hundred Maryland Continentals, three hundred North Carolina militia, and two artillery pieces to support Sumter's attack on the British supply route. Those troops might have been useful to Gates when he faced Lord Cornwallis in the Battle of Camden on August 16, 1780. Instead Gates was routed, his army decimated, and he fled the battlefield on horseback in humiliation, not stopping until he reached Hillsboro, North Carolina, four days later, far ahead of his decimated troops.

Sumter, meanwhile, moved against the British supply lines as promised, capturing the Wateree River passes south of Camden along with considerable stores of horses, rum, cattle, grain, and British baggage on August 15.[36] But Sumter's nemesis, Banastre Tarleton, was soon in pursuit, leaving the Camden area on August 17 with 350 soldiers of the

British Legion. Learning of Gates's defeat, Sumter now retreated along the west bank of the Catawba River (the name of the "Wateree River" turns to "Catawba River" north of the Great Falls, about 30 miles north of Camden), though his movements were slowed by loot and British prisoners.

Although Sumter had intelligence of Tarleton's pursuit, he ordered his men to make camp at Fishing Creek on August 18, apparently believing Tarleton was on the other side of the river. The day was blistering hot and the men parched, quenching their thirst with captured British rum. Sumter undressed and rested under the shade of a wagon without setting up proper security around the camp. But Tarleton had crossed the river earlier that day and caught the Patriots by surprise, killing or wounding 150 and capturing 310, including all of the Maryland Continentals. The half-dressed Sumter fled the British rout on an unsaddled horse, arriving alone at the Continental camp in Charlotte two days later.[37]

The defeat at Fishing Creek showcased Sumter's deficiencies in discipline, security, and military tactics, along with a healthy enchantment for capturing British stores that repeatedly brought him to the brink of disaster and insubordination. But it did not undermine his support among the region's Patriots nor his enthusiasm for their cause. It is probably from around this time he garnered his famous nickname.

Sumter missed the Battle of King's Mountain on October 7, 1780, perhaps due to a leadership dispute with Patriot Colonel James Williams of the Little River District (around present-day Laurens County). Sumter was in Hillsboro, North Carolina, that first week of October, probably lobbying Governor-in-Exile John Rutledge for a formal commission over all South Carolina militia after learning Rutledge had allegedly granted Williams a similar commission following the Patriot victory over Loyalist forces at Musgrove Mill on August 19, 1780. The dispute was settled when Rutledge commissioned Sumter brigadier general of the South Carolina militia on October 6, 1780, and Williams was killed at King's Mountain. Though Sumter's absence from King's Mountain would later become a black mark on his wartime legacy, Rutledge's commission left him South Carolina's undisputed wartime leader, increasing the political complexities of the Southern Campaign for Nathanael Greene and forever irritating other rivals such as Francis Marion.

A month later, Sumter was in the field again, operating provocatively close to the British headquarters in Winnsboro, South Carolina, with a body of about three hundred men. British Major James Wemyss received intelligence Sumter was camped on Moore's Creek, about 30 miles northwest, and requested permission to launch a raid on the camp to either kill or capture Sumter. "As the defeating so daring and troublesome a man as Sumpter [sic], and dispersing such a banditti, was a great object, I consented to his [Wemyss] making the trial on the 9th at day break, and gave him forty of the dragoons which Tarleton had left with me, desiring him, however, to put them neither in the front, nor to make any use of them during the night," Cornwallis later reported.[38] At this time, Tarleton and the main body of his Legion were fighting Francis Marion in eastern South Carolina.

Wemyss never relayed Cornwallis's orders to Lieutenant John Stark, his second in command. Wemyss left Winnsboro on the night of November 8 with the detachment from Tarleton's Legion and about a hundred men from his own regiment, arriving at Moore's Creek by midnight only to discover Sumter had moved earlier that day. The small force set off in the night to find Sumter's new location.

Sumter's new camp was at Fishdam Ford on the Broad River, the site of an old Cherokee fish dam, used to force fish into nets. Sumter is said to have again undressed and gone to sleep without setting up proper defenses around the camp, but at least some of his men remained on guard. Meanwhile, Wemyss blundered into Sumter's camp searching for it in the night. The watchful Patriots heard the British approach and fired at the unsuspecting British, seriously wounding Wemyss. Unaware of Cornwallis's orders not to attack at night, Stark continued the nighttime assault. During the melee, British assassins found Sumter's tent, but their quarry is said to have slipped out the back of the tent while they entered from the front. According to some accounts, Sumter hid from the killers under a bank along the Broad River while the fighting raged, returning to camp the next morning still in his bedclothes. Other accounts say he returned to camp within two hours, apparently unabashed.[39]

Aside from this humiliation, the British raid on Sumter at Fishdam Ford was a debacle. The British lost four dead and left twenty wounded on the field, including Wemyss, who was captured by the Patriots. Cornwallis

was furious with Wemyss for dis-
obeying his orders, while Sumter
made the dubious claim of defeating a force of British regulars,
drawing even more men to his
command, including Georgian
partisans under the command of
Elijah Clarke. Within a few days,
Sumter's militia army reached
approximately one thousand men.

As Sumter's army grew,
Cornwallis grew fearful for the
safety of the British garrison at
Ninety-Six in the western corner
of South Carolina, not far from
the region west of the Broad
River where Sumter was now
operating. He urgently recalled
Tarleton from his operations
against Marion in the east, com-

Charles, Lord Cornwallis. The British
general, depicted later in life. Cornwallis
would be offended by Greene's
unconventional tactics, though not enough
to delay his invasion of Virginia to follow
Greene south after Guilford Courthouse.
(Library of Congress)

manding him instead to pursue Sumter. Tarleton moved into the Broad
River basin searching for Sumter. Although his force of 520 men was
considerably smaller than the Gamecock's, they were all trained and
seasoned British regulars. Tarleton's scouts soon discovered Sumter's
location south of the Enoree River near present-day Union, South
Carolina. The hard-charging Tarleton immediately set out in pursuit,
but Sumter received word that Tarleton was coming.

Colonel Thomas Brandon, who was from the region, suggested the
Patriots set up a defensive position at Captain William Blackstock's farm
on the Tyger River. The farm was on a hill overlooking the main road
leading from the south, the direction from which Tarleton would be
pursuing. Brandon's suggestion was approved, and Sumter's army raced
there to set up for the oncoming attack.

With the Tyger River to its rear, preventing Sumter's large but mostly
untrained army from fleeing the British attack, and several outbuildings

along with a sturdy pasture fence, made not of split rails but uncut logs, providing cover, Blackstocks proved an excellent defensive position. The hard-charging Tarleton reached Blackstocks on the evening of November 20, though to hasten the chase he had left behind his unmounted infantry and artillery earlier in the day. He now had with him about 270 mounted troops facing Sumter's force of a thousand.

Sumter ordered a small group forward from their defensive positions to provoke an attack. The gambit worked. Tarleton ordered his cavalry forward in a frontal attack, with disastrous results. In fierce fighting that lasted approximately two hours, Tarleton lost 92 killed and 76 wounded— roughly two-thirds of his force. Rebel casualties were estimated at three dead and four wounded.

Fearing the arrival of the remainder of Tarleton's infantry and artillery, the Patriot force fled in the night, allowing Tarleton to claim victory when he took the field the next morning. In reality, Blackstocks was one of Tarleton's greatest defeats, rendered at the hands of his arch nemesis, the Carolina Gamecock. In turn, Blackstocks was Sumter's greatest victory, a decisive triumph over the hated "Bloody Ban," and not coincidentally, the only major action Sumter fought from a defensive position.

But the Gamecock had little opportunity for celebration, for he had been seriously wounded in the closing moments of the battle. As he rode out to survey the field, he was shot in the chest and shoulder. The semi-conscious Sumter was rushed from the battlefield to safety, while his subordinates ordered the Patriot retreat, leaving their campfires burning in the night to mask their withdrawal.[40]

CHAPTER 2

Quaker General

Before Nathanael Greene ever took command of the Southern Army in early December 1780, he heard about the Gamecock's legend. At the least, Greene was informed of Sumter's operations against the British supply lines during the disastrous Camden campaign, and informed of the Gamecock's victory against Tarleton at the Blackstocks.[1] Yet the major general from Rhode Island, a man who had served in the Continental Army since its very foundation, was no fan of the militia operations Sumter embodied. "What is to become of our Southern affairs?" Greene wrote in fall of 1780. "Shall we able to oppose the Enemy or not? If we are it must be with Regular troops and not with militia."[2]

The battle at Camden, South Carolina, on August 16, 1780, where the Patriot militia under command of Continental Army General Horatio Gates broke and ran against a British bayonet charge, deeply influenced Greene's opinion of the Southern militia. "It is high time for America to raise an Army for the war, and not distress the Country by short enlistments and hazzard the liberties of the State with an order of men whose feelings, let their principles be ever so good, cannot be like those who have been long in the field," he wrote in response to accounts of the battle.[3]

To Governor Thomas Jefferson of Virginia he complained, "It affords me great Satisfaction to see the Enterprize and Spirit with which the Militia have turned out lately in all Quarters … But if you depend on them as a Principal, the very Nature of War must become so ruinous to the Country ... It must be extreme of Folly to hazard our Liberties upon such a precarious Tenure."[4]

Throughout the Southern Campaign, Greene's attitude toward militia would change and change again. What he dubbed the "extreme of Folly" before taking command of the Southern Army, his opinions shaped by the more conventional nature of the Revolutionary War in the North, would transform due to strategic necessity on more than one occasion after coming south. And although today we tend to castigate political leaders for changing their minds, labelling them "wafflers," Greene's pragmatic instincts may well have been the basis for his success in the Southern Campaign. Over the next two years, he would come to understand the Southern war was no conventional war, and that Thomas Sumter was no conventional general.

Some have attributed this unique capacity for reevaluation and adjustment to Greene's Quaker heritage, which emphasizes the individual's centered search for truth through listening and speaking with discipline and circumspection.[5] If it's true Greene has been dubbed by history the "Quaker General" in an ironic attempt to contrast the faith's well-known pacifist principles against his military success, it's equally true Greene's relationship with the faith of his birth was complex, that it continued to deeply influence his thoughts and actions long after he formally denounced it.

He was born on August 7, 1742, in Warwick, Rhode Island. Nathanael's great-great-grandfather, John Greene, was a disciple of Roger Williams, a charismatic religious leader who preached the then-radical principle of separation between church and state. Williams had emigrated from England to the Massachusetts Bay Colony in 1631. With his wife and five children, John Greene left his hometown of Salisbury, England, to follow Williams to the New World shortly thereafter. But Massachusetts's Puritan leadership found Williams's radical theology of religious tolerance and individual conscience unacceptably heretical. So it was on to Rhode Island, where Williams and his followers, including Greene, established the new settlement of Providence in 1636.

The new Rhode Island colony soon became a haven for religious radicals. Later John Greene would find new religious inspiration in the teachings of John Gorton, whose beliefs included the spiritual equality of men and women, a notion too radical even for John Williams. When Gorton established his own settlement in Warwick, John Greene and his family moved with him.[6]

By the time of Nathanael Greene's birth on August 7, 1742, the family had converted to Quakerism, still considered a radical and insular group in the New World, but by that time well established in the hierarchy of Rhode Island political and economic power. His father, Nathanael Greene Sr., was a strict adherent to Quaker doctrine, including pacifism and rudimentary education for children, serving as the spiritual leader of the nearby Quaker congregation in East Greenwich. Greene Sr. was also a prosperous merchant and entrepreneur, overseeing a family business that included farming, shipping, an iron forge, and a sawmill. In 1763, Greene Sr. was the highest tax payer in Warwick, Rhode Island.[7]

Nathanael Greene's early life was dominated by his father's masculine influence; his mother, Mary, died in 1753, when Greene was only 11 years old. The young Nathanael chafed against his devout Quaker household but still found in his father a character and philosophy of life to be admired. "My Father was a man [of] great Piety, had an excellent understanding; and was govern'd in his conduct by Humanity and kind Benevolence," Nathanael Greene would later recall.[8]

Yet the young Greene could never accept the Quaker repudiation of education and learning, nor his father's endorsement of these values. The Quakers believed education was an indulgence leading to temptation and sin, and though Greene received basic tutoring, he was not allowed to attend grammar school or college. This deficiency took a toll on Nathanael Greene's psyche, leading to his vigorous pursuit of self-education and knowledge, but also perhaps an inferiority complex that contributed to later personality conflicts.

Balking at his father's prohibitions on learning, Greene read widely, devoting himself to the study of Euclid and the Latin poets, though he worked industriously in the family business. Displaying a propensity for mentorship that would serve him well throughout life, he sought the guidance of older academics, including Ezra Stiles, the future president of Yale, and grammarian Lindley Murray, finally convincing his father to hire a local schoolmaster to train him in Latin and mathematics. He became an inveterate collector of books on various subjects, including military affairs and strategy.[9]

These intellectual pursuits remained an avocation; as Greene passed into early manhood, he established himself as a forge master and merchant in the family's business empire, displaying little interest in the political controversies of the day. But Greene's outlook changed in 1770, when his father died. Then 28 and still single, his attendance at Quaker meetings waned, and on July 5, 1773, he was suspended from his Quaker fellowship.

Greene's 19th-century biographers long asserted this expulsion was the result of his participation in a military parade, prohibited under the Quaker doctrine of passivism. The monthly meeting minutes of the East Greenwich (R.I.) Society of Friends for July 5, 1773, state Greene and his cousin, Griffin Greene, were expelled for being at "a Place in Coneticut of *Publick Resort* where they had No Proper Business," and the editors of his papers argue convincingly this was a tavern or some other establishment of "questionable repute," *not* a military exercise.[10]

Whatever the case, Greene apparently expressed little remorse; his feelings toward his religious heritage were made explicit in a letter to his friend Samuel Ward dated October 9, 1772: "I lament the want of a liberal Education. I feel the mist [of] Ignorance to surround me, for my own part I was Educated a Quaker and amongst the most Supersticious sort, and that of its self is a sufficient Obstacle to cramp the best of Geniuses; much more mine."[11]

A defining issue from this time was the seizure of the merchant trading vessel *Fortune*, owned by Nathanael Greene & Company—a family enterprise established by Nathanael Sr. and now run by Nathanael, his brothers, and cousins. The seafaring merchant class of Rhode Island was notorious for surreptitiously avoiding British taxes or tariffs. On February 17, 1772, British Lieutenant William Dudingston, commanding the British navy schooner *Gaspee*, seized the *Fortune* and her cargo of rum, sugar, and "Jamaican spirits" to make an example of her, ordering the confiscated ship sent to Boston in violation of local law.

Greene and his family were furious, filing a lawsuit against Dudingston himself, a provocative action raising Nathanael Greene's profile in the burgeoning Patriot movement. Meanwhile Dudingston went on a series of raids during the spring and summer of 1772 against colonial merchant vessels, farms, and businesses, enraging the local populace. When the *Gaspee* ran aground on June 9, 1772, a vigilante mob boarded the ship, shot Dudingston in the groin, seized his crew, and burned the *Gaspee*.[12]

Nathanael Greene was falsely accused of being among the raiding party, further inflaming his new political fury. By the time the First Continental Congress convened in 1774, Greene was an active revolutionary, foreseeing a violent resolution to the ongoing political disputes with Mother England. He traveled to Boston frequently, seeking out the company of fellow revolutionaries, keeping an eye on the city's growing political turmoil, and increasingly turning his intellectual studies to the strategy of war.

But life was not all politics and turmoil for Nathanael Greene at this time, for he also fell in love with Catherine Littlefield, the cousin of family friend and former Rhode Island governor Samuel Ward. That "Caty" Littlefield was vivacious and beautiful the historians agree; perhaps too much so at times, for rumors of infidelity, never substantiated, would hound their marriage. Though smart and charming, Caty was not well educated. Twelve years her senior, Greene had known Caty since she was a young child, but in the full bloom of young womanhood she captured his heart. After a relatively short engagement, they married on July 20, 1774, and settled happily into Greene's home in Coventry.[13]

From early youth, Greene had walked with a slight limp, perhaps the result of long hours spent working the forge. Asthma attacks bothered him throughout his life. These physical infirmities never subdued young Nathanael Greene, but they now contributed to a serious setback in his military career. Shortly after his marriage to Caty, Greene became one of the principal organizers of a new militia unit, eventually known as the Kentish Guards. When the unit elected its officers, Greene was passed over due to his limp. "I was informd the Gentlemen of East Greenwich said that I was a blemish to the company," Greene wrote after the election on October 31, 1774. "I confess it is my misfortune to limp a little ... I feel more mortification than resentment, but I think it would manifested a more generous temper to have given me their Oppinions in private than to make proclamation of it in publick."[14]

Greene considered resigning but continued to serve as a private in the unit despite his injured feelings, sublimating them through intensive readings of all the military treatises he could find. Then, something of a mystery occurred. On May 8, 1775, six months after the humiliating rejection, and shortly after the clash between the Redcoats and Minutemen in Lexington and Concord that April, Greene was appointed brigadier general of Rhode Island's newly organized "Army of Observation." And when the Continental Congress established the Continental Army a month later, on June 14, 1775, Greene's Rhode Island rank transferred to it, making him its youngest and most junior brigadier general.[15]

The mysterious circumstances regarding this remarkable promotion—from private to brigadier general in five weeks—remain lost to time, but undoubtedly pertain to his family's political connections and Greene's talent for cultivating important patrons, along with timing and good luck. Perhaps Greene's stalwart character, perceptive intellect, and obvious leadership skills also played a role. Successful careers have been built on far less than Greene's considerable and innate talents.

Greene was now one of eight brigadier generals in the newly formed Continental Army, part of a senior officer corps that included four major generals, a quartermaster general, adjutant general, paymaster general, commissary general, and George Washington, its commander in chief. Whatever force or circumstance guided Greene to this unlikely status, it was a job for which he was naturally gifted. His penchant for military administration and discipline quickly attracted the attention of Washington, who arrived at Cambridge on July 3, 1775, to take command of his new army and conduct what would become the siege of Boston following the Battle of Bunker Hill.

Greene was soon a perennial member at Washington's many councils of war, where he learned how to act like a general. "He came to us the rawest, most untutored being I ever met with," recalled Henry Knox, the Boston bookseller who had bonded with Greene prior to the war and eventually became the Secretary of War. Within a year, however,

Greene was "equal, in military knowledge, to any General officers in the army, and very superior to most of them."[16]

From this experience Greene also learned councils of war usually advise caution, not attack. It was a lesson that served him well during the Southern Campaign, where he typically kept his own council, especially when his instincts told him to fight.

But if Greene was to eventually emerge as one of Washington's most trusted and able officers, he was first to undergo a rough apprenticeship, including two serious mistakes during the British attack on New York in 1776. The first was his refusal to evacuate Fort Washington, overlooking the Hudson River in what is today the Washington Heights section of New York City. Washington had urged the earthen fort abandoned on November 8, 1776, following the British Army's successful invasion of Manhattan Island. But Greene demurred, supporting the opinion of the fort's commanding officer, Colonel Robert Magaw, who assured Greene he could hold the fort if the British attacked. They did, launching an overwhelming assault of ten thousand men on November 14. Magaw's optimism proved incorrect. The massive British assault overwhelmed the American fort, forcing Magaw to surrender. Over 2,800 American men and officers were captured, along with 53 dead.[17]

Greene's losing streak continued when a week later the British sacked Fort Lee, also under his command. Built on the New Jersey side of the Hudson opposite Fort Washington in an unsuccessful attempt to deter British naval traffic on the river, Fort Lee was attacked on the morning of November 20, when British troops under Charles, Lord Cornwallis, crossed the Hudson from the New York side and scaled the New Jersey Heights. Still smarting from their defeat at Fort Washington, Greene and Washington ordered the fort abandoned and retreated in haste all the way across the Delaware River into Pennsylvania, where the British Army finally gave up their chase. The fort was lost but its defenders were saved, a pyrrhic victory for an army that had been decimated by the disastrous New York campaign and was now reduced to five thousand ragged and poorly supplied men.[18]

Yet the disastrous campaign would solidify the relationship between George Washington and Nathanael Greene, a political patronage that would serve to Greene's advantage in what would soon become his ongoing tiffs with the Continental Congress. The first part of this drama revolved around the proposed commission of Frenchman Philippe Charles Jean Baptiste Tronson de Coudray to major general in the Continental Army, a political appointment made as part of the diplomatic effort to gain French support for the American cause. By this time Greene himself was also a major general, his commission dated to August 9, 1776.[19] The problem was that under the terms of the agreement, de Coudray's commission would be backdated to supersede Greene's, nominally placing de Coudray ahead of Greene in rank. Greene was furious and threatened to resign in a petulant letter many in Congress found deeply offensive. When John Adams urged his friend Nathanael Greene to apologize, Greene refused, effectively ending their relationship.[20]

It was a circumstance that would arise again and again as the war progressed and settled into morass—Greene perceiving in Congress some slight to his command or reputation and reacting angrily, further undermining his political support. Was it sensitivity about his uneducated childhood that led to these temperamental reactions? If so, perhaps he had good reason. Greene must have realized the American Revolution was the great opportunity in his life; without it he would have forever remained a New England merchant, not someone we analyze and revere today. Yet Greene lacked "nothing but an education to have made him the first man in the United States," his friend and fellow wartime opportunist Alexander Hamilton would later assert,[21] suggesting his prospects remained forever limited at some level by his educational status. Whatever the underlying psychological motivation for these outbursts, Washington's patronage would again and again save Greene's political neck from these outbursts.

Despite his occasional petulance, Greene's emergence as one of the Continental Army's ablest officers also protected his status. Greene fought well at Trenton and Princeton in January 1777, leading one of the two principal attack columns at Trenton following Washington's famous crossing of the Delaware River. The next fall he performed well again in the Philadelphia campaign, maintaining the army in good military order following the retreats at Brandywine and Germantown. Though the campaign was a disaster for the Continentals, leading to the loss of Philadelphia, Greene gained a reputation for coolness in battle and an ability to move a large force quickly under hazardous circumstances.

Greene's talents for discipline, logistics, and supply hadn't gone unnoticed. The editors of his papers attribute these talents to his early career as a manager and businessman. In a petition written in 1769, Greene notes that he has "upwards of one Hundred" dependents working at his forge, a business training that would serve him well as an

Continental Major General Nathanael Greene, from a portrait by Charles Wilson Peale. (Library of Congress)

army general.[22] At Valley Forge during the winter quarters of 1777–78, Greene showed resolve in scouring the countryside for every last morsel of food for his men, earning Washington's admiration. The honor was a dubious one. When political intrigue led to a vacancy in the quartermaster general's position, the main supply officer for the entire Continental Army, Washington lobbied for Greene to assume the role. Though it was a position Greene found detestable, complaining that "No body every heard of a quarter Master in History," he could not deny the man he called "His Excellency." His appointment to quartermaster general was approved on March 2, 1778.[23]

If Greene prospered financially from his new position, for he had negotiated a personal commission on all goods purchased on behalf of the army, as was customary at the time, it is also true he was never satisfied with it, and longed for a return to combat. At two times during his service in the role, Greene negotiated a temporary return to combat, once during the Monmouth campaign in June and July 1778, and again at Newport, Rhode Island, later that summer.

At the assault on Monmouth, Greene took charge of the American right while General Charles Lee's troops retreated in disarray. Sensing an opportunity to demolish the Continental Army, General Cornwallis launched a massive attack on Greene's position with several of the British Army's most elite units, but Greene kept his army headstrong, repelling two furious attacks.

Later that summer, hoping for a respite with his beloved Caty and his first trip home after three long years of war, Greene lobbied for a command at the planned assault on the British position at Newport, Rhode Island. The assault was to be a combined land and sea operation coordinated between the Continental Army and the French Navy. But following a bout of bad weather, the French Navy decided to abandon the attack. With the French fleet departed, the Americans broke their siege. The British sensed an advantage and attacked the retiring Americans on August 29, 1778. Though the Battle of Rhode Island ended in stalemate, Greene performed well, leading a counterattack that captured an important defensive position.[24]

★ ★ ★

As the Revolutionary War settled into stalemate, both Greene's fellow officers and their wives noted some peculiar characteristics of Greene's marriage. During the war, Nathanael and Caty were together as much as they could arrange, primarily during the defense of New York in 1776 and the Continental Army's long winter quarters at Valley Forge in winter 1778, but also at Middlebrook, New Jersey, in winter 1779, Greene's visit to Philadelphia later that spring, and the winter camp in Morristown, New Jersey, in winter 1780.

That these sojourns typically left Caty pregnant suggests the passionate nature of the couple's marriage, but they also revealed stresses in the relationship. As noted, Caty Greene was an intelligent and vivacious young woman, though like Greene, she lacked any formal education. Just 20 when she married in 1774, she enjoyed the attention of Continental officers almost as much as she enjoyed the social outings of camp life, where rumors often fueled otherwise dreary winters. This was especially true during the winter camp at Valley Forge, where Caty flirted a bit too much with several of the officers, including the Marquis de Lafayette, General Anthony Wayne, and the army's commissary general, Jeremiah Wadsworth.

Her behavior became the subject of much gossip that winter, especially among the other officers' wives. And Greene's correspondence from this period occasionally makes mention to a strain in their marriage. Though there is not one shred of historical evidence Caty Greene's behavior that winter ever crossed the line into adultery, both Wayne and Wadsworth became her lovers after Greene's untimely death.[25]

Still, the vivacious Caty could be an asset as well as a liability. Both George and Martha Washington became subject to her charms during preparations for the defense of New York City in summer 1776, a relationship Nathanael encouraged and which undoubtedly helped seal the protégé-mentor bond he enjoyed with Washington. At one memorable officers' dance during the winter camp in Middlebrook during winter 1779, Washington and Caty danced memorably. "His Excellency and Mrs. Greene danced upwards of three hours without once sitting down," noted Nathanael. "Upon the whole we had a pretty good frisk."[26] If Greene's innate pride and insecurities enhanced his petulant reputation among the members of the Continental Congress during his lobbying visit to Philadelphia later that spring, then Caty's insistence that they attend the balls and salons of the city softened his quarrelsome reputation.

Ultimately, we are left with the portrait of a marriage between Nathanael and Caty much like any other—passionate, sometimes contentious, complex. Just as Caty could be demanding and impetuous, Greene could be controlling and imperious. That they loved one another, in all the complicated connotations of the word, there can be no doubt.

★   ★   ★

After Rhode Island, it was back to the drudgeries of quartermaster, where Greene found himself increasingly discontent, despite his success at the position's technicalities. He bore its political challenges poorly, chafing at the gossip of his fellow officers and politicians regarding the commissions he and his staff had negotiated as the terms of their appointments. If it is true Greene profited handsomely as quartermaster general, earning approximately $170,000 in commissions, then it is also true these terms were common.

Yet even Greene acknowledged the unseemly nature of this arrangement, in action if not in words, through deliberate efforts to hide the business enterprises he financed with these commissions. Of one venture he formed with the army's commissary general, Jeremiah Wadsworth, and a prominent merchant named Barnabas Deane, Greene wrote: "[It] is my wish that no Mortal should be acquainted with the persons forming the Company except us three ... I think it is prudent to appear as little in trade as possible. For however just and upright our conduct may be, the World will have suspicions to our advantage."

About this venture, named "Barnabas Deane & Company," Greene wrote in codes. To another venture, named "Jacob Greene & Company" formed with Greene's brother, Jacob, he even awarded himself Continental Army contracts. Though not technically illegal, these contracts were, at the least, a conflict of interest. Congress had responded to America's compounding wartime debt and expenses, in part, by printing more and more Continental dollars, fueling drastic inflation. As a hedge, Greene invested his commissions in real estate, shipping, and industry almost as soon as he earned them. This personal gain would be considered scandalous by today's standards; however, it was then an accepted enticement for an otherwise thankless job. And it's worth noting almost all these investments turned sour: despite some initial successes, the firm of "Barnabas Deane & Company" would be worth only 5,000 pounds just two years after it was formed.[27]

In July 1778, just prior to the action at Newport, Greene had offered his resignation from the quartermaster general's position in a long, petulant letter to George Washington. Washington refused. Later that same year, in December 1778, Greene traveled to Philadelphia to confer with Congress about army matters but found himself both disgusted by the city's lavish parties and entertainments, and also increasingly sensitive to rumors of his financial improprieties. By April 1779, the rumors became too much to bear, and Greene again offered to resign as quartermaster general. This time Washington was vague in his response. "I am sorry for the difficulties you have to encounter in the department of Quarter Master, especially as I have been in some degree responsible in bringing you to it. Under these circumstances I [cannot] undertake to give advice, or even to hazard an opinion on the measures best for you to adopt," Washington warned Greene.[28]

The incident over the atttempted resignation passed, though rumors and grumblings about Greene's conduct persisted. For the next year, Greene occupied himself with the drudgeries of his job, but by the summer of 1780, his congressional feud reached a climax. That July, Congress announced a reorganization of the quartermaster's office, decreasing its staff size, salaries, and administrative oversight. Once more Greene was furious, again submitting his resignation. "My rank is high in the line of the Army, and the sacrifices on this account I have made, together with the fatigue and anxiety I have undergone, far overbalance all the emoluments I have received," he complained in his July 26 letter of resignation. This time Greene had gone too far. An angry Congress not only accepted his resignation, but many of its members also wanted him suspended from the army. Once more Washington stepped in, saving Greene from his most serious self-inflicted wound yet.[29]

Meanwhile, Congress had appointed Washington's rival Horatio Gates to command the Southern Army, following the British capture of Charleston in May 1780. A former British Army officer whose real talents lay in administration, Gates commanded at the important American victory at Saratoga, although history suggests the real heroes were his subordinate officers, including Benedict Arnold and Daniel Morgan. Nevertheless, the Saratoga victory bolstered Gates's claim that he, not Washington, should be in command of the Continental Army. Following Washington's disastrous Philadelphia campaign in 1777, members of Congress and some senior officers conspired to replace Washington with Gates, a controversy now known as the "Conway Cabal." The incident created ill will between Gates and some of Washington's most loyal officers, notably including Nathanael Greene. But Gates's claim on supreme command of the Continental Army dissipated after the disastrous defeat at Camden on July 25, 1780, which saw the Southern Army decimated and Gates humiliated by a cowardly flight from the battlefield.

The elderly, perfunctory Gates was a poor choice to bear the hardships and deprivations of the South. His failings as a field general who practically destroyed the Southern Army were cold comfort to Washington, who finally saw Gates eliminated as a political rival at what appeared to be the expense of the southern colonies. Washington needed a new general to take over for Gates ... and fast. Like the circumstances that propelled Greene from buck private to general in a blink of an eye, his availability at the precise moment when America needed a tough, dependable, and experienced general was perfectly timed to overcome the ill feelings harbored against him by many in Congress. With their political leverage decimated by Gates's failure, Congress authorized Washington to appoint whom he wished to the southern command.[30] On October 14, 1780, he wrote to friend and protégé Nathanael Greene: "As the congress have been pleased leave the officer to command [the Southern Army] on this occasion, to my choice, it is my wish to appoint you."[31]

There is little doubt Greene recognized the providence of this moment. "I beg your Excellency to be perswaded that I am fully sensible of the honor you do me and will endeavour to manifest my gratitude by a conduct that will not disgrace the appointment," he responded to Washington, even as an irrepressible satisfaction with the independent command through which he would seal his historic legacy tempered his humility. "I only lament that my abilities are not more competent to the duties that will be required of me," he continued. "But as far as zeal and attention can supply the defect, I flatter myself my Country will have little cause to complain."[32]

★   ★   ★

That Greene was a talented and dedicated general is beyond doubt. That he could be petulant, pedantic, insecure, and self-serving we have already seen. These qualities, along with his undeniable intelligence, could lead him to pronunciations he would later regret, or be forced to renounce, such as his contempt for the South's irregular militia army. But in the circumstance that sent Greene to the southern theater in that dark fall of 1780—with the British in command of Georgia and South Carolina, the

Continentals' Southern Army decimated following its disastrous defeat at Camden under Gates, and the southern gateway to North Carolina, Virginia, and the eastern seaboard virtually wide open to Cornwallis and his seasoned British Army—fate smiled on the American cause, just as it smiled on the historic legacy of Nathanael Greene. Indeed, his country would not complain but come to hail him as one of its greatest military heroes for his leadership in the South.

In these dire circumstances Greene managed to summon his best qualities, not only as a field commander and military tactician, not only as a preternatural genius at military logistics and supply, but also as a student of human nature and psychology. It is true he was no Napoleon on the battlefield. "In battle he was brave and decisive but neither a gifted tactician nor an inspirational battle captain," notes the historian John Buchanan.[33] But it is equally true he understood both through intellect and instinct the peculiar circumstances of the war he was fated to fight in the South, and fought it with a unique sense of cunning, grit, and strategic vision, including several unorthodox decisions now seemingly brilliant in hindsight. To this we must give at least some credit to his Quaker roots. For if tolerance of dissent, discernment, and the equality of all persons are characteristic hallmarks of the faith, these same qualities served Greene well during the difficult days of the Southern Campaign. Like many a devout Quaker before and since, Greene trusted his own interior revelation, believing truth is revealed directly through the intellect rather than dogma and conventions. And even if he rejected the faith's theological beliefs in reaction to his father's strict discipline, he would rely on his father's Quaker values to lead him through the trying times to come, becoming a great American general in the process.

Let us leave this portrait of him then with a character study by a man who knew him well, Henry Lee, who will come to play a leading role in the story of the Quaker and the Gamecock. In this passage from Lee's Revolutionary War memoir, Lee describes Greene near the time our narrative commences, when Greene first took command in the South:

> This illustrious man had now reached his thirty-eighth year. In person, he was rather corpulent, and above the common size. His complexion was fair and florid; his countenance serene and mild, indicating a goodness which

seemed to shade and soften the fire and greatness of its expression. His health was delicate, but preserved by temperance and exercise...Capable of doing much with little, Green was not discouraged by this unfavorable prospect [of commanding in the South]. His vivid plastic genius soon operated on the latent elements of martial capacity in his army, invigorated by its weakness, turned its confusion into order, and its despondency into ardor. A wide sphere of intellectual resource enabled him to inspire confidence, to rekindle courage, to decide hesitation, and infuse a spirit of exalted patriotism in the citizens of the State. By his own example, he showed the incalculable value of obedience, of patience, of vigilance, and temperance. Dispensing justice, with an even hand, to citizen and soldier; benign in heart, and happy in manners; he acquired the durable attachment and esteem of all. He collected around his person able and respectable officers; and selected, for the several departments, those who were best qualified to fill them. His operations were then commenced with a boldness of design, well calculated to raise the drooping hopes of his country, and to excite the respect of his enemy.[34]

His intellect obvious, his values and demeanor influenced by his Quaker upbringing, his command of the Southern Army shaped as much by unlikely circumstance as by his military talents, Nathanael Greene's destiny was now before him. And history tells us he was the right man for the job. But Greene's many admirable qualities would soon be tested by friend and foe alike in the complex landscape of the Southern Campaign.

CHAPTER 3

Winter of Discontent

Let us presume Brigadier General Thomas Sumter failed to reflect on the historic significance of his circumstance as he lay on the bed of Captain William Blackstock, the knife of field surgeon Dr. Robert Brownfield probing his left shoulder for the buckshot lodged there. Brownfield was without anesthetic, and Sumter's wounds so severe, the pain of the crude field surgery so intense, Sumter was barely conscious at all.[1]

Only a few moments before, Sumter had been surveying the field of what many consider the famed "Carolina Gamecock's" greatest victory, the action now known as the Battle of Blackstock's Farm, or simply the "Blackstocks." On November 20, 1780, Sumter and over one thousand South Carolina and Georgia militia battled the infamous British Lt. Col. Banastre Tarleton and his feared British Legion, which had never before been defeated by Patriot militia. But it was a record that fell that day, with Tarleton's casualties estimated at 92 killed and 76 wounded, while Sumter's Patriot militia lost only three killed and four wounded.[2]

Yet as day turned to dusk, this glorious outcome was still unknown. Tarleton's British were retreating, though possibly only to re-form for another attack. As Sumter ventured onto the field to survey the situation with his aide-de-camp, Captain Robert McElvey, and a few other officers, they came within range of elements of the British 63rd Regiment still remaining on the field. Sumter saw the 63rd firing at him, but not in time. The 18th-century documentarian Lyman Draper wrote, "Sumter got a good view, and was in the act of turning when he received the wound in the shoulder."[3]

Sumter was hit by six buckshot, five lodging in the side of his chest, the sixth entering his right shoulder and chipping his spine as it passed through his body until finally lodging under his left shoulder.[4]

He attempted to disregard his wounds, until McKelvey heard the sound of blood falling on dry leaves. "General, you are wounded," McKelvey exclaimed. "I am wounded," Sumter replied, "say nothing of it."[5]

Still trying to hide his condition, Sumter was taken to Blackstock's farmhouse, where he called for Soldier Tom, his manservant and slave. "I'm badly wounded. Get the doctor."[6]

After Brownfield removed the buckshot, with Sumter semiconscious from the trauma, the Gamecock was placed on a raw bull's hide attached to poles and slung between two horses, then ridden by a militia escort to Steel Creek in present-day York County, South Carolina, a partisan camp about 75 miles away.[7]

Whether or not the wounded Sumter realized it as he lay on the surgeon's table, Blackstocks would become a watershed moment in the Revolutionary War's southern theater, though not necessarily for its strategic achievements. True, many of the militia who fought with Sumter at Blackstocks would fight with General Daniel Morgan at Cowpens on January 17, 1781, their success against Tarleton two months earlier instilling in them a sense of confidence as they faced him again that cold January morning. True, Morgan must have heard from those men how Sumter lured the hard-charging Tarleton into a trap with an advance detachment at Blackstocks, a strategy so closely echoing Morgan's brilliant double-envelopment at Cowpens that Sumter, arguably, deserves some sliver of credit for its conception. And true, Blackstocks was the first time the feared Tarleton and his British regulars had been beaten by irregular militia in the Carolina backcountry, an important turning point in the minds of the region's populace.

The most significant outcome of Blackstocks was not the battle, but Sumter's wound, which would keep him in convalescence and away from the field for the next three months, the crucial period when Nathanael Greene took command of the Continental Army. For if Sumter had been healthy and active, Greene's authority over the Continental Army and the local militia would have been compromised by the rank and status of the Gamecock, jeopardizing the circumstances that led to the American victory at Cowpens. Though Sumter had rendered valiant service to the Patriot resistance, and would do so again, his injury just prior to Greene's arrival would prove fortuitous for the American cause.[8]

This hindsight, of course, would take decades and centuries to develop. At the time, the only people sanguine about Sumter's wound were the British, who were practically overjoyed. Sumter had been an infectious thorn in their side since early that summer. Just a few weeks before Blackstocks, Cornwallis had authorized a failed assassination attempt on the Gamecock at Fishdam Ford, when British assassins entered Sumter's tent as he escaped out the back in his bedclothes on November 9, 1780. After Blackstocks, Tarleton pursued the wounded Sumter for three days in an unsuccessful attempt to finish the job, pausing only when he learned Sumter "was removed out of danger."[9] Still, Cornwallis rejoiced as intelligence on the severity of Sumter's wounds filtered back to his headquarters in Winnsboro, South Carolina. "I saw two North Carolina men who met some of Sumpter's [sic] fugitives, and who learned from them that he was speechless, and certainly past all hopes," Cornwallis wrote gleefully to Lieutenant Colonel Nisbet Balfour on November 25, 1780.[10]

Sumter was down, seriously down, but not "past all hopes," nor past maintaining his correspondence. As November turned to December, Sumter kept busy in his convalescence supervising his active network of spies, organizing supply, directing his troops, and receiving visitors. South Carolina Governor-in-Exile John Rutledge, now in nearby Charlotte with Horatio Gates and the Continental Army, paid respects to Sumter on November 29, as did Doctor William Read, of the Continental hospital in Salisbury, who was chased by the enemy on his return.[11]

Sumter wrote to Gates in Charlotte on November 25 and December 1, arguing that Cornwallis's troop detachments to outlying areas left his headquarters at Winnsboro vulnerable to attack.[12] "I have this moment received from undoubted authority, that Earl Cornwallis still lies at Winnsborough with less than five hundred and much exposed," reads his letter of December 1, his reliable instincts for bold attack hardly the sentiments of someone lying at death's door.[13]

Gates would not have the opportunity to act on Sumter's intelligence, for he was relieved of command by Nathanael Greene on December 3, 1781. Greene's enmity toward Gates over his efforts to usurp Washington's command was well known, the occasion of this transfer the subject of much gossip and speculation among the Continental Army officers and troops. But of the transfer of command wrote Colonel Otho Holland Williams, "General Greene observed a plain, candid, respectful manner, neither betraying compassion nor the want of it—nothing like the pride of official consequence even *seemed* [italic from original]. In short, the officers who were present, had an elegant lesson of propriety exhibited on a most delicate and interesting occasion."[14]

Greene quickly turned his attention toward Sumter and the local militia. The alliance between Greene and Sumter began harmoniously enough, perhaps due to Sumter's diminished state. On December 8, Greene and Rutledge traveled to the nearby home of John Price near the Tuckasseegee Ford on the Catawba River where Sumter was now convalescing, a site deemed more secure than his previous one in York County, from which Read had been pursued by Loyalists as he departed. During this meeting, Sumter argued again for an attack on Cornwallis at Winnsboro.[15]

"I proposed to General's [William] Smallwood and [Daniel] Morgan the attack upon Lord Cornwallis," Greene wrote to Sumter on December 12 in a follow-up to that initial meeting. "They are both pointedly against it as being impracticable. I am not altogether of their opinion and therefore wish you keep up a communication of intelligence, and of any changes of their disposition that may take place."[16] Major General Robert Smallwood was the ranking general of Maryland Continental Line and also serving at that time as general over all North Carolina militia. He was unhappy with his status under Greene's command and would not remain long there, returning to Maryland on December 18.[17] Morgan was a skilled and experienced battlefield commander who had joined Gates's command in late September and subsequently received a long-desired promotion to brigadier general on October 13, 1780.[18] Gates had placed Morgan in command of his light forces, a position he would retain under Greene, who trusted Morgan implicitly.

Since Greene had pointedly rejected any offensive operations after his arrival at Charlotte due to the "wretched and distressing" condition of the troops he inherited there, this expression of support for Sumter's plan was probably made in courtesy, although sometimes with Greene it was hard to tell. Like many great leaders, Greene was capable of endorsing opposing viewpoints at the same time, his assessments and interior deliberations constantly in flux as new information was received and processed.

In private, Greene's initial assessment of the Carolina militia endorsed his already low opinion of irregular forces. "As I expected, so I find the great bodies of militia that have been in the field and the manner in which they came out, being all on horse back, has laid waste all the Country in such a manner that I am really afraid it will be impossible to subsist the few troops we have," he complained in a letter to George Washington on December 7. "The inhabitants of this country are too remote from one another to be animated into great exertions; and the people appear notwithstanding their danger, very intent upon their own private affairs."[19]

The militia's devotion to their horses, and the problems with both forage and plunder such devotion entailed, would become an enduring theme of Greene's Southern Campaign. But as December 1780 progressed, Greene changed his opinion about mounting an expedition with militia support to threaten Cornwallis's flank west of the Catawba River, a region Sumter considered his own province.

Historians debate whether Greene's famous decision to split his command, sending a mounted, "flying army" to the west under the command of Daniel Morgan while moving east to the Pee Dee with the bulk of the Continental Army, was inspired by Sumter or a strategic initiative of Greene's own design. Though perhaps tedious to the casual reader, the debate is not inconsequential for the American Revolution historian, for in it lay the seeds of Morgan's momentous victory at Cowpens on January 17, which in turn, the argument goes, created the circumstances that led to Cornwallis's surrender at Yorktown 10 months later. Writing of Morgan's victory at Cowpens, the 18th-century historian David Ramsay opines: "The glory and importance of this action resounded from one end of the continent to the other. It re-animated the desponding friends of America, and seemed to be like a resurrection from the dead to the southern states."[20]

Historian John Buchanan gives credit for the decision to Greene, pointing as evidence to Greene's letter of November 2, 1780, to Samuel Huntington, then the president of the Continental Congress:

> As it must be some time before the southern Army can be collected and equipped in sufficient force to contend with the Enemy in that quarter upon equal ground, it will be my first object to endeavour to form a flying army to consist of Infantry and horse. It appears to me that Cavalry and Partizan Corps are best adapted to the make of the Country and the state of the war in that quarter, both for heading and encouraging the Militia as well as protecting the persons and property of the Inhabitants.[21]

But Sumter's biographer and frequent defender Robert D. Bass argues the plan was Sumter's inspiration, citing Greene's letter to Sumter of December 15, 1780:

> Governor Rutledge shew me a couple of notes which you sent him, wherein you express a desire to have a detachment made from this Army on the other side of the Catawba. The measure you wish I have been preparing for Ever since I was with you, and shall have the troops in readiness in a day or two at farthest. The constitution of the Corps I mean to employ in that quarter, and the position I intend they shall take, are part of a plan I have had in contemplation ever since I came to this ground.[22]

Even North Carolina militia general William Davidson has a claim on its inspiration. In a council of war held by Gates in Charlotte on November 25, and again to the North Carolina Board of War in a letter dated November 27, Davidson argued for a plan close to the one Greene eventually adopted: "My scheme is to send Genl. Morgan to the Westward with his light Troops & Rifle men, 1000 volunteer Militia which I can raise in 20 days & the Refugees from South Carolina and Georgia ... and proceed immediately to 96 and possess ourselves of the western part of South Carolina, at the Same time the main Army to move down to the Waxhaws which will oblige the Enemy to divide."[23]

The likely truth is that Greene amalgamated the advice of Sumter, Davidson, Morgan, and others, along with his own experiences from earlier in the war and his impressions of the situation he inherited from

Gates, into the plan's conception. Undoubtedly, Greene's strategies of November evolved through December as he encountered the personalities and conditions on the ground. Like many writers, Greene would frequently draft proposed strategies in his letters, changing and modifying them from correspondence to correspondence, as if the process of putting them on paper helped him to refine and consider their contingencies. And his political instincts made him prone to flattery, exaggerating the influence of others to curry their favor. But whatever the inspiration, his later failure to give Sumter due recognition for the idea, the glory of Cowpens falling on Morgan, not Sumter, became part of a growing list of indignities Sumter kept tally of in his head.

Not debatable is the difference in objectives between Greene's and Sumter's plans. At their meeting in early December, Sumter advocated for a direct attack on Cornwallis's headquarters at Winnsboro, an action that, if executed, would have been one of the major battles of the campaign. Greene's objectives were primarily logistical, based on the need for provisioning his troops and keeping the western populace agitated against their British occupiers. His orders to Morgan were to "spirit up the people, to annoy the enemy in that quarter," and "collect the provisions and forage out of the way of the enemy." Morgan was not prohibited from engaging the enemy but was to act "with caution" and avoid "surprises by every possible precaution."[24] As Greene well knew, thanks in part to Sumter's intelligence network, Cornwallis was being reinforced with troops from Virginia and England, and would soon be preparing for a winter campaign; he would need the Patriot militias of the west in the fighting to come.[25]

Greene's decision ignored the military maxim of not dividing one's force in the face of a superior enemy. The British, not for the last time, were baffled by Greene's unconventional tactics. In his memoirs of the war, Sir Henry Clinton remarked that Greene's army "thus separated" was "certainly not in a situation to encourage any hopes of success from its operations."[26] Indeed, the decision was fraught with peril, though made out of a necessity for feeding his troops, and may well have ended in disaster if not for the brilliant leadership of Daniel Morgan at Cowpens, along with the inexperience of the 26-year-old Banastre Tarleton. Despite its inherent dangers, the decision has been identified as one of the most important and consequential of the war,[27] blessed by good fortune perhaps, but all the more miraculous for it.

Nor is it debatable that Thomas Sumter and Nathanael Greene had fundamentally different opinions about the hierarchy of command for this "flying army." Greene's orders to Morgan seemingly left little room for interpretation:

> You are appointed to the command of a Corps of Light Infantry, a detachment of Militia and Lt. Col. [William] Washingtons Regiment of Light Dragoons. With these troops you will proceed to the West side of the Catawba River where you will be joined by a body of Volunteer Militia under the command of Brig'r Genl [William L.] Davidson of this State, and by Militia lately under the command of Brig'r Genl [Thomas] Sumter … For the present I give you entire command in that quarter, and do hereby require all Officers and Soldiers engaged in the American cause to be subject to your orders and command.[28]

But if Greene expected the former Continental officer Sumter to acquiesce to these orders, subjugating his own rank and command to that of Morgan's, John Rutledge knew better. Rutledge had already adjudicated in one power struggle involving Sumter, ruling for Sumter over his rival, militia colonel James Williams. As a result, Sumter missed the battle at King's Mountain in October 1780 but obtained the rank of brigadier general and command over all the South Carolina militia. Rutledge knew Sumter's temperament far better than Greene at this point and worried about the consequences of Greene's orders on the Gamecock. On December 20, 1780, he wrote Sumter, advising him that Morgan would call on his way to the Catawba, cautioning his prickly general, "I wish he may have what Aid he wants, from the South Carolina Militia, westward of the Catawba."[29]

Rutledge soon wrote Sumter again, apparently in response to Sumter's complaints over the matter: "General Greene and you understand the matter with respect to you not having any command at present in a very different way—as I perceived on speaking to him a few days ago on that point."[30]

The Gamecock, however, would not be placated, although complications of his wounds kept him bedridden and mostly pacified. By

January 8, 1781, if not sooner, news of the Gamecock's indignation filtered back to Greene. "I am impatient to hear of your perfect recovery of seeing you again at the head of the Militia," Greene wrote to Sumter. "General Morgan has gone over to the West side of the Catawba ... But I expect he will have but few men from your Brigade until you are in a condition to appear at the head of them ... If Genl Morgan don't meet with any misfortune until you are ready to join him I shall be happy, as your knowledge of the country and the people will afford him great security against a surprise."

Whatever reconciliations Greene attempted with these platitudes, he likely undid with a curious diatribe against the capabilities of militia operations later in the same letter:

> Partizan strokes in war are like the garnish of a table, they give splendor to the Army and reputation to the Officers, but they afford no substantial national security ... You may strike a hundred strokes, and reap little benefit from them, unless you have go(od) Army to take advantage of your success ... It is not a war of posts but a contest for States dependent upon opinion. If we can introduce into the field a greater army than the Enemy, all their posts will fall of themselves; and without this they will reestablish them though we should take them twenty times.

He also criticized the pillage plaguing the Carolina countryside, perpetrated by Patriot and Loyalist alike, insinuating Sumter had some influence in the matter: "Plunder and deprivation prevails so in every quarter [that] I am not little apprehensive all this Country will be laid to waste. Most people appear to be in pursuit of private gain or personal glory. I persuade myself though you may set a just value upon reputation, your soul if filled with a more noble ambition."[31]

For a man who'd spent the last seven months fighting the British, with little support from the Continental Army, and was currently suffering from a life-threatening wound in that service, Sumter had good reason to find this letter offensive. Greene's letters could often be pedantic. A voluminous correspondent, Greene sometimes was too eager to show off his innate intelligence, but these letters could also reveal his human flaws: an inferiority complex inbred from a lack of formal education; the need to be considered worthy by subordinate and superior alike. "General Greene brought with him to his new command an unfortunate habit. He was a voluminous writer and moralizer," fumes the historian and South Carolinian Edward McCrady, writing in 1902. McCrady continues:

> He wrote, not military reports—clear and succinct ... but long personal letters, going into personal details, and criticisms and discussions, usually of complaint ... Such also was the character of his communications to his subordinates; and indeed to these latter there was withal an assumption and tone of superiority and patronage which must have been galling to men who were his seniors in years and of greater military experience.[32]

Not surprisingly, Greene's letter did little to assuage Sumter's wounded pride. But it is this letter's overt denunciation of a "war of posts" strategy that has confounded Sumter's defenders most. Finding the provisions for his growing army scarce in the region west of the Broad River, Morgan proposed an expedition into Georgia. "If you think Ninety-Six, Augusta or even Savannah, can be surprised, and your force will admit of a detachment for the purpose and leave you sufficiency to keep up a good countenance you may attempt it," Greene responded,[33] appearing to endorse exactly the type of military operations Sumter had initially proposed.

Later, after Greene's return to South Carolina following the Battle of Guilford Courthouse on March 15, 1781, he would make a "war of posts"—capturing the British outposts in the South Carolina interior one by one to slowly drive the British Army back to Charleston—the central tenet of his strategy. That Greene would disregard Sumter's suggestions in January, only to wholeheartedly embrace them a few months later, without giving Sumter any due recognition, has maddened Sumter's biographers ever since. That he would rely heavily on Sumter and other elements of the South Carolina militia to enact that strategy is simply adding insult to injury.

In Greene's defense, a Walt Whitman quote might serve: "Do I contradict myself? Very well, then I contradict myself. I am large. I contain multitudes." His disregard of a strategy that he later adopts proves only that Greene could be as exasperating as he could be brilliant. To hold him to one viewpoint only ignores these complexities. He was a contemplative man operating in an ever-shifting environment; his contradictions prove as much.

If Greene believed these entreaties placated Sumter, he soon received word otherwise. Writing on January 15, General Morgan, now camped on Thicketty Creek near the Broad River, on Cornwallis's western flank, complained:

> I dispatched Captain [C.K.] Chitty, (whom I have appointed as commissary of purchases for my command,) with orders to collect and store all the provisions that could be obtained between the Catawba and Broad rivers. I gave him directions to call on Colonel [William] Hill, who commands a regiment of militia in that quarter, to furnish him with a proper number of men to assist him in the execution of this commission, but he, to my great surprise, has just returned without effecting any thing. He tells me that his failure proceeded from the want of countenance and assistance of Colonel Hill, who assured him that General Sumter directed him to obey no orders from me, unless they came through him.[34]

The incident between Chitty and Hill was of inconsequential historic merit, a dustup between officers of regular and irregular troops, as is perhaps common in war, civil or otherwise. Morgan was asking Hill, through Chitty, to use his militia to raise provisions for Morgan's army, an unpopular task in any situation. To do so would have required Hill's militia to canvass the already depleted local populace, requesting or alternatively taking their meager goods and provisions in the heart of winter. It doesn't even rate a mention in William Hill's memoir, which has otherwise become notable, at least among Revolutionary War historians, for its unsubstantiated yet circumstantially plausible account of another Sumter feud—the Gamecock's rivalry with militia colonel James Williams.

Yet in the troubled relationship between Greene and Sumter, this moment looms large. Greene's pedantic tendencies cannot be ignored as a cause for their difficulties, though in his response to Morgan he urged appeasement. "I am surprised General Sumter should give such an order as you mention to Col. [William] Hill; nor can I persuade myself that there must be some mistake in the matter," he admits to Morgan in his letter of January 19. "I will write to General Sumter on the subject, but as it is better to conciliate than aggravate matters, where every thing depends so much upon voluntary principles."[35]

In his promised response to Sumter written that same day, Greene attempts to act on his own advice, starting in a conciliatory tone:

> I have just received letters from General Morgan informing me of his situation, and representing the difficulty he meets with collecting provisions, and among other things he mentions some embarrassment which has arisen from an order of yours to Colonel [William] Hill, not to obey an order from him, unless it came through you. I imagine there must be some misapprehension about the matter; for I cannot suppose you could give an improper order, or that you have the most distant wish to embarrass the public affairs.

All well and good, and perhaps appeasement enough for the temperamental Gamecock if Greene had ended the letter there. Unfortunately, the next paragraph again veers into hubris, with Greene lecturing the elder and experienced Sumter on order of command:

> It is certainly right that all orders should go through the principal to the dependants ... This is a general rule and should never be deviated from but in cases of necessity ... In that case the order should be directed to the branches and not the principal; and as the head is subject to the order the branches are of course: for it would be very extraordinary if a Captain should presume to dispute an order from his General because it was not communicated through his Colonel.[36]

Though Greene's conciliatory motives were admirable, his message to Sumter was clear: Morgan was his superior, at least in terms of order of command. The Gamecock obviously took umbrage, though his answer would manifest itself in action, not words. Writing on January 29, informing Greene he had only just received Greene's letters of both January 8 and January 19 (along with an inconsequential letter dated January 15), Sumter replied: "I confess I have been under some embaressment respecting Gen. Morgans command, & the orders he has given. As I have been concerned but little in either trust, & believe I have been guilty of no Impropriety, and shall always make a point to correspond & act upon such principles with Gen Morgan, as is most likely to tend to the publick Good ... therefore will not stand upon punctilos. to the prejudice of the service."[37]

This passage reveals Sumter as Greene's equal in prose, if not his master in the art of irony. The word *punctilio* means "a fine point, particular, or detail." Sumter may have misspelled it here but otherwise employs it masterfully, implying the matter between Morgan and Hill is hardly worth the huff Greene has made of it.

Nevertheless, the letter appears concessionary. It was around this time that Sumter received notice of a resolution of thanks for his victories at Hanging Rock, Fishdam Ford, and Blackstocks passed by the Continental Congress on January 13 at the suggestion of a letter from Nathanael Greene, sent shortly after Greene's arrival in the Carolinas in December.[38] Perhaps this recognition by Congress mollified Sumter's resentment. Or perhaps he was simply exhausted by Greene's sermonizing and ready to move on.

He does, however, appear to address Greene's concerns about plundering sincerely, though admitting no simple solution to this unfortunate characteristic of civil war. He continued:

> When I had the Honour of a conference with [you,] if I discovered [i.e. displayed] any injudicious thirst for enterprise, private gain, or personal Glory, I am sorry for it, and shall be doubly Mortified to find that my endeavours, together with the Good people of South Carolina, have not tended the least Degree to promote the Publick Good; I lament that private Gain is the primary Object with too many, and as much lament that the desire of Fame is not more sought after. As to the Former the world I think will acquit me, but the latter reason & Conscience convinces I have not been arrogant & designing but allways meant to conduct myself & demean myself, so as to tend most to Publick Good, & the satisfaction of my superior officers.[39]

Sumter writes optimistically here: history does not acquit him for his assent of plunder, though the realist might acknowledge his finer point, that it is an unfortunate but necessary tool of war. Nevertheless, this passage takes on greater depth and meaning as the story of Sumter and Greene unfolds. By the time this letter was written on January 29, Morgan had won his stunning victory at Cowpens, and Greene had mobilized his army in the strategic retreat known by history as the "Race to the Dan." Cornwallis and his army of approximately 2,500 mobilized on January 18 and were by now attempting to cross the swollen Catawba River in North Carolina, which they achieved in a perilous crossing at Cowan's Ford, north of Charlotte, on February 1, 1781.

Greene responded to Sumter on January 30, 1781, admitting he had been "so much engaged" that he has not had time to "congratulate" Sumter on Morgan's victory at Cowpens, his thoughts obviously concentrated on Cornwallis.[40] How Sumter responded to this backhanded congratulations we can only speculate. Though they continued their correspondence throughout the rest of the winter and early spring, with Greene constantly inquiring about Sumter's recovery, the Race to the Dan brought to a close the opening act in their story. Sumter would soon recover sufficiently enough to return to the field; Greene would play cat-and-mouse with Cornwallis across central North Carolina, until meeting him on the battlefield at Guilford Courthouse on March 15. But Act Two would commence shortly, with the themes of rank and plunder taking on deeper implications.

CHAPTER 4

Sumter's Rounds

In February 1781, Thomas Sumter emerged from his three-month convalescence to begin his next campaign in the South Carolina interior. Though not yet completely healed from the wounds he received at Blackstocks, he had good reasons to hurry a return to the field.

As Sumter's biographer Anne King Gregorie notes, the planning of a militia campaign in the South Carolina backcountry often depended on the crop cycle and the contingencies of a six-week enlistment, and Sumter understood instinctively he needed to muster his militia in February if he hoped to campaign before the spring planting season. He also believed Cornwallis's foray into North Carolina had left the British forces remaining in South Carolina vulnerable to a decisive attack. Informing his men erroneously that Francis, Lord Rawdon, had only three hundred men enforcing the British garrison in Camden, Sumter proposed a lightning strike on the Congaree and Santee outposts guarding the British supply line between Camden and Charleston, an objective he had targeted before with some success during the Battle of Camden the previous August. With Rawdon's reduced force unable to adequately reinforce these outposts, he argued, a successful campaign could isolate the British garrisons at Camden and Ninety-Six, forcing Rawdon to abandon the South Carolina interior. That these outposts also contained considerable stores of British supply and captured loot was a fact not lost on Sumter, who knew his men would be as motivated by these spoils as they were by a chance to deliver a decisive blow against their enemy.[1] A consummate student of backcountry psychology, he understood the promise of material gain only increased his militia's motivation to campaign against the British.

Greene unfortunately suggested as much in his letter to Sumter of January 8: "Plunder and depradation prevails so in every quarter [that] I am not a little apprehensive all the Country will be laid to waste. Most people appear to be in pursuit of private gain or personal glory. I persuade myself though you may set a just value upon reputation, your soul is filled with more noble ambition."[2]

Diplomatic blunders aside, Greene had good reason to be concerned about the prevalence of looting and plundering in the Patriot forces, both regular and irregular. This crisis would only deepen as the Southern Campaign continued. With Greene moved on to North Carolina during the winter of 1781, both Marion and Sumter complained of plunderous behavior within their own ranks. "I ... lament the great probability of this country being laid waste by plundering parties, as people Dayly discover a greater avidity to that shameful practice," Sumter wrote to Greene at the end of January.[3] In a similar letter to Continental General Isaac Huger, Marion expressed concern about dispatching a subordinate officer named William Clay Snipes on a mission to collect recruits in Georgia because he was certain Snipes "will do no other Service than plunder the inhabitants."[4]

Writing to Greene on March 10, François Lellorquis, the Marquis de Malmédy, a French officer commissioned a colonel in the Continental Army and assigned to Greene during the Guilford Courthouse campaign, begged Greene to issue an order against plundering to the Continental Army, the crime becoming so prevalent among his troops. Greene complied though the order apparently did little good.[5]

And though Thomas Sumter no doubt recognized the inherent depravity of looting private property, he was a pragmatist at heart, capable of rationalizing immoral behavior when it suited his objectives. And plundering the stores and supply of the British Army was another matter altogether, fair game as far as he, and for that matter Greene, were concerned.

If Sumter used the implicit promise of plunder to rally his troops, his rushed return to the field was explicitly encouraged by Greene, who had been in correspondence with Sumter throughout the winter. Writing to

Sumter on February 3, 1781, Greene noted: "It is true I wish to see you again in the field; and I have ever considered it a great misfortune that you was wounded on my first coming to the command ... I am sorry your wound continues troublesome. I was in hopes from the account of several people that you would be in the field in a few days."[6]

And as genuinely anxious as Greene was for Sumter's partisan campaigning to resume, this letter was also an attempt at diplomacy, for by now Greene was well aware the famed "Carolina Gamecock" had been deeply offended by General Daniel Morgan's command in the western theater during Sumter's convalescence, even if it had resulted in the stunning American victory at Cowpens. In the same letter, Greene admits, "In what respect General Morgans command embarrassed you I am at a loss to Imagine; but dare say I cou'd explain it to your perfect satisfaction in a few minutes, could I have the happiness to see you."[7]

For all his faults and flaws, Sumter was no mere plunderer. To label him as such is to discredit the complexity of both his character and his motivations. Recall it wasn't the Patriot cause or the promise of plunder that drew Sumter back into the war the previous summer, but his quest for revenge against Banastre Tarleton, who burned his home on May 27, 1780. Sumter had resigned his commission in the Continental Army two years before and was by then, at the age of 46, considered elderly, settling into a comfortable life of managing his not inconsiderable estate. Yet clearly the American cause was one he took seriously, risking his life for it many times since on the battlefield, and one he remained committed to in his later service as both a United States congressman and senator.

Yet like many men, both powerful and insignificant, Sumter's ego could wreak havoc with his better natures, and in his campaigns of 1780–81, these human shortcomings were often on display. A talented recruiter who could inspire near-fanatical loyalty in his men, Sumter clearly possessed some natural charisma, a spirit of animation that drew men to him. And this spirit is evident in his correspondence, a sense of energy and magnetism in the prose, particularly when possessed of some enterprise for which he wanted his colleague's approval or assistance.

However, his correspondence could also turn dour and sullen, especially when asked to do something against his own initiative or self-interest, and also when he felt the fates had conspired against him, or when a colleague failed to offer him due recognition. He was capable of odd, sometimes bizarre, behavior. At both Fishdam Ford and Fishing Creek, he ignored credible intelligence of the enemy's pursuit, failed to post guards around camp, and abruptly disrobed to his long johns to sleep despite tangible threats. Both encounters ended in calamity, with Sumter slipping out of camp in his nightclothes, leaving his men to be slaughtered by the attacking British.

And in his power struggle for command with James Williams, which resulted in Sumter missing the battle at King's Mountain, as well as the umbrage he displayed over Morgan's expedition west of the Broad River, we have seen hints of the personality conflicts that would become more pronounced as the war progressed and his influence diminished.

From a modern perspective, these incidents of reckless behavior, general irritability, and conflicts with colleagues suggest some evidence of bipolar disorder. Of course, the 1780s were a long time before the era of modern psychoanalysis, and bipolar disorder requires a medical diagnosis, making any such conclusion pure speculation, even if this evidence persists as our narrative progresses, his manic and depressive episodes becoming more pronounced after Blackstocks.

In this case, his fractious behavior would gain him command over all the South Carolina militia once more. With Morgan now retired from the field due to ongoing health issues, and Greene eager for Sumter to commence a spring campaign against the British forces remaining in South Carolina, Greene's letter of February 3 conveyed as much: "It is my ardent wish that you shoud embody your Militia as soon as your health will permit. This force I think may be usefully employed against the enemy in South Carolina; and whether it is employed there or with the continental Army when collected, you will have command of the whole."[8]

"Command of the whole" was a return to the status he enjoyed in the fall of 1780, when South Carolina Governor John Rutledge had appointed him the colony's sole brigadier general of militia. Yet both Sumter and Greene undoubtedly realized that at some level things were not precisely as they had been before: in December, South Carolina Governor John Rutledge had promoted Francis Marion brigadier general, equaling Sumter's rank, and following his heroics at the Battle of Cowpens, Andrew Pickens achieved the same. Though Sumter still enjoyed seniority over his fellow brigadier generals, and the assurances of Greene, he would never again enjoy their unquestioned devotion, particularly Marion's.

And so, as eager to reestablish his authority as he was to seize a strategic advantage before the spring planting season, Sumter once more mustered his militia. Answering the call were men such as James Gill from the Chester District (south of current-day Rock Hill, South Carolina), who had fought with Sumter at both Rocky Mount and Fishing Creek. Like Gill, Hamilton Brown was from the Chester District and had campaigned with Sumter during the previous summer. Zachary Kitchens also served at Sumter's defeat at Fishing Creek on August 18, 1780, and returned for this mission. "Sumpter [sic] called us together and examined the strength of the British Outposts," Kitchen recalled in his pension application.[9]

Yet the muster was as notable for its absences as for those who answered the call. Only 280 men assembled at Sumter's old camp ground in the Waxhaws. In contrast, Sumter had fought with over a thousand men at the Blackstocks.[10] With both Pickens and Marion having grown more powerful during Sumter's convalescence, the Gamecock's drawing power was now diminished. And as usual, Sumter's men were poorly provisioned, though motivated for a try at the British stores. Deciding, as he often did, that speed was more strategically expedient than caution, Sumter disregarded the diminished state of his force and launched the campaign described by many who fought with him as "Sumter's Rounds," marching out from the Waxhaws on February 16.[11]

Sumter's first objective was Fort Granby (also known as Fort Congaree), which guarded an important trading post and ferry on the Congaree River.[12] The fort was located in the settlement of Granby at the home of James Cayce, a two-story structure built in 1770 and fortified by the British in 1780 with a square earthworks redoubt that included bastions, strong parapets, and a surrounding ditch with abatis—logs carved to a point and protruding from the earthworks.[13]

Granby's commander was Major Andrew Maxwell, a Maryland Tory and notorious plunderer himself who commanded about three hundred Provincials and Loyalist militia inside the fort.[14] Arriving at Fort Granby on February 19, 1781, Sumter attempted to deceive the garrison into surrender by painting logs and tobacco hogsheads black to disguise them as artillery—a *ruse de guerre* known as "Quaker guns," which had been used successfully before in the Carolina backcountry, most notably by Continental Colonel William Washington at Rugeley's Mill near Camden on December 4, 1780. But the ruse failed because Maxwell knew of both Sumter's approach and his lack of artillery. After an unsuccessful attack, Sumter set up a siege of the fort, laying down a slow, continuous rifle fire to harass the garrison's inhabitants.[15]

During the siege, Sumter's men erected a crude tower from which they could fire down into the fort from a covered position. With more thoughtful engineering and construction, this same device would be perfected by South Carolina Major Hezekiah Maham during the successful siege of Fort Watson by forces under the command of Francis Marion and Lieutenant Colonel Henry Lee in April 1781, becoming forever immortalized as the "Maham Tower," though Sumter and his men deserve some credit for its conception.[16]

Learning of Sumter's attack, Lord Rawdon dispatched a force of seven hundred men and two artillery pieces under the command of Lieutenant Colonel Welbore Doyle to relieve Granby. Fearing such an attack, though apparently still unaware of the true strength of Rawdon's force, Sumter wrote to Marion on February 20, 1781, requesting reinforcement: "I arrived at this place [Fort Granby] yesterday morning … Every thing hitherto favourable, and have no doubt but I shall succeed, if not interrupted by Lord Rawdon … It is my wish that you would be pleased to move in such a direction as to attract his attention, and thereby prevent his designs … If you can, with propriety, advance Southwardly so as to cooperate, or correspond with me, it might have the best of consequences."[17]

Whether by fate or design, Marion did not answer Sumter's call for reinforcement. On February 28, he wrote to Sumter with excuses about the paucity of his troops and the strength of the enemy in his theater.[18]

Doyle assumed Sumter would retreat northwards, up the Broad River, and seized all the fords in that direction. Learning of Doyle's approach, Sumter broke the siege and marched south toward Marion, futilely seeking a rendezvous with the Swamp Fox. Meanwhile Rawdon, sensing perhaps a long-awaited endgame to the British Army's exhausting attempts to rid themselves of Sumter, dispatched the 64th Regiment of New York Volunteers and a fieldpiece under the command of Major McLeroth toward Sumter's new position. A force of regulars and militia also set out from Ninety-Six in pursuit of Sumter.[19]

With British forces closing in from three sides, his men outnumbered and poorly provisioned, a more cautious commander might have dispersed his forces into the wilderness. But not the Gamecock, who optimistically believed Patriot militia from the region would be drawn to his command and still awaited reinforcement from Marion. Instead he crossed the Congaree and traveled 35 miles downriver to the British outpost at Belleville.

Another link in the chain guarding supply and communications from Charleston to the British interior, Belleville was located at the home of Colonel William Thomson, a Patriot who had been captured at the fall of Charleston. The home had been fortified by a stockade, with plantation outbuildings comprising part of the defensive works. In command of the outpost was Lieutenant John Stuart of the 71st Highlanders.

Arriving at the fort on February 22, a day after leaving Granby, Sumter ordered a direct attack on the fort across an open field, where his men endured heavy fire before burning some of the outbuildings. But Stuart's men strongly resisted the attack and successfully doused the fire, causing Sumter to disengage after only 30 minutes. His men exhausted and hungry, Sumter left detachments to surround the fort but retreated with the bulk of his force to Manigault's Ferry, approximately 2 miles away on the Santee River.[20]

At Manigault's, fortune finally smiled on Sumter's otherwise ill-fated campaign, however briefly. On the morning of February 23, Sumter received intelligence that a convoy of British supply wagons was approaching his position from the south. He moved quickly to a rising piece of ground a short distance away known at Big Savannah, setting up his ambush just as the convoy appeared in the distance. Sumter successfully outflanked the convoy's 80 British regulars under Major David McIntosh, and after a skirmish that resulted in several British deaths, captured the British wagons, including not only a large supply of arms, ammunition, and clothing, but also several locked chests thought to contain British gold.[21]

The capture was a windfall for the small partisan band. Perhaps that is why it was remembered so vividly by many of the soldiers with Sumter during this campaign in their pension applications, many of which were transcribed 50 years later. But Sumter's luck quickly shifted again: with Rawdon's British forces still in hot pursuit, Sumter had the supplies and British chests loaded onto boats and floated down the Santee River; but whether by mistake or treachery, the pilot of the boat, a man named Robert Livingstone, steered the flotilla to the British outpost at Fort Watson, where they were retaken by the British.[22]

"Hearing of a reinforcement [after the action at Bellville], we marched to meet them [the British]. It turned out to be a small detachment of British guarding some British wagons loaded with clothing & money for the soldiers. These surrendered & the loading was put on a barge & soon retaken at Wright's Bluff [Fort Watson] with some of our men," recalled James Gill.

At least one of Sumter's soldiers believed Sumter was complicit in Livingstone's presumed treachery. "A suspicion was then entertained that Sumpter [sic] used the money—the deponent believes so yet," reads the pension application of Zachary Kitchens.[23]

After Sumter's army sent off the boats, a fresh detachment of British forces from Camden, including cavalry and a field gun, approached their position. Sumter formed for battle but the British withdrew, unaware of Sumter's precarious plight. Hoping to rendezvous with his boats carrying the captured British stores, Sumter retreated to the Santee River, but instead learned of the supply convoy's recapture. Now trapped against the river, Sumter and his men searched desperately for boats hidden in the adjoining swamps. Finally finding two canoes, they spent the next two days crossing the Santee, three men to each canoe, their horses swimming beside them.[24]

Having escaped Rawdon's men in the desperate river crossing, Sumter now decided to attack the British outpost at Fort Watson to regain the lost wagon convoy. Built the previous year by Colonel John Watson, the fort was at a place called Wright's Bluff along the Santee River, just below its junction with the Congaree River, roughly 50 miles due south of Camden. Colonel Watson constructed the fort on a Santee Indian ritual mound, rising about 50 feet above the surrounding swamp. Though not a large outpost, the fort's defenses were considerable, with fosse (a defensive ditch), parapet (a defensive, earthen wall), and abatis (logs sharpened to a point protruding outward from the defenses).[25]

Fort Watson had recently been reinforced with about four hundred Provincial troops, but with characteristic alacrity and a failure to do any reconnaissance, Sumter ordered his tiny band of two hundred to directly assault the well-defended outpost around noon on February 28, 1781. The results were predictable: the British account of the battle listed Sumter's casualties as 18 killed, with some prisoners and many horses taken.[26]

After the unsuccessful attack on Fort Watson, Sumter withdrew to a place called Farr's Plantation on the swamps of the Black River, near his own mills and property. Sumter's biographer Anne King Gregorie describes this as a "dark time for the Americans." Discouraged and exhausted officers and men fled the camp. Some North Carolina militia fighting with Sumter's South Carolinians attempted to desert en masse and were held at bayonet point.[27]

Marion, responding to Sumter's entreaties for troops and support on March 2, answered again that his own force was too weak, the enemy opposition too strong, to provide any. Still hoping to solicit the Swamp Fox's assistance, Sumter responded to Marion on March 4, 1781:

> I am very sorry to be so far out of the way of meeting with you at a time when there is the greatest occasion for it … My horses are so worn out that I can scarce move at all, and officers and men quite discouraged—finding no force in these parts, not even men enough to join to guide me through the country. But, notwithstanding little may be done now, yet much good might be expected to result hereafter from a personal consultation, which I hope to have the favour of by tomorrow night.[28]

Such consultations would never come; Marion continued to find reasons not to come to Sumter's assistance. Sumter's biographer Robert D. Bass insists Marion's failure to respond was due to circumstance, not recalcitrance. "Although there was little co-operation between the Gamecock and the Swamp Fox, there was no animosity between these Partisans," he writes with Pollyannaish optimism.[29] But the earlier South Carolina historian Edward R. McCrady acknowledges something more nefarious in Marion's actions. "Still, it is strange that, within a day's journey of Sumter, he [Marion] does not appear to have made any response to the earnest appeal for a conference."[30]

While recuperating and waiting for reinforcement, Sumter's militia captured four of Watson's men at Nelson's Ferry and Sumter attempted to negotiate an exchange. In a letter dated to Marion on March 15, 1781, Watson reported to Marion that he offered an exchange, but that Sumter never completed it, presumably because he was once more being pursued by the British, this time by Major Thomas Fraser and his force of South Carolina loyalists.[31]

Sumter now moved to his own plantation at the High Hills of the Santee to collect his wife and son, before fleeing Fraser's pursuit by way of friendly settlements near the swamps of Black River, hoping to escape to safety in the Waxhaws. According to documentary history collected by the 19th-century historian Lyman Draper and reported in several contemporary sources, it was a fraught and terrifying escape. Sumter's paralytic wife, Mary, was mounted on horseback with a featherbed for a saddle and a negro woman behind her to hold her in place, while the Sumters' sole child, Tom, then only 12 years old, and many of the family's slaves, either walked or rode along within the ranks of what was left of Sumter's ragtag militia.

On March 6, 1781, Fraser apprehended Sumter's party near a place called Ratcliff's Bridge over the Lynches River. Sumter sent his family and slaves into the swamps, and turned to face Fraser's Loyalists, though many of his men also fled. An account from Draper tells of Sumter frantically calling out to his son, "Lay down Tom! Lay down Tom!" as the British attacked.[32]

In a running battle, Sumter was able to collect his family and retreat to Ratcliffe's Bridge, burning it to prevent further pursuit by Fraser. "Fraser yesterday fell in with Sumter (who was advancing this way) between Scape Hoar and Radcliffe's Bridge," Rawdon informed Watson in a letter dated March 7, 1781. "A smart action ensued, in which the enemy were completely routed, leaving ten dead on the field and about forty wounded. Unfortunately none of our Dragoons had joined Fraser, so that he could not pursue his victory. Sumter fled across Lynches Creek and continued his retreat northward; he had his family with him, so that I think he has entirely abandoned the lower country."[33]

Sumter's tattered, hungry, discouraged army finally returned to the Waxhaws after their perilous escape at Ratcliff's Bridge. During the disastrous three-week campaign, they lost approximately a quarter of their force. Not surprisingly, perhaps, the men were dejected and angry. Many of them felt deceived by Sumter, who had so clearly misinformed them about the strength of Rawdon's force. Some believed Sumter put their lives in peril to rescue his own family. Men like Zachary Kitchens believed Sumter had employed some sort of deception in the loss of the briefly captured British supply wagon. Sumter had captured many slaves during the expedition, and apparently this, too, caused resentment. Colonel Robert Gray, a prominent Loyalist from the Camden area who wrote a reminiscence of the Revolutionary War in 1782, recounted:

> They [Sumter's men] were now exceedingly dejected ... Sumter, who had carried off a number of Negroes, offered one to every person who would enlist for ten months as a dragoon to form a body of state cavalry, he could hardly procure a single recruit and he began to grow extremely unpopular. They raised so great a clamor against him for deceiving them with regard to Lord Rawdon's strength that he was obliged at a muster to enter into a long vindication of his conduct. All of this however was ineffectual.[34]

Though it was conducted at the urging of Nathanael Greene and was successful in eliciting a massive response from Rawdon, who perhaps might have been able to support Cornwallis's operations in North Carolina if not engaged in his pursuit of the Gamecock, Sumter's Rounds failed in its other strategic objectives: capturing the British outposts supporting the supply lines to Camden, if not the supplies themselves, and raising militia along the Congaree–Santee basin for more extensive action against the British occupation.

More significantly, Sumter's Rounds portended the personality conflicts between Marion and Sumter that would hamper the Patriots spring campaign, once Greene made his strategic decision to return to

South Carolina following the battle at Guilford Courthouse. Sumter's ongoing personality conflicts in 1781 have led some historians to suggest he underwent some fundamental psychological schism during his convalescence, a selfishness not apparent during his campaigns of 1780. "Did this experience [his serious wound at Blackstocks] sap some of the bold courage of the Gamecock? Did he not press his attack with the same hard courage he had once displayed?" asks the historian John S. Pancake. "Probably Thomas Sumter himself could not have answered such questions, but the terrible wound and its painful aftermath may have affected his fighting spirit in ways of which he himself was not aware."[35]

Regardless of his psychological state, Sumter was still the brigadier general over all South Carolina militia, a man to be reckoned with by British and Continental alike.

CHAPTER 5

Sumter's Law

The judicial districts that emerged from the Regulator Movement of the late 1760s brought with them some sense of societal order to the South Carolina backcountry. The Circuit Court Act of 1769 provided funding for land, courthouses, judges, and jails in Camden, Cheraw, Orangeburg, and Ninety-Six, along with Beaufort and Georgetown on the coast. Though these circuit courts did not begin functioning until 1772, rudimentary law and order was finally established in the South Carolina interior, diminishing both the vigilante influence of the Regulators and the lawless terror that had given them rise.[1]

Though sectarian and ethnic tensions still smoldered, the backcountry gentry could now focus on their farming and business enterprises. By the beginning of the American Revolution, Thomas Sumter had accumulated considerable property and business interests through investment, marriage, and his own industry. And he was far from alone. Joseph Kershaw of Camden owned a prominent mercantile trade with Charleston and more than a thousand acres of land. South Carolina historian Walter Edgar reports his Camden home "was as elegant as any Charleston mansion."[2]

Sumter's rival James Williams, colonel of the Little River militia from the Ninety-Six District, owned a mercantile business, a mill, and at least 3,600 acres of land.[3] Sumter's loyal subordinate William Hill owned a prosperous iron mine and mill that produced everything from farm and household implements to ammunition and weaponry.[4] That these successful planters and businessmen were also militia leaders was common for the time. In Colonial-era South Carolina, economic status conveyed with it authority in the political, religious, and military realms. With minimal government authority in the backcountry, the settlements and clans typically looked to their most prominent citizens for all forms of leadership.

The South Carolina economy had long run on its slavery system. Edgar reports South Carolina's rice planters of the early 1700s estimated the need for 30–50 slaves per thousand acres for a good annual return. By the 1770s, a backcountry planter with nine to 12 hands could earn an annual income of £250 to £500 sterling (roughly $22,000 to $44,000 in today's dollars) planting indigo and hemp.[5] In 1770 slaves comprised 61 percent of the colony's population, and Charleston was the American Southeast's primary slave market.[6]

Therefore, it's not surprising slave ownership became a mark of social and economic status for the backcountry planter. James Williams listed ownership of 33 slaves in his 1780 will.[7] William Hill owned 90 slaves by the late 1770s, and Joseph Kershaw one hundred.[8] Nor is it surprising that many of those who aspired to the economic status of a Williams, Hill, Sumter, or Kershaw saw in slave ownership a path toward it.

Historians have long noted the bitter irony inherent in the fact that the founding fathers' creed of "Life, Liberty, and the Pursuit of Happiness" did not apply to America's slaves. During the American Revolution, neither South Carolina's low country elite nor its backcountry bourgeois had any interest in acknowledging such ironies, though Henry and John Laurens were two notable exceptions. Born in 1724, Henry Laurens was a merchant, rice planter, and politician who became one of South Carolina's richest men, in part through the slave trade. Laurens would serve as president of the Continental Congress from November 1777 to December 1781, but by the time of the American Revolution he had become a staunch opponent of the slavery system, both on humanitarian and religious grounds.

His son, John Laurens, born in 1754, shared his father's views on slavery. With the help of his father's political influence, John Laurens joined the staff of George Washington in 1777 after receiving a formal education in Europe. As the war progressed, and Laurens earned the rank of lieutenant colonel, he proposed to Washington and his father a plan to create units of African-American slaves in the Continental Army. The units would be commanded by white officers. Slave-owners would be compensated "at a rate not exceeding one thousand dollars" for each slave not over thirty-five years of age. The slave himself would receive no pay but "would be clothed and subsisted at the expense of the United States." At the end of the war, the slave would be free and receive a 50 dollar bonus. Congress approved Laurens's plan, but only contingent on the prior approval of Georgia and South Carolina. In May 1779, Laurens's proposal was placed before both houses of the South Carolina General Assembly, where it was promptly voted down. In recent years, John Laurens's historic legacy has reemerged thanks to his prominent role as a character in the musical *Hamilton*, which mentions his progressive positions on slavery.

South Carolina's slaves did serve in the American military, but only as nameless laborers, earning seven shillings, six pence a day on behalf of their masters. South Carolina's famous Fort Moultrie on Sullivan's Island, whose palmetto defenses withstood British bombardment during their assault on Charleston in 1776, is the most prominent example of this practice. Today the palmetto tree adorns the South Carolina state flag in Fort Moultrie's honor, but few who sport the iconic symbol on t-shirts, hats, and bumper stickers probably realize the famous fort was constructed mostly with slave labor.

Most South Carolinians were more interested in guarding against uprisings or escape attempts of slaves than enlisting and arming them. When the British threatened to invade Georgia and South Carolina in 1779, both colonies sent Continental Army General Isaac Huger to Congress to solicit additional military support. There, Huger argued, the local militias could do little to oppose the pending British invasion because they were needed to "remain home to prevent insurrection against the negroes, and to prevent the desertion of them to the enemy."[9]

Slave insurrections were always a concern in South Carolina, where African Americans outnumbered whites since the earliest days of the colony, but the fear heightened after a Continental Congress agent in London warned American authorities a "plan was already laid before" the Crown for inciting slaves to revolt if the colonies should rebel. In response, South Carolina's Council of Safety issued warnings in 1775 against "insurrections by our negroes."[10]

While there were no slave insurrections in South Carolina during the American Revolution, the British Army did steal slaves and encouraged them to flee their Patriot masters. Prior to his invasion of South Carolina, General Henry Clinton issued a proclamation promising "every Negro who shall desert the Rebel Standard ... full security within these Lines [and] any Occupation which [they] shall think proper," though he was careful to distinguish that such guarantees did not apply to any slaves belonging to white Loyalists. Upon his capture of Charleston, Clinton repeated his promise to liberate any slave belonging to a rebel master, prompting the escape of thousands of slaves to Charleston.[11] Historian David Ramsey estimated 25,000 South Carolina slaves were either captured by the British or sought refuge with them during the war, though other historians propose more moderate numbers. Some of these slaves served as laborers or servants in the British Army. The "Black Pioneers" were a provincial regiment of freedmen and runaway slaves who served as engineers. Others served as guides, pilots, or messengers for the British Army.[12]

As the war drew to a close, the disposition of these slaves became a primary concern of the South Carolina government. "When the long expected evacuation of Charleston really drew nigh, it was apprehended by the inhabitants, that the British army, on its departure, would carry off with them some thousands of negroes which were within their lines," writes Ramsay. Negotiating his withdrawal from the city, British General Alexander Leslie agreed to the following provision: "That all the slaves of the citizens of South Carolina, now in the power of the honourable lieutenant-general Leslie, shall be restored to their former owners, as far as is practicable, except such slaves as may have rendered themselves particularly obnoxious on account of the their attachment and services to the British troops, and such as had specific promises of freedom."[13] British records indicate that approximately five thousand African Americans evacuated Charleston with the British Army in December 1782, although only a small portion of those ever received their freedom; most were the slaves of Loyalist refugees and were resettled on plantations in the West Indies or British Florida.[14]

★   ★   ★

The British Army's slave policy only exacerbated the partisan civil war engulfing South Carolina in the winter of 1780 and 1781. Issues of race, class, economic status, and religion now erupted in a toxic conflagration. Slaves were captured and/or stolen by both sides, Patriot and British alike. When Patriot forces captured a slave escaped or taken from a Patriot master, they were typically returned to their owners. But a Tory's slaves were considered fair game, a spoil of war.

This lawless civil war drove Greene to the pits of despair. In a downcast letter to Samuel Huntington, president of the Continental Congress, written on December 28, 1780, from his camp on the Pee Dee River, he complains:

> I am sorry it is not possible to give your Excellency more flattering accounts from this quarter, but our situation is not less disagreeable than I have represented. And the spirit of plundering which prevails among the Inhabitants adds not a little to our difficulties. The whole country is in danger of being laid to waste by the Whigs and Tories, who pursue each other with as much relentless fury as beasts of prey. People between this and the Santee are frequently murdered as they ride along the road.[15]

In a letter to his fellow Continental officer, the North Carolinian Robert Howe, written around this same time, on December 29, 1780, Greene complains similarly:

> The Whigs and Tories pursue one another with the most relent[less] Fury killing and destroying each other wherever they meet. Indeed a great Part of this Country is already laid Waste & in the utmost Danger of becoming a Desert. The great Bodies of Militia that have been in Service this year employed against the Enemy & in quelling the Tories have almost laid Waste the Country & so corrupted the Principles of the People that they think nothing of plundering one another.[16]

Yet when it came to the capture of slaves, Greene's morals appear more transactional. In his exuberant letter to wife Catherine reporting the victory at Cowpens, he lists "60 negroes" among the many spoils captured by Morgan during the battle.[17] And presumably he did not return the "50 negros" Francis Marion collected on the Continental Army's behalf to move rice he collected on the Pee Dee and Waccamaw rivers "out of the enemy's power."[18]

The plundering of the countryside also disturbed the British officers in South Carolina, who reported on it often, though typically without any acknowledgment of their own complicity. In a letter to Lord Cornwallis dated December 5, 1780, Lord Francis Rawdon, writing from Camden, complains:

> Small parties of the enemy are committing every barbarity around us. Two brothers of Major Harrison's, who were ill of small pox, lay at a house about eight miles in our rear. Last night a scouting party of rebels burst into the house, shot both sick men in their beds, tho' they were incapable of making the least defence, and afterwards murdered the old man of the house in the same manner. This day an officer whom I had sent to patrole in my front reported to me that, having come up to a house which a party of rebels had just quitted, he found it stripped of every thing that could be carried off … the woman was left standing in her shift, even her stockings and shoes having been pulled off her and her four children were stripped stark naked. These are the enemies who talk of the laws and usages of war.[19]

The British were no wide-eyed innocents when it came to the practice of terror, or capturing slaves. In his memoir of the Revolutionary War, Colonel William R. Davie condemned the British practice of burning Patriot houses. "This barbarous practice was uniformly enacted by the British officers in the Southern States," he wrote. "However casual the rencounter might be, when it happened at a plantation, their remaining in possession of the ground was always marked by committing the Houses to flames."[20]

In his letter responding to news of Andrew Pickens revoking his parole and joining the Patriot forces, Cornwallis ordered, "If Colonel Pickens has left any Negroes, cattle or other property that may be usefull … I would have it seized and applied accordingly, and I desire that his houses may be burnt, and his plantations, as far as it lies in your power, totally destroyed."[21]

The British might burn houses and capture slaves, but to Cornwallis and the other British officers of the southern theater, Sumter and his men were nothing more than "banditti," the name "Gamecock" practically synonymous with the pillage and plunder ravishing the South Carolina countryside.[22] Part of this British disdain was attributable to Sumter's success against them. Sumter was a talented and resourceful partisan commander fighting an unconventional war, not "banditti." But perhaps it is fair to attribute a portion of his success to a cunning we might today call "street smarts," not dissimilar to the intelligence of U.S. President Donald Trump—an innate understanding for the psychology of the common man.

As Thomas Sumter surveyed the backcountry theater in the wake of his disastrous February 1781 campaign, he recognized the need for a more substantial commitment among his militia troops. During the "Sumter's Rounds" campaign, he had been forced to detain part of his force at gunpoint and saw others walk away in disgust, all the while waiting for an influx of volunteers from the surrounding countryside that never materialized. Worse, perhaps, were the circumventions of Francis Marion, whose support seemed curiously unavailable, the Swamp Fox unresponsive, whenever Sumter needed him most.

Meanwhile, Greene urged Sumter to "rouse the people of South Carolina" for military operations in Cornwallis's rear.[23] Writing to Sumter on March 8, 1781, from Hillsboro, Governor John Rutledge urged Sumter to "pursue such measures as may be most serviceable to the State." He also addressed the apparent rift with Francis Marion, along with expectations for militia leader Andrew Pickens, who was returning to the state after serving with Greene in North Carolina: "I doubt not that Gen. Marion (to whom I have wrote) & Gen. Pickens (to whom I have spoke on the subject) will forward your views to the utmost of their power."[24]

To Marion, on the same subject, Rutledge wrote, "I am persuaded of the continuance of your utmost attention, and hope you will cultivate a good understanding with Gen'ls Sumter and Pickens, and do everything in your power to forward the former's views."[25]

But Sumter was too wily to rely on Marion's obedience. Fool him once, perhaps, but there was too much of the Gamecock in the Swamp Fox, and vice versa, for their trust to ever be complete. What he needed, Sumter decided, were regular troops under his deliberate command—troops that would not abandon him at their personal whim or inspiration, as volunteer militia tended to do, or fail to answer his commands. The troops he desired would be of a prolonged commitment, not the four- to six-week militia term, which was really no commitment at all. They would serve for a regular enlistment, so that the Gamecock could undertake the type of protracted campaign he envisioned against the British outposts, the type of campaign his superiors were demanding.

By rank and by innate authority, by the pleadings of Greene and the tacit approval of Rutledge, he was authorized to organize such a body. The trouble was he had no incentive for their commitment, no way to pay or otherwise reward their service. But it is true that desperation breeds inspiration, and as Sumter pondered his dilemma, we can imagine his mind returned to the black day at the end of Sumter's Rounds, when he had desperately offered his disgruntled militia captured slaves as an enticement for their continued support. Surely this cunning man recognized the economic status slave ownership conveyed and its appeal to the type of young man who might enlist for military service. Though his scheme had not been effective then, some seed of inspiration emerged there, and for reasons we cannot now know, he decided to institute it on a broader scale.

And so, sometime after the end of Sumter's Rounds, on or about March 8, 1781, and before March 28 of that same month, Sumter formulated and announced his plan for what would become known as "Sumter's Law": a plan to raise a regular, standing militia of 10-month enlistments. This body would, of course, report directly to him, and be comprised of officers, noncommissioned officers, and enlisted men.

On March 28, still clearly smarting from Marion's failure to support him during "Sumter's Rounds," Sumter wrote to Marion:

> It was exceedingly mortifying for me, after so much pains taken to be deprived of a conference with you, a circumstance much to be lamented ... My unfortunate failing herein and withal finding contrary to my expectation, that you had neither men, or surplus of any kind, and the force I had with me but small and from many causes decreasing, rendered my retreat at once both necessary and difficult. I find that disorders are prevalent in your Brigade ... To obviate which evil as far as possible, I have adopted measures truly disagreeable, such as can only be justified by our circumstance and the necessity of the case ... to which I propose raising several Regiments of Light Dragoons upon the State establishment, agreeably to the enclosed sketch of a plan for that purposes.[26]

The proposal Sumter enclosed to Marion has been lost to time, but from a letter written by Colonel Richard Hampton to Major John Hampton on April 2, 1781, we have the terms consistent with what Sumter must have sent:

> Bro. Wade has joined Gen'l. Sumter, and has left all his property in the possession of the British and Tories; he now fights them hard. Bro. Henry is raising a regular Regiment of Light Horse, as also Col. Middleton, Hawthorn hill. I have accepted the Majority in Middleton's Regiment. Bro. Wade I believe will also raise a regiment. It will not be amiss to mention the terms on which they are to be raised, and the number each Regiment is to consist of. The troops are to enlist for ten months, each Regiment to have one Lieut. Colonel, one Major, five Sergeants, ten Lieutenants; each company two Serg'ts, twenty-five privates—the pay to be as follows:
>
> > Each Colonel to receive three grown negroes and one small negro;
> > Major to receive three grown negroes;
> > Captain, two grown negroes;
> > Lieutenants, one large and one small negro;
> > The Staff, one large and one small negro;
> > The Sergeants, one and a quarter negro;
> > Each private, one grown negro;
>
> And to be furnished with one coat, two waistcoats, two pair overalls, two shirts, two pair stockings, one pair shoes and spurs; one horseman's cap, one blanket, (and one half bushel salt, to those who have families); with two-thirds of all articles captured from the enemy except negroes and military stores; and salvage allowed them for all the articles belonging to our friends which we may capture from the enemy, and to be equipped with a sword, pistols, horse, saddle and bridle, &c. Should you meet with any young men who are willing to turn into this kind of service, you may assure them that the terms will be strictly complyed with, and the General directs that any who may think proper to come out with the waggons in order to join the said service, are to be served with provisions for themselves and horses.[27]

Sumter's Law proposed a wage paid in human bondage, the bounty to be paid by slaves captured from Loyalists. Horses, arms, clothing, and other supplies were also to be "furnished" from the countryside. At essence, it was a plan of sanctioned "looting," with pillage and marauding an unfortunate byproduct. If Sumter's Law wasn't responsible for introducing sinister elements of class struggle into the Revolutionary cause through its confiscation of slaves without due process of law, it certainly exacerbated it. And aside from its official adoption of thievery and plundering as a policy of the state, its tearing apart of families was simply inhumane, at least from our modern perspective.

Sumter's Law illustrates the role of slave ownership as a pathway to socioeconomic status in South Carolina, along with other regions of the Antebellum South. Among its many issues, Sumter expected Marion, Pickens, and other militia leaders to recruit his State Troops from within their own ranks, infuriating Marion.

In a letter dated May 6, 1781, Sumter addresses Marion's opposition, referencing Marion's protest to some unnamed third party, and taking umbrage at Marion's questioning of his authority:

> I revere the citizen who is tenacious of the laws of his country. I lament their being so much abused. If I have done it, I think myself accountable and shall no doubt be called upon by the gentleman to whom you say you shall represent the matter, and if he is unacquainted with my motives and the step I have taken, should be happy to have his opinion upon that head ... but I have not a doubt but he and all impartial men, will applaud an undertaking which promised so much good to the United States ... especially as it was the last and only measure that could be adopted for its security ... As to the powers by which I act, they ought not to be called in question by any man, until gentlemen whom it might concern, had used proper means to obtain information.[28]

For all his preaching on the moral outrage of plunder and pillage, Greene tacitly approved the terms of Sumter's Law, no doubt because he was by now plotting his return to South Carolina and was relying on the Gamecock for support. "Altho' I am a great enemy to plundering, yet I think the horses belonging to the Inhabitants within the Enemy's lines should be taken from them," he agreed, explicitly refusing to include the word "slave" in his correspondence. He tried to insist Sumter issue "certificates" for captured goods: "Indeed any horses, or any other kind of property whether taken from Whig or Tory, certificates ought to be given, that justice may be done to the inhabitants hereafter; and if any discrimination is necessary with the people, Government may make it when the certificates are presented for payment."[29] How a human being, stolen from his home, ripped from his family, and awarded to someone else as their personal property in return for services rendered could be reimbursed through a certificate, he does not explain. In the moment, Greene needed reliable soldiers to fight the British; the thorny details of Sumter's Law would have to be sorted out later.

Ultimately, Sumter's Law created more harm than good, and as we shall see, haunted Sumter, not only in the continued deterioration of his relationship with Marion, but also long after the Revolutionary War. Though Andrew Pickens contributed his quota of State Troops, and Governor Rutledge gave his tacit approval, Sumter's Law only raised three regiments, and those undersized.[30] If its tepid response contributed somehow to Sumter's recalcitrance of April and May, such evidence is lost to the tides of time. But certainly Sumter's Law in some way added fuel to the boiling cauldron that would soon bubble over in the aftermath of Hobkirk's Hill.

CHAPTER 6

War of Posts

After Cornwallis's pyrrhic victory at Guilford Courthouse, Nathanael Greene was eager to draw him once more into battle. Cornwallis lost 25 percent of his army on March 15, 1781, more than five hundred men dead or wounded. Greene sensed Cornwallis was ripe for the *coup de grace*. But his senses were driven by need. With expiring militia enrollments, his own army equally battered, and little prospect for resupply in the Haw River basin where he now pursued Cornwallis, Greene knew this opportunity would soon pass him by. But after chasing Greene across the Carolinas for most of the winter, Cornwallis was not about to fall into another of the Continental general's traps. Cornwallis steadily retreated toward Wilmington, North Carolina, where he could resupply and seek naval transport to more advantageous theaters.

Realizing Cornwallis could not be caught, Greene reassessed his strategy. His options were limited. Desperate for supplies, and with no naval support, a protracted siege of Cornwallis at Wilmington was impossible. He considered joining his comrade the Marquis de Lafayette in Virginia, where Lafayette was engaged with a British raiding expedition initially under turncoat Benedict Arnold. In hindsight, a move toward Virginia seems his most prudent option. Prior to the "Race to the Dan," his brilliant strategic retreat across central North Carolina, Greene established a system of supply depots in southern Virginia that could now be employed to his advantage. A unification with Lafayette's Continental Army reinforcements promised a more reliable fighting force than the Carolinas' erratic volunteer militia. And Virginia was the most powerful and important colony in America, a stage more suitable for military glory than the Carolina wilderness.

As Greene pondered these contingencies, Lafayette sent word that Admiral Mariot Arbuthnot had reinforced the British in Virginia. Writing from North Carolina's Deep River on March 29, Greene wrote to Washington of Lafayette's intelligence: "If this report is true our flattering prospects are at an end in that quarter ... I am at a loss what is best to be done ... In this critical and distressing situation I am determined to carry the War immediately into South Carolina. The Enemy will be obliged to follow us or give up their posts in that State."[1]

Like his decision to split his army in December 1780, sending Daniel Morgan west of the Broad River for his fated encounter with Banastre Tarleton at Cowpens, Greene's return to South Carolina in April 1781 is one of the legendary decisions in American military history. Yet it was a gamble defying the laws of military strategy, then and now. The decision violated established military protocol by leaving an enemy army unchallenged, exposing himself to attack in the rear from Cornwallis. Although Greene's interior logic now makes sense, it was fraught with strategic peril. Well aware of his transgressions, Greene revealed his method, if not his madness, in a letter to North Carolina officer James Emmet: "Don't be surprised if my movements don't correspond with your Ideas of military propriety. War is an intricate business, and people are often saved by ways and means they least look for or expect."[2]

Greene hoped to deliberately confuse Cornwallis, perhaps provoking him into another trap. To his confidante the Baron von Steuben, the Prussian military officer famous for drilling the army into the Continental Army at Valley Forge in 1778, Greene wrote: "[The] boldness [of my plan] will make [the British] think I have secret reasons which they cannot comprehend."[3]

Henry Lee wrote approvingly of his commander's unconventional tactics. "If, as I believe, a general is sure to act wisely when he takes the course most dreaded by his adversary, the late decision of General Greene was indubitably correct," wrote Lee.[4]

For his part, Cornwallis seemed offended. "Greene took advantage of my being obliged to come to this place [Wilmington], and has marched into South Carolina," he wrote huffily. But not offended enough to strike at his opponent's bait. Long obsessed with a domino strategy for seizing the South, Cornwallis believed that by moving northward through South and North Carolina to Virginia in force, he could leave the states in his wake subjugated. That this strategy was a failure, Cornwallis would by now well admit, but that didn't mean he was in a mood to turn around. A return to South Carolina meant a long march involving numerous river crossings in spring rain, with Patriot partisans sniping at his flanks. His thoughts increasingly turned to Virginia, where he believed the war's final play could be made.

"If we mean an offensive war in America we must abandon New York and bring our whole force into Virginia, we must then have a stake to fight for, and a successful battle may give us America," he wrote to British General William Phillips, now serving with Benedict Arnold in the Chesapeake. "[Let] us quit the Carolinas (which cannot be held defensively while Virginia can so easily be armed against us)."[5]

Though Henry Lee was no confidante of Cornwallis, he was a participant in these events, and claimed some insight on Cornwallis's dilemma: "For never was a leader more affected than Cornwallis was, by the disclosure of the enemy's object. Day after day did his lordship revolve in his mind the difficulties of his situation ... Sometimes he determined to follow Greene ... at other times he would proceed into Virginia ... At length he decided on the latter measure."[6]

Cornwallis's decision proved disastrous, leading to the surrender of his army at Yorktown on October 19, 1781. In the bargain, he ignited a bitter, years-long feud with Henry Clinton, commander-in-chief of the British Army in the American colonies, though it was a feud that had smoldered for years.

Clinton's orders to Cornwallis in June 1780 were clear: leaving Charleston to return to New York in June 1780, Clinton had commanded Cornwallis "to secure the South and recover North Carolina." Cornwallis might "assist in operations" in Virginia only when the Carolinas are safe from any attack."[7]

Cornwallis's move to Virginia now disregarded those orders. Not coincidentally, he didn't request Clinton's approval to invade Virginia, one of several transgressions the two would debate ad nauseam after the war. Yet Cornwallis had solicited the support of Lord Germain, Secretary of State for America in the British cabinet, with overall authority over administration of the American war, in a secret correspondence. Germain himself believed control of the Chesapeake Bay was the key to ending the long American conflict. Cornwallis surely suspected his insubordination would please his masters back in England, even if it infuriated Clinton. In this assumption, he guessed wrong twice. Though he ultimately went on to a distinguished career in the British Army, serving successfully in the Napoleonic Wars and as Governor-General of India, his unauthorized move to Virginia was a black mark on his career following the war, as was his disgraceful public feud with Clinton.

Greene would remain wary of Cornwallis as he turned his Continental Army back toward South Carolina, but the famous earl, dubiously regarded as Britain's greatest Revolutionary War field commander, would never more dominate his strategic priorities. Instead Greene would initiate his famous "War of Posts" by returning with his army of 1,500 to South Carolina and attack its British outposts one by one.

For support he would rely on Thomas Sumter and the South Carolina militia. "I … have written Genl. Sumter to collect the Militia and aid the operations," he wrote to George Washington in his letter explaining his decision to return to South Carolina.[8]

To Sumter he wrote on March 30, explaining his strategy. The militia was deserting him, he explained. He could not provision his army in North Carolina, nor could he hope to fight Cornwallis "upon equal terms after our Militia leave us. All these considerations have determined me to change my route, and push directly into South Carolina; and if our Army can be subsisted there we can fight them upon as good terms with your aid as we can here." If the British reinforced one outpost by drawing from the others, those weakened outposts would be vulnerable to the militia of Andrew Pickens and Francis Marion, commanding in the west and east, respectively. "I beg you will therefore give orders to Genls Pickens and Merion [Francis Marion, bracket from Greene's editor] to collect all the Militia they can to co-operate with us."[9]

Meanwhile, Sumter's main militia would support his attack against Greene's first and most important objective—the British outpost at Camden. Or so he hoped.

As previously noted, that Greene now advocated precisely the type of partisan campaign he had eschewed in his letter to Sumter of January 8, 1781, is a point of contention for defenders of Sumter's legacy. In that letter he wrote, "Partizan strokes in war are like the garnish of a table … You may strike a hundred strokes, and reap little benefit from them, unless you have go(od) Army to take advantage of your success … It is not a war of posts but a contest for States dependent upon opinion."[10] We can surmise the hypersensitive Sumter also recognized this paradox, though his response to Greene, written on April 7, makes no mention of it.[11]

Debating Greene's capricious nature, however, only leads us to the conclusion he was prone to change his mind. More relevant is to question whether, given Sumter's mercurial disposition, and his well-known indignation over Morgan's command at Cowpens, Greene was naïve to now rely on Sumter's cooperation just three months later. Anne King Gregorie, a defender of his legacy, argues as much. But it is also possible Greene simply miscalculated Sumter's disposition. During the course of the war, again and again, Greene was disappointed by those who put their own interests above the great Patriot cause. If Greene's commitment to the cause was absolute, he assumed as much from others.

And since his conciliatory letter on February 3, the one that reads in part, "In what respect General Morgan's command embarrassed you I am at a loss to imagine; but I dare say I cou'd explain it to your perfect satisfaction in a few minutes, could I have the happiness to see you,"[12] Greene had enjoyed a cordial correspondence with Sumter, perhaps convincing himself the Gamecock was willing to forgive and forget. "Nothing in the Summit of my Power Shall be Neglected that may in the least tend to further your operations against the Enemy," Sumter wrote to Greene on April 7, 1781.[13]

In return Greene promised Sumter troops—approximately five hundred North Carolina militia to be raised around Salisbury, North

Carolina, would be placed under Sumter's command—and a cannon. On April 13, Sumter wrote Greene a cautionary letter outlining difficulties in raising troops but still spoke optimistically of supporting Greene upon his arrival at Camden.[14] "Am happy to understand that our plan of operations agrees with your sentiments," Greene responded to Sumter on April 14.[15]

With Greene's army destitute, his strategic options limited, and Sumter committing his support in writing, Greene likely assumed Sumter's bruised ego was now healed with his recently wounded body. He had no reason to believe Sumter's letters betrayed anything other than his true intentions.

Perhaps Greene *needed* to believe Sumter's commitment, for if the return to South Carolina was to be a military success, Greene must have food and supplies for his troops. Thanks to his successful but unhappy service as quartermaster general, Greene possessed a keen understanding of the important role logistics and supply played in the success of any military campaign.

In a letter to Thomas Jefferson on March 23, 1781, before his decision to return to South Carolina, Greene warned the Virginia governor his army would be forced to "fall back" from his pursuit of Cornwallis unless it receives provisions "immediately."[16] In another letter to Jefferson on March 27, 1781, he complains of militia support: "Since I wrote I find a considerable part of the Militia claim their discharge at an earlier period than I expected ... The struggle here is great, the situation of the Army precarious. The least misfortune will bring the war to your doors. You will feel the necessity, therefore of giving me immediate support."[17] Greene would find sympathy but little support from the future United States president. In a similar letter to North Carolina Governor Abner Nash on March 29, Greene wrote: "I wish it was in my power to pursue them [Cornwallis's Army] farther, but want of provisions and a considerable part of the Virginia Militias time of service being expird, will prevent our further pursuit."[18]

A world-class complainer, Greene undoubtedly suspected there was little even Thomas Jefferson could do to feed his army. The active militia of South Carolina seemed his most promising hope. And it is from this period that a dubious incident from Thomas Sumter's spring campaign seemed much on Greene's mind. In a correspondence to Samuel Huntington on March 23, 1781, Greene makes reference to Sumter's capture of a British supply train during "Sumter's Rounds," the one containing banded chests thought to contain British gold. Though that expedition ended disastrously, the capture of British supply in the South Carolina interior might answer at least part of his logistical miseries. And there was no better bandit of British supply than Thomas Sumter.[19]

Greene now turned his army toward Camden, approximately 150 miles from his position on North Carolina's Deep River. Located on a spur of the "Great Wagon Road" where it touched the Wateree River, Camden was the closest thing to a "town" in the north-central portion of the South Carolina colony, strategically located to serve as a dumping off point for settlers in the colony's central interior. That it was also on one of the main trading routes to the Port of Charleston made it an important north–south meeting point in this increasingly populated region of the South Carolina backcountry.

Continental General Horatio Gates certainly found it so back in August 1780, when his southward bound Continental Army collided with the north-bound Cornwallis there on August 16. Gates's ill-conceived encounter, known to history as the "Battle of Camden," was disastrous for the American cause. Of the three thousand members of Gates's Southern Army, between nine hundred and one thousand men were wounded and/or taken prisoner in the battle. Estimates of the Continental dead were from 250 to eight hundred. With his army in chaos, Gates mounted a horse and rode to Charlotte, North Carolina, 70 miles away, then found a fresh mount and rode the final 120 miles to his headquarters in Hillsboro, North Carolina, without stopping.[20]

We can imagine that the shattered, decimated, ruined Continental Army of only seven hundred men that finally arrived in Hillsboro days and weeks later was none too happy to find Gates waiting for them there. This same seven hundred that still comprised the heart of Greene's Army must have found their leadership now much improved, if their stomachs just as hungry.

By 1781, several roads spurred off from the Camden settlement in all directions; Greene likely followed the same route down from the Pee Dee River in April 1781 that Gates had followed down from Hillsboro a mere seven months before. The modern-day equivalent would be U.S. Highway 1, which connects the North Carolina Triangle area to Southern Pines, North Carolina, then proceeds on to Camden, a part of the Carolinas called the "Pine Barrens." On both occasions—Gate's march to Camden and Greene's—this desolate name would prove to be an accurate description of the supply and forage to be found along the route.

"The little provisions and forage which were produced on the banks of its small streams were exhausted or taken away by the enemy, and by the hoards of banditti, what little might remain, out of his way," recalled Colonel Otho Holland Williams, the Maryland officer who had the misfortune of serving as Horatio Gates's adjutant general, or chief administrative officer, during Gates's disastrous Camden campaign.[21]

During his journey along this same route eight months later, Greene found the Pine Barrens equally inhospitable. His correspondence during the march to Camden is a litany of complaints about lack of horses, shoes, ammunition, food, rum, and most importantly, troops. "We began our march from Deep River on the 7th [of April 1781], and arrived in the neighbourhood of Camden on the 19th," Greene wrote to Samuel Huntington on April 22, 1781. "All the Country through which we past is disaffected, and the same Guards and escorts were necessary to collect Provisions and forage, as if in an open and avowed Enemies Country."[22] To Thomas Sumter, writing on April 19, Greene complained, "The Country is barren, and promises us no hope of support. My greatest dependence is on you for supplies and Corn and Meal."[23]

As he marched toward Camden, Greene dispatched Henry Lee's "Legion," a mixed force of about three hundred cavalry and light infantry, to reconnoiter with Francis Marion. Their objective was British Lieutenant Colonel John Watson and his British expeditionary force of about five hundred men operating in the eastern portion of South Carolina. Lee's orders were to keep Watson from reinforcing Rawdon at Camden. Lee found Marion at his lair in the swamps of the Black River on April 14. "Active operations now became practicable," wrote Lee, "and on the evening of the 15th, Marion and Lee [writing of himself in third person] took a position in the open country, with Watson to their left, considerably below them, and on the route for the fort called by his name, which he had erected."[24]

Lee was born into a prominent Virginia family that dated its ancestry back to the earliest days of the English monarchy. His ancestor Lionel Lee, the first Earl of Lichfield, raised a company of gentlemen cavaliers that accompanied Richard the Lion Hearted in the Third Crusade. Henry Lee was born on January 29, 1756, to Henry and Lucy Lee and lived a young life of privilege, becoming an outstanding horseman and attending Princeton College (then the College of New Jersey). He was preparing to study law in England when the Revolutionary War erupted. Commissioned a captain in the Virginia cavalry when he was just 20 years old, Lee's company joined the 1st Continental Dragoons in 1776, where he soon became intimate with George Washington, who often sought the company of his fellow Virginians. They were lifelong friends: it was Lee who wrote of Washington, "First in war, first in peace, first in the hearts of his countrymen," for the founding father's funeral oration.

Lee distinguished himself in service with Washington, displaying a mastery of the partisan fighting that would later characterize his service in the Southern Campaign. His skillful horsemanship earned him the nickname "Light Horse Harry." Promoted to major in 1778 and given his first command, Lee scored one of the great victories of the war with his surprise attack on the British garrison at Paulus Hook, New Jersey, in August 1779. Though a relatively minor victory, it boosted American morale and earned him one of only eight gold medals awarded by the Continental Congress during the war for bravery and valor.

He was promoted to lieutenant colonel on November 30, 1780 and given command of his "Legion," the three cavalry companies already under his command plus three infantry companies. The Legion's original strength was one hundred cavalry and 180 infantry. Lee outfitted his cavalry in short green jackets, similar to the jackets worn by Banastre

Tarleton's British Legion, and insisted on the finest quality horses for his men.

Lee was well known to Nathanael Greene through his service with Washington, and when Greene was transferred to the Southern Army in fall 1780, he requested Lee join him. During the Southern Campaign, he was arguably Greene's most trusted officer, usually acting with unusual autonomy, often in conjunction with Marion's partisans. After the war, however, his fortunes turned. Though he would serve one term as governor of Virginia from 1792 to 1795, he was a poor businessman, speculating in bad real estate and living beyond his means. He declared bankruptcy and, beginning in 1808, served a year in debtor's prison. But Lee's misfortune was America's gain, for it was during this time that he wrote his memoirs, published in 1812, as an effort to get out of debt.

Unfortunately for Lee, the memoir was not a financial success during his time, though it has endured as a lively and essential account of the Revolutionary War, especially the Southern Campaign. Lee's biographer Charles Royster notes, "Lee was not always a reliable storyteller, but he made his narrative irresistible. For many dramatic episodes his account is the only surviving one or the one with the most vivid details." An 1869 edition of the memoir was edited by Lee's son, Robert E. Lee, the only significant writing published by the Confederate general outside of his military correspondence.[25]

An interesting footnote to Lee's memoirs is that, in it, he takes credit for Greene's decision to turn the Continental Army from its pursuit of Cornwallis back to South Carolina. Again referring to himself in the third person, Lee writes: "The proposer suggested, that leaving Cornwallis to act as he might choose, the army should be led back to South Carolina … From the first moment the substitute was presented to the mind of Greene, it received his decided preference."[26]

The editors of Greene's papers cast doubt on Lee's claim, noting Greene's first written reference to his "War of Posts" strategy appeared in a letter to George Washington dated March 29, almost a week before Lee claimed to have proposed the plan himself.[27] Nevertheless, Lee's description of this discussion provides a flattering account of Greene's strategic mind at work:

> General Greene gave to the subject that full and critical investigation which
> it merited, and which, by long habit, had become familiar to his mind. He
> perceived advantages and disadvantages attendant upon either course ... and
> convinced that he had much to hope, and little to apprehend, from returning
> to South Carolina, he determined to carry the war into that State. No sooner
> had he decided, than he commenced operations.[28]

Watson was campaigning on the coast around Georgetown, South
Carolina, leaving the eponymously named Fort Watson a prime
target for Lee and Marion's combined force. This was the same
well-constructed fort Sumter attacked in February in a futile attempt
to recapture the lost British supply train. On April 15, the day after
their meeting on Black River, Marion and Lee arrived at Fort Watson
and initiated a siege, cutting off the fort's water supply. With Watson
and the majority of his force still away, the fort was lightly manned;
only about 140 men under the command of British Lieutenant James
McKay were inside. However, the Patriots had no artillery, and McKay
was amply provisioned. And after McKay constructed a well inside
the stockade, the fort appeared impenetrable. Meanwhile, a smallpox
epidemic struck Marion's militia, demoralizing the men and causing
many to desert.[29]

With time running out, and the return of Watson an ever-present
threat, South Carolina militia colonel Hezekiah Maham suggested a
novel approach to the dilemma: he would construct a raised tower from
which the Patriots could fire inside the fort. Atop the tower would
be a platform with a log parapet (wall) providing defensive cover for
sharpshooters. Marion and Lee approved the plan, waiting five days for
Maham and his crew to cut and fit the logs. On the night of April 22,
the prefabricated structure was raised outside the fort.[30]

At daylight on April 23, Marion's sharpshooters climbed the tower
and started pouring rifle fire into Fort Watson through small loopholes
in the floor. The fire from above gave cover to militia and Continental
volunteers, who stormed the fort and began tearing down the abatis.
McKay surrendered as he saw the assault party ready to storm the fort.
Lee and Marion offered generous terms to the men inside: officers were
granted parole and could take their swords and possessions with them to
Charleston, where they were to await regular exchange.

As the first post to fall in Greene's "War of Posts" strategy, Fort Watson's capture boosted the morale of an otherwise depleted army. More importantly, its capture played a role in effectively delaying Watson from reinforcing Camden. After learning of Lee and Marion's union, Watson fell back to Georgetown before initiating a circuitous route to Camden, first diverting south to the British garrison at Monck's Corner for additional troops before resuming his course north. With Marion and Lee's combined force now in pursuit, Watson was forced to cross six creeks, build a 60-foot bridge over a seventh, and cut roads through swamps of thick river cane in his efforts to reach Camden.[31] The diversion cost precious time; Watson and his reinforcements did not arrive at Camden until May 7, well after they were needed there.[32]

While Marion and Lee succeeded wildly in diverting Watson to the east, Andrew Pickens was finding more measured success in the west. Pickens was a long-time militia leader from the Long Cane settlement on Long Cane Creek in the southwestern corner of South Carolina. After fighting with distinction during the early part of the war, he'd taken parole when Clinton captured Charleston, but returned to action in late 1780 after Tory raiders burned his settlement. Pickens commanded the militia ably under Morgan at Cowpens and continued to campaign with Greene during the famous "Race to the Dan," but had petitioned Greene for a return home shortly before the battle at Guilford Courthouse. Sorry to lose his most loyal and obedient militia commander, Greene agreed on the condition Pickens would continue militia operations in the region surrounding the British outpost at Ninety-Six in western South Carolina.[33] In a correspondence after the war, Pickens recalled his orders from Greene were to "harass the foraging parties at Ninety-Six and Augusta [GA] and as much as possible encourage the desponding inhabitants."

It was a promise Pickens struggled to uphold. In a letter to Greene written April 8, 1781, Pickens complained, "it will be difficult to maintain even a small party for lack of provisions."[34] As April continued, Pickens's partisans from the Long Cane settlement in western South Carolina increasingly deserted him—no surprise given their distance from Camden and the upcoming planting season. On April 13, Sumter advised Greene he had detached four regiments to support Pickens, with orders to "Move Down & Take a position on the Tyger River Near the Fish Dam Foard to indeavour to Cover the Country & Collect Provision, & if hard pressed by the enemy to pass Broad River to this Side, [the eastern side] Rather than Retreat to wards the enemy."[35]

By April 25, however, Pickens was in camp with Sumter on the Broad River. "He has none of his brigade with him," reported Sumter, who ordered Pickens back to the Ninety-Six region with a militia regiment under Colonel Hays, "to take command of the troops in that quarter."[36] Despite Pickens's mixed success at raising a militia body, his efforts did keep British Lieutenant Colonel John Harris Cruger, commanding at Ninety-Six, from reinforcing Camden due to fear of partisan attack.

Finally arriving at Camden after the desolate march, Greene was disheartened by the garrison's considerable defenses. Commanded by Francis, Lord Rawdon, Camden's four corners were guarded by earthwork fortifications, with a fifth placed at the "Great Wagon Road." A large stockade defended the town's center.[37]

Rawdon was one of Cornwallis's ablest officers. Now only 26 years old, the Irish nobleman had distinguished himself as a combat officer in several campaigns. By 1778, the young Rawdon had earned the rank of lieutenant colonel and later became adjutant general when Henry Clinton assumed command of the British Army later that same year. Recognizing that many of the Americans willing to enlist in the British forces were recent Irish immigrants, Clinton commanded Rawdon to raise the "Volunteers of Ireland," which became one of the British Army's ablest provincial corps during the remainder of the war. But Rawdon's forthright honesty soon put him in conflict with the temperamental Clinton, and he had resigned his adjutant general position in September 1779, informing Clinton he had "no longer the honour of being upon those terms of mutual confidence in a station whose duties are most irksome to me."[38]

Rawdon would serve as a formidable foe to Greene throughout the Southern Campaign. Following his service in America, he would command with distinction during the Napoleonic Wars. Later he would serve as Governor General of India beginning in 1813, securing British domination of the Indian subcontinent. For his distinguished service in India, he eventually would be made the "Marquess of Hastings."[39]

Though Rawdon was in overall command of the approximately eight thousand soldiers defending Britain's interest in the South Carolina and Georgia interiors, with him at Camden were only nine hundred troops. Greene's ragtag army of 1,500—comprised mostly of 1,200 Continental regulars from Virginia and Maryland, along with approximately 250 North Carolina militia and William Washington's cavalry of fewer than a hundred men—outnumbered Rawdon's, but Camden's formidable defenses made an attack on the post infeasible.[40]

Now it was time for Sumter's help. As his army approached Camden, Greene's pleas to the Gamecock for assistance grew increasingly strident. "If we can get provisions, and you can raise a considerable force to co-operate with us, I think we shall perplex the enemy not a little, and perhaps do them an irreparable injury," he wrote on April 7.[41] Then, on April 19, his anxiety obviously increasing, he wrote to Sumter: "The Army has arrived and taken position within three miles of Camden ... The Country is barren, and promises us no hope of support. My greatest dependence is on you for supplies of Corn and Meal ... I want to know very much your situation, and how you have disposed yourself, so as to cooperate with our Army on any particular emergency."[42] And again on April 23: "I wrote you a day or two ago of our arrival in the neighborhood of Camden, and desired to know your strength and situation, to which I have received no answer ... I long to hear from you that I may know how to take my measures respecting Provisions and other matters."[43]

While Greene was maneuvering around Camden, Sumter had moved to the west and established camp on the Broad River to cut off supplies and reinforcement from Ninety-Six. Admittedly, Greene assented to this movement. "You will collect your force with all possible speed, and endeavour to take a position ... where you may be enabled to cut off, or interrupt the communication between Camden and other posts of the Enemy, keeping it in your power to cooperate with, or *join* [italics in original] this Army," read Greene's letter to Sumter of April 14.[44]

Greene evidently hoped to keep Sumter close enough to support him if necessary, without once more offending the prickly Gamecock. Though he did have enough troops on hand to scourge the Tories in the Mobley's and Sandy River settlements, and to dispatch a brigade with Pickens to Ninety-Six, Sumter was otherwise incapable of responding to Greene's requests, or at least that's what he later argued.[45]

More infuriating than his future excuses, however, was his lack of response. The once sanguine and seemingly cooperative Thomas Sumter now turned suspiciously silent, the force of up to a thousand men he had optimistically offered for Greene's aid nowhere in sight. "General Sumter I have not heard of," Greene complained to Lee on April 22. "I wish you could learn where he is and inform me."[46] And again on April 24, he complained to Lee: "General Sumter has not joined the operations as early by about a week as he promised, which lays me under many disadvantages."[47]

With Sumter's reinforcements nowhere in sight, his provisions growing more depleted by the day, and Camden's defenses seemingly impenetrable, Greene desperately sought some strategic advantage against Rawdon. Late in the evening of April 19, Greene ordered Captain Robert Kirkwood and his band of Delaware Continentals to probe Logtown, a small cluster of log homes about a mile north of Camden. Kirkwood captured the settlement but endured heavy fire from Camden's advance works. Deeming the British defenses too stout for assault, Greene decided to establish camp the next day not at Logtown but on Hobkirk's Hill, a slightly higher ridge about another mile north.[48]

Greene began setting up for a siege of Camden by securing the surrounding area, the only solution he saw for taking the outpost without the manpower for an assault. On April 21, he ordered Kirkwood and William Washington's Continental cavalry to raid British positions west of Camden. Kirkwood and Washington burned a house in one of the British redoubts, but more significantly returned with 40 horses and 50 head of cattle.[49]

Receiving a false report Watson was approaching from the southeast, Greene moved his army across Big and Little Pine Tree Creeks to cut off Watson's rumored approach. After an arduous journey—Greene's army forced to build a road and bridge through the swamp—they camped on Paint Hill for two days until Greene received word Watson was not, in fact, approaching. As Greene ordered his troops back to Hobkirk's Hill, he received the welcome news that a repaired cannon was returning to him from Lynches Creek, 20 miles to the northeast. This intelligence would prove critical in the battle to come.[50]

CHAPTER 7

Fight, Get Beat, Rise, Fight Again

On the night of April 24, 1781, Lieutenant Colonel Francis, Lord Rawdon, received an American deserter at his Camden headquarters.

The deserter reported to Rawdon the American army was without artillery and dangerously low on supplies. "I had procured information that the enemy with a view of hazarding an assault had sent their cannon and baggage a day's march in their rear, but that abandoning the resolution, they had detached all their militia to bring up again their artillery," Rawdon later reported to Cornwallis.[1]

Though the news suggested Greene was vulnerable, Rawdon had his own concerns. His force of approximately nine hundred men was comprised primarily of American volunteers, mostly Provincials, recruited in the northeast and trained by the British Army, including Rawdon's own unit, the Volunteers of Ireland, along with a few hundred South Carolina royalists. His only regular British Army company was the 63rd Regiment.[2]

Like Greene's, Rawdon's "stock of provisions was but scanty." He had hoped for reinforcement from Lieutenant Colonel John Watson, commanding a force of about five hundred men, "who had long been detached with a considerable corps for the purpose of dispersing the plunderers that infested our eastern frontier," but now had news that the position of Francis Marion, fighting with Lieutenant Colonel Henry Lee's mounted Legion, "precluded the hope of Lt. Colonel Watson joining me."[3]

An able and industrious officer, Rawdon decided to capitalize on Greene's weakened state, hoping to surprise the Continental general before his artillery returned. "Altho' my intelligence was somewhat tardy, I hoped I should still be in time to avail myself of this conjuncture." He planned an attack for early the following morning, April 25. "By arming our musicians, our drummers and in short every thing that could carry a firelock, I mustered about nine hundred for the field, sixty of whom were dragoons. With this force and two six pounders we marched about 10 o'clock ... leaving our redoubts to the care of the militia and a few sick soldiers."[4]

Rawdon hoped to initiate his attack early that morning but was delayed because part of his cavalry was out foraging. At his redoubts in Camden, Rawdon left only "Negroes and Tories," reported Samuel Mathis, a resident of Camden who had been captured by the British during the fall of Charleston and paroled back to his hometown. Mathis continued:

> ... and every man of his whole army, in the most silent and secret manner, without any drums, fife horn or any noise or general parade all went off as they got ready, the cavalry first, then men and officers all on foot leading their horses, the infantry following in open order and trailed arms, taking down the valley in the Southeast corner of the town, in the opposite direction from where the American Troops lay ... The weather had been dry and it was a beautiful clear sunshiny day rather warm for the season of the year.[5]

Greene had set up his camp at Hobkirk's Hill in battle formation, hoping to goad the British into just such an attack. Desertions continued to plague Greene, and it is likely his army was now a few hundred men smaller than the 1,500 or so who had arrived at Camden on April 19. To maintain discipline and battle readiness, Greene ordered, "Roll is to be taken at least three times a day, and absentees reported and punished ... Every part of the army must be ready to stand to arms at a Moments warning."[6]

At the front of a defensive formation of three lines he had placed two companies of pickets, the 1st Virginia and the 2nd Maryland Companies, some of his most seasoned and experienced Continental troops. Captain Robert Kirkwood and his company of Delaware Continentals were positioned in the woods to support the pickets. Straddling both sides of the Waxhaws Road was his main line of defense, with Colonel Otho Williams commanding the 1st and 2nd Maryland Regiments on the left side of the road in a line that extended eastward into the swamps of Pine Tree Creek. Brigadier General Isaac Huger commanded the 1st and 2nd Virginia Regiments on the right side of the road. To the rear, and held in reserve, were William Washington's Continental Light Dragoons of about 87 soldiers and North Carolina militia. Also in reserve were "Irish Light Infantry," a force of hand-picked men from the 1st and 2nd Maryland Regiments, nicknamed for the Irish heritage of most of its soldiers.[7]

Conspicuously absent were Thomas Sumter's South Carolina partisans, despite Greene's repeated pleas for assistance. But if Sumter's absence contributed to Greene's desperate lack of supply, as the deserter reported, Rawdon's intelligence was now outdated by about three hours. As Greene maneuvered around Camden in the days leading up to the battle, he *had* sent his baggage to his rear with Colonel Edward Carrington.[8] But Carrington had arrived with a fresh supply of provisions just that morning, which was quickly dispersed to the men for their first hearty meal in several days. Greene had with him one 6-pound cannon, and arriving with Carrington were two more 6-pounders under the command of Charles Harrison and a company of Virginia artillerymen, making Rawdon's intelligence obsolete. As Rawdon approached Greene's position, two of the cannon were positioned along the main road, facing Log Town, and the third between the two Maryland regiments on the left (east) side of Greene's main line.[9]

With the British regulars of the 63rd Regiment in the vanguard, Rawdon's approach was concealed by the thick woods and terrain to the east of Camden. Under this cover, they swung around to the left (east) flank of Greene's line, reaching the east side of Hobkirk's Hill before encountering Continental pickets.[10]

As the picket fire alerted them of the attack, Greene's men were enjoying a repose, cleaning up from their breakfast and washing in a nearby stream. Greene himself was said to be enjoying his breakfast.[11] "The British marched on until discovered by Kirkwood who attacked and fought them with great resolution until overwhelmed," Mathis reported. "Kirkwood's muskets gave the first alarm to the Americans, several of whom were at the spring cooking and washing and had to run a considerable distance before they got to their arms which were stacked in the very line they had to form. However, most if not all of them did get to their arms and were regularly formed in battle array."

Rawdon formed his line with the British 63rd Regiment and the King's American Regiments under Lieutenant Colonel George Campbell. "As the Enemy were found to be advancing only with a small front, Lieut Col. Ford with the 2nd Maryland Regiment had orders to advance and flank them upon the left, Lieut Col. Campbell had orders to do the like upon the right," Greene recalled in his official

Francis, Lord Rawdon. A later image. Though aged only 27 during the 1781 Southern Campaign, he was one of Britain's most able and industrious officers. (Library of Congress)

report on the battle. "Col. Gunby with the first Maryland Regiment, and Lieut Col. Hawes with the second Virginia Regiment, had orders to advance down the hill and charge them in front."[12]

Seized with the initial element of surprise, the British under Campbell initially turned the American left. Rawdon's cavalry reached the road on his left flank and were advancing in close order when Harrison's artillery, having just arrived, opened up on them. "A well directed fire with canister and grape did great execution and soon cleared the road so that all their doctors were sent to take care of the wounded," Mathis recalled.[13]

The artillery fire caught Rawdon by surprise. "Their artillery (three six pounders) had unluckily arrived a few minutes before the attack began, of which circumstances they gave us notice by heavy showers of grape shot," he recalled.[14] This artillery fire, coupled with the orderly formation of Greene's main line and their initial flanking maneuvers, quelled the initial momentum of the British attack. In response, Rawdon called up the Volunteers of Ireland, his own regiment, and the King's American Regiment, extending his own front line to counter the American attack. The fighting now became an intense standoff along the east side of the road.

At this point, two lapses caused the American attack to falter. Washington's light dragoons, heretofore still in reserve behind the main line, swept around the Continental right flank in an attempt to get behind the left side of Rawdon's line, but immediately encountered the remnants of British cavalry on the main road, where they had been mangled by the American artillery and were being attended to by British medical staff. Instead of continuing his attack to the British rear, Washington stopped to capture about two hundred British wounded and medical staff, along with other British noncombatants.

Meanwhile, the left side of the Continental line was yielding slightly to the attack of the Volunteers of Ireland, but the right side was advancing, anchored by the 1st Maryland Continentals at the interior of the line. But elements of the 1st Maryland fell into confusion due to the death of one of their officers, Captain William Beatty. Seeing their disorder, Colonel John Gunby ordered the rest of the 1st Maryland Regiment to halt, then back up so they could reorganize, but the British seized this moment of opportunity by pressing their attack with a bayonet charge, causing the 1st Maryland to break in confusion. When Lieutenant Colonel Benjamin Ford, commanding the 2nd Maryland Regiment, was shot, that regiment also began to withdraw. Confusion quickly took hold in the Continental line, and Greene was forced to order a general retreat.[15]

At this moment occurred an incident of some historical debate. With the Continental line in retreat, the American artillery was in danger of being overrun by the British. According to his 19th-century biographer, William Johnson, Greene recognized the danger and rushed to the artillery's assistance. "Greene galloped alone, (for his aids were dispensing his orders) and dismounting and seizing the drag-ropes with one hand, whilst he held his horse with the other, exhibited an example which the most timid could not resist." No eyewitness or contemporary account mentions Greene's singular heroics in this incident; the account is likely apocryphal.[16] In the account by Samuel Mathis, Greene ordered to the defense of the threatened artillery Captain John Smith, who defended them heroically until they could be removed from the field, aided by Colonel William Washington, whose cavalry had now returned from their ignominious mission in Rawdon's rear to defend the Continental retreat.[17]

Greene reported, "we retired about two or three Miles without any loss of Artillery or Ammunition Waggons, the Baggage having been sent off at the beginning of the battle." Washington's late actions with his cavalry were sufficient to cut off the British pursuit. Though Greene had surrendered the field, the casualty figures suggested yet another stalemate. Greene reported 270 American casualties, half of whom were listed as "missing." Rawdon reported 33 killed, 151 wounded, and 39 missing. American casualties are estimated at 21 killed, 113 wounded, 47 captured, and 89 missing.[18]

In his report on the battle, Greene somewhat unfairly laid blame for the defeat on Gunby's orders to reorganize the 1st Maryland.[19] Greene immediately granted Gunby's request for a court-martial, which found "Colonel Gunby's spirit and activity were unexceptionable. But his order for the regiment to retire, which broke the line, was extremely unpopular and unmilitary, and in all probability the only cause why we did not obtain a complete victory."[20]

A fairer assessment was made by Henry Lee, writing in his memoirs almost 30 years later:

> Had the horse [i.e. Washington's cavalry] been still in reserve, not only would the forward movement of the enemy, which followed the recession of the first regiment of Maryland been delayed, but that regiment would have been restored to order, and the battle renewed with every reason still to conclude that its events would have been restored to order, and the battle renewed with every reason still to conclude that its events would have been auspicious to America. The maxim in war, that your enemy is to be dreaded until at your feet, ought to be held inviolate; nor should a commander permit the gratifying seductions of brilliant prospects to turn him from the course which this maxim enjoins.[21]

Writing in his own memoir, William R. Davie concurs, suggesting the battle was lost for lack of sufficient reserve, not Gunby's battlefield mistake.[22]

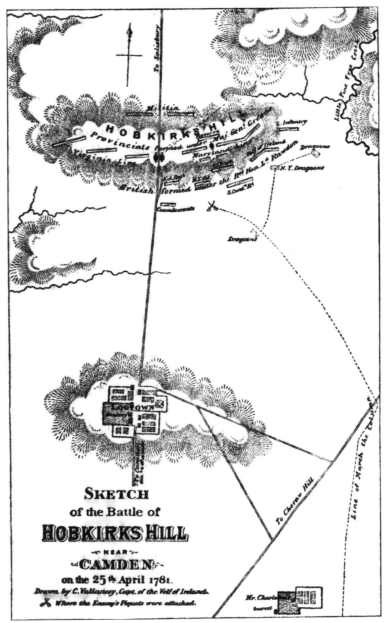

This map depicts Nathanael Greene's defenses at Hobkirk's Hill on the morning of April 25, 1781. Rawdon's attack is depicted by the dotted line on the right. (McCrady, Edward. *The History of South Carolina in the Revolution, 1780–1783.* New York: The Macmillan Company, 1902)

A fairer assessment still might lay the blame on Greene himself, whose forces were sufficiently aligned, superior in number, and amply supported by his artillery. Why not fight from a defensive position, blasting Rawdon into submission with his three cannon? Clearly, Rawdon's surprise attack led to some disarray both in Greene's ranks and in Greene's tactical calculations. When historians claim Greene was no genius as a battlefield conductor, here is evidence to the claim.

Whoever was to blame, Greene reserved the bulk of his resentment for Thomas Sumter. Having lost yet another battlefield confrontation with the British barely more than a month after the defeat at Guilford's Courthouse, and despondent over the deficient support of Sumter's South Carolina militia, Greene fell into a deep depression. "General Greene, heretofore soured by the failure of his expected succor from Sumter, now deeply chagrined by the inglorious behavior of a favorite regiment … became for awhile discontented with his advances to the South," Lee recalled in his memoir.[23]

In a more vivid account, Davie recalled:

> General Greene was deeply disgusted with the conduct of General Sumter, who had repeatedly refused to obey his express and urgent orders to join him before Camden; to this strange and unmilitary conduct of Sumter he justly attributed to his incapacity to effect the complete investment of Camden, the loss of the action on the 25th … and considering him as a mere Pandour or freebooter, whose sole object was plunder and who therefore would neither act under him nor in concert with him, he would certainly have arrested him, but from considerations arising from the State of the Country at the time, and the hope that these rambling expeditions of Sumter might arrest the attention of the enemy.[24]

Perhaps adding to Greene's despondency was Sumter's long-delayed response to his entreaties for reinforcement. Writing on April 25, the same day as Greene's defeat, the Gamecock admitted guilefully, "My movements are very slow … The trouble and perplexity I have had to get the militia out inconceivable, but think them pretty well subdued. I hope you have not suffered for supplies, and that your expectations and wishes may be fully and speedily answered."[25]

Sumter's biographer Anne King Gregorie suggests Greene's expectations of Sumter were unrealistic. She argues Sumter's volunteer troops likely had little taste for a protracted siege of Camden, as seemed Greene's only option for dislodging Rawdon from his strongly fortified position, especially in April, when there was so much to do at their homesteads. "New England Quaker that Greene was, with his tactics from Caesar and Turenne, and with his position achieved through experience with regulars, he could not be expected to understand the problems of a commander of frontier militia," she writes. She notes that, having organized a standing state militia at Greene's request, Sumter now had an obligation to supply and compensate these men, a reference to the morally questionable provisions of Sumter's Law. She observes, "Greene did not have a dollar to advance in place of the promised pay in negroes." Furthermore, she questions how Washington's fabled and experienced quartermaster general could expect Sumter to feed the Continental Army in a region already cleaned bare by warfare and pillage, especially if he expected Sumter's foragers to join his own troops.[26]

She notes Greene cast no aspersions about Sumter's culpability for the defeat at Hobkirk's Hill in his correspondence with Sumter immediately following the battle. Though true, it is also true Greene still desperately needed Sumter's assistance. Given his unfortunate conflict with Sumter over the winter, Greene likely wouldn't risk a similar confrontation by provoking the Gamecock now.

Also true is that he didn't hesitate to cast his aspersions on Sumter in correspondence with others. Greene's true state of mind was probably best expressed in a letter to his old friend Joseph Reed, with whom he had served on Washington's staff earlier in the war. "The love of pleasure and the want of principle among many of those who are our friends renders the exertions very languid in support of our cause," Greene wrote to Reed on May 4. He continued:

> The war here is upon a very different scale to what it is to the Northward. It is a plain business there ... Some of the [southern] States when ruin approach[es] them, exert themselves; but the difficulties and dangers no sooner subsides, than they sink down into their former sloth and inattention ... You frequently hear of great things from Generals [Francis] Marion and [Thomas] Sumter. These are brave good Officers; but the people that are with them come and go as they please, and are more allurd from the hopes of plunder than from a desire to serve the public, at least this is the case with many, if not all their followers ... The prospects here are so unpromising,

and the difficulties so great, that I am sick of the service, and wish my self out of the Department. When I made this last Movement I expected 2000 Virginia militia to operate with us, and 1000 Men with Sumter but both have faild me; and I am in the greatest distress.[27]

The letter is a brutal and forthright assessment, born out of obvious despondence, the type of correspondence many of us have written at a low point only to later regret, or hopefully shove deep in a drawer. That it would have a profound impact on Greene's legacy and his future relationship with Sumter is not surprising, as we will eventually see. Greene was only 38 at this time, still prone to express thoughts and opinions in his correspondence and conversations a wiser man might keep to himself. As with Sumter, his innate pride and insecurities could wreak havoc on his judgment. In this case, it would cost him.

Greene's dismal opinions of Sumter's character couldn't have been helped by the fact Sumter and his army moved to the vicinity south of Camden almost immediately following Hobkirk's Hill. Suddenly, with timing that suggested more than coincidence, he once more had adequate troops for campaigning. Sweeping the Broad River valley for food, horses, and slaves as he traveled, Sumter made his way toward the Congaree in the last days of April 1781 and the first of May, his objective a return to the British outpost at Fort Granby and its cache of captured loot.

Realizing he had little control over the Gamecock's actions, Greene acquiesced reluctantly to Sumter's plan. "I find you think it will be prejudicial to the publick service for you to cross the Wateree and join me [at his new camp at Rugeley's Mill, about 10 miles north of Camden]. Our situation requires it; but as you press so many objections, and I am so desirous to rouse the people in that quarter, I have thought it most adviseable to revoke the order, and leave you at liberty to prosecute your original plan."[28]

With a renewed sense of vigor and industry, Sumter replied on May 2, "I am Glad You are So Circumstanced as to permit the Troops With me to Remain in this Quarter, Which I have No doubt but you will find it have an exceeding Good Effect, as it Will tend to increase our force Very much, & Lessen that of the Enemy excessively, & Secoure Resources for our army Which otherways must have been Lost." And as if to prove his point, that his presence at Camden was detrimental to the Patriot cause, Sumter's letter goes on to list a bounty of horses and meal he intends to send Greene's way. "I Can have Sent forward any Quantity of Meal that you May have occasion for," he boasts optimistically. He also mentions the capture of "Several Negroes" and requests for his operations on the Congaree one of Greene's 6-pounders.[29] This same day, May 2, Sumter initiated his second attempt to capture Fort Granby.

If Greene felt despondent in the aftermath of Hobkirk's Hill, he wasn't the only one. Rawdon grew increasingly dismayed about his position at Camden. His losses at Hobkirk's Hill had been considerable, and his supply situation grew desperate in the following days. On May 7, Lieutenant Colonel John Watson finally reached Camden, his arrival long delayed by the efforts of Francis Marion and Henry Lee to deter him. But Rawdon found Watson's original force of five hundred men "much reduced in number through casualties, sickness, and a reinforcement which he had left to strengthen the garrison at Georgetown," not enough to replace what he had lost at Hobkirk's.[30]

Meanwhile, Sumter had captured the Congaree River crossing at Friday's Ferry in preparation for his siege on Fort Granby. Just a few days later, Marion and Lee captured McCord's Ferry on the Santee as they initiated their attack on Fort Motte on May 6. With these captures, Rawdon's supply line was imperiled, not to mention his escape route. Nelson's Ferry, even further down the Santee, was now his only secure crossing. Seeing no other option for maintaining his precarious position at Camden, Rawdon initiated another daring maneuver against Greene.

"On the night of the 7th I crossed the Wateree at Camden ferry, proposing to turn the flank and attack the rear of Greene's army, where the ground was not strong, though it was very much so in front," Rawdon later reported to Cornwallis.[31]

At this time, Greene was contemplating a move of his own, back into North Carolina. On May 3, he received a report that Cornwallis was on the move toward Cross Creek, North Carolina (modern-day Fayetteville), and was thought to be "coming towards Camden," though "it is possible he may be pushing for our Stores on the upper route."[32] To Sumter he wrote on May 4, "The movement of Lord Cornwallis will oblige us to

collect all our regular force," and on
May 5 he wrote to Sumter:

> I wrote you yesterday that Lord Cornwallis
> was advancing into the Country on the
> East side of Cape Fear River ... His
> object and future route remains to be
> explained. Should he come this way or
> go up into the upper Country towards
> Salisbury ... it would be my wish to
> collect our force and fight him. On this
> presumption I beg you to inform me
> what force you think you could join me
> with for the purpose; and how far you
> can depend upon the people you have
> with you, to fight with regular troops.[33]

William R. Davie. After a brilliant
career as a partisan commander,
Davie reluctantly served as Nathanael
Greene's commissary officer, where
he was privy to some of Greene's
intimate thoughts on Sumter. Later
he would go on to serve as governor
of North Carolina and help found the
University of North Carolina. (Library
of Congress)

Not surprisingly, with the British
outposts at Fort Granby and Fort Motte
firmly in his sights, Sumter was less than
enthusiastic about a campaign in North
Carolina. And though Greene soon
learned Cornwallis was continuing
into Virginia, not turning back toward
North Carolina, Sumter's reluctance
to join him provided further evidence
of the Gamecock's apathy toward the American cause. Meanwhile,
Greene's own men were deserting him. "The time of service of many
of the Maryland troops is expired, and we are daily discharging them,"
Greene complained to Samuel Huntington on May 5. "Sometimes not
less than eight or ten in a day, and these some of the best soldiers in the
field." Long-promised reinforcements from Virginia had not arrived, and
he had no assurances they ever would. "I can see no place where an
Army of considerable force can subsist for any length of time ... The
Country is so laid to waste and the means of transportation so unequal
to the business of collecting supplies from a distance for an Army, that
it is difficult for me to conceive how an Army is to be subsisted in this
Country any longer."[34]

And so, as Rawdon launched his desperate attack on the night of May 7, Greene had little will or desire to meet him. Greene's army had been decimated at Hobkirk's Hill, his best troops were deserting him, and he had little hope of reinforcement. He could not rely on the support of Thomas Sumter's South Carolina militia, of that he knew well, and his supply situation was desperate, again. The only thing to do was fall back.

"The troops had scarcely crossed the river, when I received notice that Greene had moved early in the evening ... I followed him by the direct road, and found him posted behind Sawney's creek," Rawdon continued in his report to Cornwallis. "Having driven in his pickets, I examined every point of his situation: I found it everywhere so strong, that I could not hope to force it without suffering such loss as must have crippled my force for further enterprise."[35]

After falling back in the face of Rawdon's advance on the night of May 7, Greene retreated north again on May 8, and then again on May 9. It is from the night of May 9 that we have this bleak recollection from William R. Davie:

> This evening [Greene] sent for me earlier than usual; I found the map on the table, and he introduced the business of the night with the following observations, which serve to shew the State of his mind at that trying crisis—"You see that we must again resume the partizan war, Rawdon has now a decided superiority of force, he has pushed us to a sufficient distance to leave him free to act on any object within his reach, he will strike at Lee and Marion, reinforce himself by all the troops that can be spared from the several garrisons and push me back to the mountains ... Sumter refuses to obey my orders, and carries off with him *all the active force* of this unhappy state on rambling predatory expeditions unconnected with the operations of the army ... Congress seems to have lost sight of the Southern States, and to have abandoned them to their fate, so much so, that we are even as much distressed for ammunition as men ... Rawdon will push me back to the mountains; Lord Cornwallis will establish a chain of posts along James River and *the Southern States, thus cut off, will die like the Tail of a Snake.*" These are his very words, they made a deep and melancholy impression, and I shall never forget them [italics from original].[36]

A melancholy night indeed, indicative of the usually buoyant Greene's dark mood in the days following Hobkirk's Hill. But a darkness before the dawn, for the cliché is as apt here as anywhere. On May 9, with Greene refusing to engage him again, Rawdon deemed his position at Camden untenable. "On the 9th I published to the troops, and to the militia, my design of evacuating Camden," Rawdon reported to Cornwallis. "During the ensuing night I sent off all our baggage, &c., under a strong effort, destroyed the works remaining at Camden, with the rest of the troops, till ten o'clock the next day, in order to cover the march."[37]

Upon learning of Rawdon's evacuation on the morning of May 10, Greene was jubilant. "I employed the whole night writing until an orderly Serjeant summoned me to Head-Quarters about day-light," Davie continued in his memoir.

> On entering the General's tent, I soon perceived some important change had taken place; "I have sent for you," said he, with a countenance expressing the most lively pleasure, "to inform you that Lord Rawdon has evacuated Camden—the place was the key to the Enemy's line of posts—they will now all fall or soon be evacuated—All will now go well—Burn your letters—I shall march immediately to the Congaree" ... The General's mind was of that luminous cast which gives extensive range to the mental view, and highly endowed with powers of calculation he immediately fore-saw and predicted all the mistaken movement of the British Commander and instantly changed his plan of operation and assumed the offensive.[38]

If the campaign at Hobkirk's Hill reveals the limitations of Nathanael Greene, the general, it also reveals the full depth of an extraordinary human spirit poised precariously on the fulcrum of history. Lesser men have failed in such moments, as have greater ones. Greene was no Caesar. He was a man of mistakes and doubts and insecurities operating in a complex theater of war, his allies at times as querulous and as challenging as his opponents. It is perhaps then this spirit of perseverance, coupled with his supreme understanding of military logistics, that distinguishes him as not only a great American general, but also a great American. In one of his most famous lines, written to the Chevalier de La Luzerne back on April 28, during some of the darkest days of the Southern Campaign, he summed it up best: "We fight get beat rise and fight again."[39]

CHAPTER 8

Partisan Games

Any study of the American Revolution's Southern Campaign inevitably must include a comparison between Thomas Sumter and Francis Marion. First let us acknowledge the excellence of their nicknames. In a conflict that gave us such geriatric fare as "Old Put" (General Israel Putnam), "The Old Waggoner" (General Daniel Morgan), and "Old Granny" (General Horatio Gates), "Gamecock" and "Swamp Fox" reign supreme.

As Exhibit A we have the South Carolina Gamecocks, the mascot for the University of South Carolina, but also an epithet, at times, for the entire population of the state. In South Carolina, it is a description worn proudly, for it captures the spirit of a people who are known for being proud, courageous, and a little bit prickly—with just a touch of lewdness thrown in for extra fun. Already we have learned the origin of the name, and read how British commanders uttered it with sheer contempt and disdain—the same manner, perhaps, as Georgia, Florida, or Alabama fans might utter it on an October Saturday afternoon.

But it is the "Swamp Fox" nickname that may be the true work of genius, for it captures something that is both quintessentially American—a spirit of defiance, shrewdness, and perseverance that would be as at home on the riverboats of the Mississippi, the gold fields of California, or the shores of Iwo Jima as it was in the swamps of South Carolina—and speaks to the essence of guerilla warfare. It is a nickname that, under different circumstances, we might as easily confer on Geronimo or Lawrence or Tito as we do on Marion, though it belongs indisputably to him. Let us therefore give credit where credit is due, for the name's inspiration is attributed to none other than Banastre Tarleton, who after chasing Marion for seven hours in the fall of 1780, only to lose his quarry in the "swamps and defiles," was said to pronounce, "Come my Boys! Let us go back, and we will find the Gamecock. But as for this damned old fox, the Devil himself could not catch him." Thus, at least according to American folklore, the "Swamp Fox" moniker was born.[1]

Marion himself was born at his family's settlement on the Santee River in 1732 and Sumter in 1734, making them both in their late 40s during the latter part of the war, considered "old" for their time, given an average life expectancy in Colonial America of about 35 due to disease and harsh living conditions. Both were elected to South Carolina's Provincial Congress in 1775, then elected officers in the regiments of State Troops formed by that body, Marion as an officer in the famed 2nd Regiment, Sumter in the 6th. They both served in the successful defense of Charleston in 1776 and had their commissions adopted into the Continental Army following that action. Both, at times, had "issues" with authority. And of course, in the latter stages of the war, they were both partisan commanders, fighting with volunteer and irregular troops.[2] In the mind of the casual historian, the consumer of pop culture, they might easily be considered one and the same.

But they were vastly different men—different leaders and certainly different soldiers. Marion was born to a close-knit family of Huguenots, Protestant separatists like most of the Scots-Irish, but hailing from northern France, the Huguenots lived simply and kept to themselves. By the time of Marion's birth, his family had already been settled in South Carolina for two generations. Sumter's parents were English, perhaps arriving as indentured servants.

As war activities lulled in South Carolina during the late 1770s, Sumter resigned his Continental Army commission, due in part to poor health. Marion continued to serve, though he found garrison life around Charleston dull. He gained a reputation as a strict disciplinarian, demanding order and cleanliness from his troops. He served in the siege of British-held Savannah in September and October 1779, including the disastrous main assault on the town on October 9, 1779, during which 244 American and French were killed and over six hundred wounded.

Once more garrisoned at Charleston in the spring of 1780, as the British began their siege there, Marion was invited to a dinner party at the home of Captain Alexander McQueen. After dinner McQueen locked the doors of the house, a prelude to the interminable rounds of toasts and drinking customary of the times. Never a heavy drinker, and always a bit of a social misfit, Marion escaped the party by jumping from a second story window, breaking his ankle in the fall.

If it wasn't for this accident, Marion likely would have been captured with the 2,600 other Continental Army soldiers taken prisoner by the British when Charleston fell in May 1780.[3] Instead he had been evacuated from the city in April and was recuperating with family on the Santee. His Continental commission still active, his ankle still healing, Marion rode to the Continental Army headquarters in July 1780 to offer his services, but there was little use for him there, so he asked permission to assume command of the Williamsburg militia in the eastern part of South Carolina.

Finding Marion's unusual appearance "in fact so burlesque that it was with much difficulty the diversion of the regular soldiery was restrained by the officers; and the general himself was glad of an opportunity of detaching Colonel Marion," General Horatio Gates granted Marion's request.[4] Marion would operate as a partisan commander for the remainder of the war.

Gates was not the first or last to find Marion's appearance unusual. His biographers typically describe him as "dark-visaged" and "small," with knees and ankles deformed at birth. Some note a hook nose and narrow face that made him "homely." He was known for dark moods that sometimes overtook his spirit of enterprise. Like Sumter, he could be oversensitive to issues of status and rank, though his tantrums tended to subside quickly, and overall he was governed by principles of cooperation and service to a greater cause.

If Sumter's favorite move was the straight-ahead attack, Marion preferred subterfuge and ambush, relying on the element of surprise and an intimate knowledge of his fighting terrain for tactical advantage. When the odds were against him, he vanished into the swamps. Both Sumter and Marion were excellent spymasters, employing vast and intricate intelligence networks to inform their campaigns, but Sumter was expansive in his recruitments, taking any and all into his ranks, often with a legacy of pillage and looting to show for it. Though Marion's ranks sometimes swelled into the hundreds during major engagements, he preferred to operate with a small force of family and friends, sometimes fighting with as little as a few dozen, relying on complex social networks to maintain discipline and secrecy. Sumter, it has been said, sometimes used his men's lives carelessly in pursuit of the Patriot cause; Marion guarded his soldiers' lives diligently, and therefore earned their loyalty.[5]

★　★　★

In his correspondence, Greene often expressed concerns about the reliability and temperament of militia forces. Now, the circumstances of war required their employment. Though he had learned through painful experience that Sumter, and to a lesser extent, Marion and Lee, might act on their own initiative despite his orders, he also increasingly realized the states to his north—primarily Virginia, but also Maryland, Delaware, and North Carolina—would never support him and his army the way he believed they ought.

With Cornwallis on the move, and Greene concerned he might threaten the Continental Army supply lines in North Carolina, or even attempt a reunion with Rawdon at Camden, he tried to lobby both Sumter and Marion for an expedition into North Carolina to counter Cornwallis's hypothetical attack. But their response to these entreaties was tepid at best, and with Cornwallis now on the way to Virginia, he gave up any pretense of requiring their support and instead resigned himself to supporting their individual initiatives.

Was this a failure of leadership on the part of General Nathanael Greene? Could a general with the moral standing of a George Washington or Daniel Morgan bend the South Carolina partisans to their will? Perhaps. Remember that Greene was over 10 years younger than both Sumter and Marion. Certainly, he was the alien, still in many ways learning the customs and attitudes of the American South.

Ralph Waldo Emerson said, "Common sense is genius dressed in working clothes." Winston Churchill adds, "True genius resides in the capacity for evaluation of uncertain, hazardous, and conflicting information." If Nathanael Greene was a military genius, and there are those that argue either way, it was in his capacity for evaluation and re-evaluation, a common-sense intelligence that could flex and adjust to uncertain conditions, conflicting information, and that did not remain intractable in the face of evidence to the contrary. "Greater" men have lacked it. This was the genius that inspired the division of his army in January and his turn on Cornwallis in April. Now he embraced the partisan operations he previously belittled.

Even before Rawdon evacuated Camden, Sumter was on the move, with Greene's blessing, concerns about Cornwallis aside. Sumter's "plan" was another attempt on Fort Granby, guarding Friday's Ferry on the Congaree River near present-day Columbia, an important link in the British supply chain from Charleston, especially for supplies bound to the British outposts on the western frontier—Ninety-Six and Augusta. Sumter's first attempt on Granby during "Sumter's Rounds" on February 19 had been an unmitigated disaster. Over two months later, Granby was still commanded by the notorious Tory Major Andrew Maxwell and still held a large cache of plundered loot, including slaves and horses. Collecting men, supplies, and captured slaves as he traveled down the Broad River toward the Congaree, Sumter began his second siege of Granby on May 2, securing both sides of the Congaree at the approaches to Friday's Ferry, a situation that distressed Rawdon and played no small role in his decision to evacuate Camden seven days later.

Sumter and Greene were writing daily now, Greene abandoning hope of drawing either Sumter or Marion to his reinforcement outside of Camden. Granby was defended by two 12-pounders and some smaller guns. Maxwell's command included 340 men, including 60 regulars. Though Sumter again had no fieldpiece, and little hope of taking Granby with a direct assault, he was always optimistic when operating independently and of his own accord. "Majr Maxwell Keeps pretty Close," Sumter wrote of his quarry inside Granby. "I think this place May be Taken with a Sixpounder ... The Tories are Very uneasee & Will Numbers of them Disert if opportunity Serves."

Sumter adds, "I will use my endeavours to have Some horses procured Suitable for the Purpose you intend them," for in the aftermath of Hobkirk's Hill, Greene found his army in desperate need of fresh mounts.[6]

"Do not fail to get us all the good Dragoon horses that you can, for we are in the utmost distress for want of them," Greene reminded Sumter in his letter of May 4. "Genl Marion I am told has a considerable number of them on which he has mounted his Militia. It is a pity that good horses should be given into the hands of people who are engaged for no limited ti[me]."[7]

Writing to Marion on April 27, just two days after the defeat at Hobkirk's Hill, Greene had ordered Marion and Lee to "cross the river Santee ... and direct your force as information and circumstances may direct either towards George Town or elsewhere as shall appear to be necessary keeping me constantly advised of your situation." Greene suggested, "if you cross the Santee you can take all the posts upon the Congaree and those posts that lie between Camden and that river," by which he meant Fort Granby and also Fort Motte and Belleville. For their mission, Greene dispatched to them one of his cannons.

Marion and Lee had done precisely as Greene suggested, heading for the British outpost at Fort Motte while Sumter began his siege of Granby. Located near the point where the Congaree and the Wateree rivers join to form the Santee, Fort Motte was erected around the home of Rebecca Motte, a three-story mansion on a high rolling plain overlooking the Congaree. The British seized the house in January 1781 and erected around it earthworks, a palisade, and a surrounding ditch. Two blockhouses on either corner of the palisade provided additional defense for the 120-foot enclosure. While the British occupied her home, Rebecca Motte had been forced to evacuate to her overseer's house on a nearby hill.[8]

On May 4, with Greene still invested at Camden and now worried about a possible attack from Cornwallis, he wrote Marion, once more questioning him about horses. In this letter Greene's penchant for sermonizing betrayed him again: "I am told the Militia claim all they take from the Tories; and many of the best horses are collected from the Inhabitants upon this principle. I cannot think the practice warranted either in justice or policy. If the object of the people is plunder altogether, Government can receive but little benefit from them. The horses would be of the highest importance to the public in the regular service."[9]

Marion received this letter on May 6, the day he and Lee initiated their attack on Fort Motte. According to Marion's biographer Hugh Rankin, Marion believed Greene's implication was that he was mishandling his men.[10] The frustrations of war boiled over in the occasionally temperamental Swamp Fox. "I acknowledge that you have repeatedly mention[ed] the want of Dragoon horses & wish it had been in my power to furn[is]h them but it is not nor never had been," he seethed. Marion continued:

> The few horses which has been taken from [Tories?] has been kept for the service & never for private property, but if you think it best for the service to Dismount the Malitia now with me I will direct Col. [Henry] Lee ... to do so, but am sertain we shall never git their service in future. This would not give me any uneasiness as I have somtime Determin to relinquish my command in the militia as soon as you arrived in it & I wish to do it as soon as this post is Either taken or abandoned. I Shall assist in reducing the post here and when Col. [Henry] Lee returns to you I [will] Take that oppertunity in waiting on you when I hope to get permission to go to Philadelphia.[11]

As home of the Continental Congress, Philadelphia was a popular destination for disgruntled Continental Army officers to lobby for promotion or log their complaints. Greene had acted similarly, on more than one occasion, earlier in the war. But for all his concerns about the reliability of partisan forces, for all his complaints about their plunderous behavior, Greene understood instinctively the loss of Marion would be a disaster for his campaign.

Greene went into damage control mode. On May 9, the same day, as reported later by William R. Davie, he had his long talk with Davie expressing his deep concerns about the "rambling predatory expeditions" of the South Carolina militia and his belief that Cornwallis's movements would "cut off" the Southern states so that they would die "like the tail of a snake." Greene responded to Marion's May 4 letter:

> I shall always be happy to see you at head Quarters, but cannot think you seriously mean to solicit leave to go to Philadelphia ... You have rendered important service to the public with the Militia under your command; and done great honour to yourself and I would not wish to render your situation

less agreeable with them unless it is to answer some very great purpose and this I perswade my self you would agree to from a desire to promote the common good. I wish you success at the fort you are besieging.[12]

Here, Greene capitulates at a partisan commander's tantrum. His common sense guided him toward constraint; instinctive evaluation warned him this was no time for pride or indignation. Perhaps he recognized his own tendency to press an issue too vigorously. The following morning, he would learn of Rawdon's evacuation and everything would change. He would need Sumter and Marion and the South Carolina partisans every step of the way.

To Marion's credit, the incident was already over. Rankin writes that he considered it no more, and by the time this letter was written, he and Lee were already invested at Fort Motte, placing their artillery and setting up their siege lines.

Meanwhile, Sumter's force was growing outside Fort Granby. On May 6, the same day Marion and Lee initiated their siege at Fort Motte, he reported to Greene he had with him now "five hundred Men & officers included. I expect to be Eight hundred Strong by the Middle of the Week. Perhaps in the Corse of the (month) one thousand." Among these were Sumter's "State Troops," the men he planned to pay with captured slaves, who "Mounted & equipped as Light dragoons I think will in a Short Time, that is when properly Supplyed with arm's be equally as Serviceable as the Best horse upon the Continent. The Men I think preferable to any I ever Saw. Near three hundred have Inlisted for ten Months. These men will be able to perform Good Service in a short time."[13]

Greene sent Sumter a 6-pound cannon. Indeed, the Gamecock's enthusiasm proved impossible to resist. As noted by Sumter's biographer Robert D. Bass, Sumter was almost manic with activity and stratagem as he tightened his grip on Granby. With troops flocking to his camp and the tides of war now turned his way, with Greene seemingly now resigned to Sumter's independent operations, and with his vast intelligence network again active and returning valuable information, Sumter seemed "again youthful. More like an inquisitive schoolboy than a brigadier general ruling a state."[14]

Even the news that Marion and Lee were attacking Fort Motte, which Sumter had planned to attack himself, did not distress him. Leaving Colonel Thomas Taylor in command of the bulk of his militia to continue the siege of Fort Granby, Sumter left with his State Troops and the remainder of the militia, picked up the 6-pounder sent from Greene en route, and moved toward Orangeburgh (now spelled Orangeburg), the next British garrison south of Fort Motte.

Commanding at the village of Orangeburg was Captain Henry Giesendanner. Little is known about the defensive works at the post aside from the fact the British had fortified the settlement's brick jail built in 1770 "upon the crown of the gentle hill."[15] Eager to attack the garrison before they received word of Rawdon's evacuation of Camden (in fact, Rawdon had ordered Orangeburg evacuated but Giesendanner had not yet received the order), Sumter left his artillery behind with his militia and arrived at the post on May 10 with about 120 of his mounted State Troops. Giesendanner and his men retreated into the brick jail.[16]

Serving in Sumter's militia for this action was Thomas Young, whose memoir of the Revolutionary War is an invaluable source for Revolutionary War historians. Young marched behind the advance guard, "for we had a piece of artillery to manage," but arrived in Orangeburg the next morning, May 11. "The tories were lodged in a brick house," Young recalled, "and kept up a monstrous shouting and firing to very little purpose. As soon as the piece of artillery was brought to bear upon the house, a breach was made through the gable end; then another, a little lower; then about the centre, and they surrendered."[17]

Writing on May 11, Sumter reported to Greene that the post at Orangeburg surrendered at 7 o'clock "this morning." He captured eight officers, 82 privates, a small supply of "Military Stores," and "Provisions plenty But No Conveniency of Moving It." Upon examining the garrison, he found it to be "extreemly Strong" and believed it would have been very difficult to capture if it had been "obstinately Defended."[18]

Flushed with his victory at Orangeburg, and confident about his position at Granby, Sumter set his sights on disrupting Rawdon's retreat

south. The countryside was awash
in terrified waves of Loyalists,
fleeing Patriot retribution with
their stock and whatever else they
could carry, proving too much
of an opportunity for Sumter
to resist. "Before I Return to
the Congarees I think to Move
towards Santee, and endeavour
to Alarm Lord Rawden to prevent his Crossing the River," he
wrote Greene on May 12. "An
other Motive I have for Taking
a Turn through the Country, is,
I find Many people Braking up &
Remvoing to Town, So is every
Reason to believe the Country
will be Striped of every thing

Colonel Henry Lee. Lee was a gifted officer
and horseman. His memoirs provide a colorful
account of the Southern Campaign. (Library
of Congress)

that is Valuable. I Wish to Deprive them of as Many horses as possible &
prevent the Inhabitance from Moving & Carrying off great Quantities of
Stock Which are Now Collecting."[19]

Moving quickly south on the route toward Charleston, Sumter himself
traveled within 18 miles of Monck's Corner, while his men swept a
broad swath of country between Wassamassaw and Dorchester. Though
Rawdon had traveled another way, still hoping to relieve Fort Granby
after the fall of Fort Motte, Sumter's raid so scourged the countryside
that no Tory came near Rawdon's army for five days, severely restricting
Rawdon's intelligence operations.[20]

While Sumter raced south, Marion and Lee conducted their siege of
Fort Motte. Lee's account of this action qualifies as one of his *Memoirs'*
irresistible narratives, earning the genteel Rebecca Motte a storied role
in South Carolina history. Lee writes that while Marion and his men
occupied the "eastern declivity of the ridge on which the fort stood," his
Legion set up operations in the caretaker's home where Motte was living:

Not only the lieutenant colonel [Lee, writing in the third person], but every officer in his corps, off duty, daily experienced her [Rebecca Motte's] daily hospitality ... While her richly spread table presented with taste and fashion all the luxuries of her opulent country, and her sideboard offered without reserve the best wines of Europe ... her active benevolence found its way to the sick and to the wounded; cherishing with softest kindness infirmity and misfortune, converting despair into hope, and nursing debility into strength.

By May 10 Lee's men had completed a siege trench within 400 yards of the fort. The Patriot's 6-pounder was placed on a battery in Marion's quarter for "raking the northern face of the enemy's parapet, against which Lee was preparing to advance." Inside the fort was Lieutenant Donald McPherson, an officer "highly deserved and respected," along with about 150 foot soldiers and a small detachment of dragoons.

Lee determined it was time to "summon the commandant." Under a flag of truce, Lee sent forward an envoy to McPherson, "admonishing him to avoid the disagreeable consequence of an arrogant temerity. To this the captain replied, that, disregarding consequences, he should continue to resist to the last moment."

Marion and Lee resumed work on their siege lines, preparing for an attack, but later that day they received word from Greene that Rawdon was retreating from Camden toward Fort Motte, and would be there within 48 hours. With the clock ticking, Marion and Lee decided they were left with only one course of action. On the morning of May 11, Lee informed Rebecca Motte of the "sad necessity, and assuring her of the deep regret which the unavoidable act excited in his and every breast"—they would be forced to burn down her beautiful house.

But the staunch Patriot Motte reacted with her trademark Southern gentility. "With a smile of complacency this exemplary lady listened to the embarrassed officer, and gave instant relief to his agitated feelings, by declaring, that she was gratified with the opportunity of contributing to her country." After viewing the bows and flaming arrows the Patriots had prepared for the job, she called for Lee and presented him with a bow and arrows imported from India. "She requested the substitution of these, as probably better adapted for the object than those we had provided."

Once more McPherson was offered surrender; once more he refused. Using Rebecca Motte's imported bow (according to the storyteller Lee), the Patriots launched arrows—tipped with resin and sulphur and set ablaze—onto the roof of her mansion home, which was soon on fire. As the British troops struggled to put out the flame, the Patriot 6-pounder opened fire, "raking the loft from end to end." As his men jumped from the burning roof, McPherson surrendered, and Marion quickly ordered his militia to assist in putting out the fire.

McPherson was offered honorable terms. Marion lost two men but there were no other British or American casualties. "McPherson and his officers accompanied their captors to Mrs. Motte's, and partook with them of a sumptuous dinner; soothing in the sweets of social intercourse the ire which the preceding conflict had engendered."[21]

After the dinner, Nathanael Greene and a small guard of cavalry arrived at Fort Motte. This was the first face-to-face meeting between Greene and Marion, and by several accounts, whatever tension had been created by Marion's threat to resign and take his complaints to Philadelphia made just a few days before was already forgotten by the two men, or quickly put aside in the spirit of celebration. With Rawdon and his army still approaching from Camden, the three men quickly made plans.[22] Referring to Fort Granby as "Frydays Ferry" in his official orders, Greene commanded to Lee: "You will march immediately with the van of the Army for the post at Frydays Ferry commanded by Major [Andrew] Maxwell and demand an immediate surrender of that post."[23] Greene would follow Lee with the remainder of the Continental Army, reinforcing Lee at Granby if necessary, his main objective now the British outposts at Ninety-Six and Augusta, where he planned to join Andrew Pickens. Acting with a greater degree of independence, Marion set off to the east, across the Santee. His objective was the British garrison at Georgetown, though as usual the wily Swamp Fox would only attack if the opportunity presented itself.[24]

Lee arrived at Fort Granby on May 14, with him one of Greene's 6-pounders. Both Greene and Lee believed Rawdon intended to reinforce Granby as he moved south to protect the line of retreat from the garrisons at Ninety-Six and Augusta, which were not yet evacuated.

That Sumter had initiated the attack on Granby, and some of his militia were still there, was of little or no consequence to Greene; time was of the essence. Finding the British position at Granby well defended, Lee erected a battery for his cannon to the west of the fort early the next morning, May 15. "The morning was uncommonly foggy," Lee recalled in his memoir, "which fortunate circumstance gave time to finish the battery before it was perceived by the enemy."

As the fog cleared, and with his artillery position now visible to the defenders inside the fort, Lee moved his infantry into place for attack. But first, "solicitious to hasten the surrender of the post, Lie[u] tenant-Colonel Lee determined to try the effect of negotiation with his pliable antagonist." He believed he knew how to motivate Major Andrew Maxwell: "The garrison consisted of three hundred and fifty men, chiefly loyal militia, commanded by Major Maxwell ... represented to Lee as neither experienced in his profession, nor fitted by cast of character to meet the impending crisis. He was the exact counterpart of McPherson (the commander at Fort Motte); disposed to avoid, rather than to court, the daring scenes of war."

Commencing his negotiations with Maxwell, Lee received word Rawdon was in the vicinity. Eager to reduce the garrison as quickly as possible, he offered Maxwell the most generous of terms: "Before noon, Maxwell with his garrison ... the baggage of every sort, two pieces of artillery, and two covered wagons, moved from the fort." With them was the loot plundered from the surrounding countryside, presumably stashed within the two covered wagons Lee had agreed to let pass without search. "The major with the garrison, protected by the stipulated escort, proceeded on their route to Lord Rawdon."

Greene was still approaching Fort Granby with the main body of his army as Maxwell surrendered. Lee recalled that, arriving at Granby a few hours later, Greene was "delighted with the happy event, his satisfaction ... considerably increased when he saw the strength of the fort ... He testified with much cordiality, and in most gratifying terms, his obligations to the light corps; applauding as well the rapidity of his advance as the vigor of its operations."[25]

But Sumter's militia, in siege around the fort now for 13 days, were furious as they watched Maxwell march out of the fort to safety with his plunder in tow. Word traveled fast in Sumter's militia. Even as Lee was arriving at Fort Granby, before he negotiated its surrender on May 15, Sumter was putting ink to his concerns. "I hope it may not be disagreeable to recall Colonel [Henry] Lee, as his services cannot be wanted at that place [Fort Granby] ... I cannot believe it would be your wish," Sumter wrote to Greene from Orangeburg on May 14, his sweep of the countryside south and east of Orangeburg now complete. "I have the greatest respect for Colonel Lee, yet I could wish he had not gone to that place, as it is a circumstance I never thought of ... I have been at great pains to reduce that post, I have it in my power to do it, and I think it for the good of the public to do it without regulars."[26]

The Congaree crossing guarded by Fort Granby was critical for Greene's plans to move on Ninety-Six and Augusta. With rumors of Rawdon's approach swirling through the countryside, its immediate capture was a strategic imperative. To criticize Lee for the ample terms of Granby's surrender ignores these contingencies. The historian Mark Boatner notes Lee's "good sense" in the situation with Napoleon's Maxim 46: "The keys of a fortress are well worth the freedom of the garrison."[27]

Sumter's expectation Lee abandon his attack on the fort, leaving it and its spoils for Sumter's men, was naïve at best—perhaps made without understanding Greene's strategic situation (though this seems unlikely, given Sumter's robust intelligence operations)—and rapacious at worst. Still, it is unlikely Greene received Sumter's letter of May 14 until after the fort had been taken by Lee, or until its negotiations for surrender were well underway.

Nevertheless, Sumter was furious when he arrived at the Congaree River on May 16 and heard the generous terms offered to Maxwell from his disconsolate men. The disregard he believed the action conferred on him and his troops turned the mercurial Gamecock morose once more, and seemingly exacerbated the lingering effects of the Blackstocks' wound. In the words of Sumter biographer Robert Bass: "Frustrated, stabbed anew in the wounds beyond healing, and both raging inwardly and outwardly contumacious, the Gamecock flew the pit."[28]

Writing to Greene on May 16, shortly after his reunion with his militia at Granby, he tendered Greene his resignation. Apparently referring to the generous terms of Fort Granby's surrender Greene had attempted to explain in an unfound letter, Sumter replied:

> I am convinced your Reasons are Cogent & your observations exceedingly Just ... But with deepest Regret find the discontent & disorder among the Militia So Great as to leave No hope of Subsiding Soon. My Indisposition & Want of Capacity, to be of Service to this Country Induces me as a friend to beg leave to Resign My Command and have taken Liberty to enclose My Commission Which I hope you will Receive, as I find my inability So Great that I Cant without doing the Greatest Injustice to the publick think of Serving any Longer.[29]

We can only wonder at Nathanael Greene's reaction to this letter, the Gamecock's South Carolina brigadier general commission enclosed inside. Did Greene laugh, cry, or simply shake his head in bewilderment? Surely it was similar to the same emotion he had reportedly shared with William Davie just a few nights before, when he complained about Sumter's insubordination and his "rambling predatory expedition."[30] And only 10 days before, he had received a similar letter from Marion.

Greene was no innocent in these matters. On several occasions he had offered to resign either his quartermaster general appointment or his major general commission. But that had been earlier in the war. Greene was changed now, his experience in the Southern Campaign more immersive, more challenging, more solitary than anything he experienced before. He had learned that in military command, as in other leadership arenas, one must endure the emotional outbursts of colleagues and subordinates. Indeed, one becomes inured to them. Surely he was still prone to fits of his own frustrations and disappointment. But he could control his emotions now, especially when strategically necessary. He had learned to cajole and manipulate rather than react impulsively. And he still needed Sumter, desperately, as he needed Marion and Pickens. His strategy depended on it, despite his inner doubts, his dark nights of the soul—perhaps because he had no other options.

There were also technical issues to consider. Sumter's brigadier general commission had no standing in the Continental Army, meaning Greene had no authority to accept it, though surely he was at least briefly tempted to do so. It was to South Carolina Governor John Rutledge the letter should be sent. This point would serve as the opening in his latest attempt at appeasement: "I take the liberty to return you your commission, which you forwarded me yesterday for my acceptance, & to inform you I cannot think of accepting it, & beg you to continue your command," he wrote to Sumter on May 17.

> It is unnecessary for me to tell you how important your services are to the interest & happiness of this Country; and the confidence I have in your abilities (and) Zeal for the good of the service. Your continuing in command will lay the public in general and me in particular, under a very great obligation; & tho it may be accompanied with many personal inconveniences, yet I hope you will have cause to rejoyce in the conclusion of the business from the consideration of having contributed so largely to the recovery of its Liberty.[31]

The letter is a complete apology, a blatant appeal to Sumter's ego, without the preachy corollary that soured Greene's previous apologies. But Greene didn't stop there. In a second letter, also written on May 17, he asserts Sumter's broad authority over the South Carolina militia, and specifically Francis Marion: "You will continue your command at this place, & form and encourage the militia in all parts of the State ... You will direct General Marian to take such a position, & employ him in such manner as may most effectually anoy the enemy, & at the same time co-operate with us should occasion require it." To appease Sumter's disgruntled men, he agreed to share with them the items captured at Granby, including all of the captured slaves, to be used for payment of Sumter's State Troops: "Such of the negroes as were taken at this Garrison (as are not claimed by good Whiggs, & their property proved,) belonging to the Tories or disaffected you will apply to the fulfilling of the contract."

Greene and his army were bound for Ninety-Six, and though he surely knew better, he pleads for Sumter's support: "You will carefully watch the motions of the enemy below this place [Fort Granby, by implication giving Sumter broad watch over the Congaree and Santee river basins] & advise me of all their movements, & should they come out in force towards Ninety Six, you will take such a Route as to effect a junction with us at that Place."[32]

Though we don't have a record of Sumter's written response to these letters, if there was one, Greene's capitulation was a success. Perhaps, like Marion, the Gamecock just needed time to cool off. Perhaps Greene's appeal to Sumter's patriotic ideals, his role in the recovery of "Liberty," hit home. Sumter's biographers provide little insight to his reaction. "To Sumter's credit he retained command," writes Anne King Gregorie succinctly, though she also notes other conditions precipitating a change of heart: on the day Sumter received Greene's letter, he captured 74 slaves from the estate of Andrew Lord, a rich Loyalist, along with 22 horses, one hundred sheep, one hundred cattle, and other loot and plunder. He also took 69 slaves from George and Will Ancrum, and slaves and sundries from other nearby Tories.[33]

In a letter to Marion, also written May 17, Greene pleads with Marion to accept Sumter's Law:

> Upon consulting Gen. Sumter respecting the mode of raising and paying the 10 month troops which he has been endeavoring to effect for some time past, I find ... that it originated with Governor [John] Rutledge in substance tho not in form. But upon the whole I think it will have its advantages ... As Continental troops can not be had[,] this may be the best substitute which could be adopted. I wish you therefore to give it all the countenance you can until the Governors pleasure is further known in the matter or the State has it in its own power to contribute to the support of the war upon a more permanent footing for the Militia service.[34]

The letter is a curious corollary to the incident of Sumter's resignation at Fort Granby, for it not only implies some conversation between Sumter and Greene not otherwise recorded in history, perhaps some negotiation or quid pro quo, but also a tacit approval for the terms of Sumter's Law, though clearly with some moral reservations. And clearly he understands Marion's reservations to these terms, but at least for the time being, Sumter's will would prevail. In some interior deliberation, Greene had decided appeasing Sumter was more strategically critical than risking Marion's anger.

This, of course, would change. The dynamics between Greene and Sumter and Marion were ever fluid, ever subject to the whims of war. These partisan games would continue to plague Greene, even as the prize of South Carolina was finally in his sight.

CHAPTER 9

Ninety-Six

Andrew Pickens was the remaining third in the triumvirate of great South Carolina partisan generals. Unlike either Thomas Sumter or Francis Marion, he was Scots-Irish to the core, from a family of Ulster immigrants, and a veteran of the Great Wagon Road migration. He was born in 1739 near Paxtang, Pennsylvania, and traveled south as a child, eventually settling in the Waxhaws, near present-day Charlotte.

In 1763, Pickens and his brother sold the 800-acre farm they had inherited in the Waxhaws and obtained land on Long Cane Creek in the Savannah River valley of southwestern South Carolina. He met and married Rebecca Calhoun, an aunt of the famous South Carolina politician John C. Calhoun, and they had eight children, establishing themselves as prominent citizens in the Long Cane settlement. At the time of the American Revolution, Pickens was a farmer, justice of the peace, and militia captain.

The Long Canes settlement was about 20 miles from Ninety-Six, the most important trading center in western South Carolina. Ninety-Six's unusual name derives from its location, 96 miles southeast of Keowee, an important trading center of the Lower Cherokee Towns, as determined in a prominent 1730 survey of the Cherokee Path, the main trading route from Charleston to the Cherokee nation.[1] Over the next five decades, Ninety-Six emerged as the most vibrant settlement in the South Carolina backcountry west of Camden thanks to the Cherokee trade. Pickens was among the six hundred Patriot militia attacked by 1,800 Tories at Ninety-Six on November 19, 1775, the first battle of the American

Revolution in South Carolina. Also known as the Siege of Savage's Old Fields, the Battle of Ninety-Six ended after two days of shooting, though little blood was shed. The exhausted and presumably deafened factions called a truce, and for the next five years the settlement remained under Patriot control.

Pickens campaigned in the Augusta, Georgia, area following the British capture of Savannah in late 1778, displaying his tactical skills at the Battle of Kettle Creek on February 14, 1779. There he stalked and surprised a superior force of Tories, killing or wounding between 40 and 70, and taking about 75 prisoners, while only losing about 30 of his own men.

Following the surrender of Charleston in May 1780, Cornwallis moved quickly to take Ninety-Six and establish it as one of his main British garrisons in the South Carolina interior, anchoring a line of defense which included Camden to its east and Augusta to its west. Beginning in August 1780, Ninety-Six was commanded by Lieutenant Colonel John Harris Cruger, a Loyalist officer who had led a battalion of New York Provincials south in 1778 as part of the expedition that captured Savannah, Georgia. A member of a prominent New York City family, Cruger previously had served as New York's mayor and its chamberlain, or treasurer.[2] His brother, Nicholas Cruger, managed the family's firm in St. Croix and was a sponsor of the young Alexander Hamilton's education at King's College.[3] Renowned as a stern disciplinarian but also an honorable and skilled soldier, Cruger would prove a worthy opponent to Greene, Pickens, and the Patriot forces.

With Pickens's Long Canes settlement located in between the now strongly reinforced British outposts at Ninety-Six and Augusta, further resistance appeared futile and Pickens accepted British parole. Though many lobbied for his return to the Patriot cause, he resisted their pleas throughout the fall of 1780 and was not among the South Carolina militia commanders fighting at King's Mountain; however, after a Tory raid plundered his plantation and frightened his family later that year, Pickens renounced his parole and resumed militia operations.

Like Daniel Morgan, Andrew Pickens's historical legacy was bolstered by Thomas Sumter's wound at Blackstocks. A dour, serious man, Pickens was well regarded both by his fellow South Carolina partisans and by

Morgan, into whose camp on the Pacolet River Pickens arrived on Christmas Day 1780. If the charismatic and egotistical Sumter had been healthy, it is unlikely Pickens would have played a starring role at Cowpens, just as it is unlikely Morgan would've been able to implement his famous battle plan with Sumter's interference.

At Cowpens, Pickens commanded the second line of Morgan's famous triple alignment, comprising the bulk of the North and South Carolina militia. This was the line that famously retreated after laying down a withering fire at Tarleton's troops, drawing them expertly into Morgan's trap. For his part in the glorious victory, Pickens was awarded a sword by

Andrew Pickens. Pickens was third in the triumvirate of great South Carolina generals, including Sumter and Marion. He was a gifted battlefield commander, earning the respect of Morgan and Greene. (Library of Congress)

Congress and a commission of brigadier general by South Carolina Governor John Rutledge, matching him in rank to Sumter if not quite in status. He continued to serve with the Continental Army through the Race to the Dan, earning the respect of Nathanael Greene for his command of the militia troops. In the days leading up to the Battle of Guilford Courthouse, however, Pickens requested leave to return to Long Canes, fearing for the safety of his friends and family back home. The request was granted reluctantly by Greene.[4]

During Greene's march through the Pine Barrens from Deep River in North Carolina to Camden in April, Greene wrote Pickens, ordering him now to "endeavour to collect a body of Militia to lay siege to Augusta and Ninety-Six."[5] On April 16, Georgia militia under the command of Lt. Col. Micajah Williamson established a fortified camp on the outskirts of Augusta, threatening the British garrison there commanded by Thomas "Burnfoot" Brown.

Back in August 1775, the staunch Loyalist Brown earned his nickname the hard way: he was tied to a tree by Patriot vigilantes and tortured with burning wood placed under his feet, then tarred and feathered and paraded through the streets of Augusta while ridiculed by the crowd. After fleeing to east Florida, Brown was now commissioned a lieutenant colonel of Loyalist militia commanding his own unit, called the King's Rangers. In addition to his command of the British garrison at Augusta, he also served as superintendent of British affairs with the Creek and Cherokee tribes in the region.[6] Perhaps with good reason, Burnfoot Brown nurtured a legacy of terror, hanging, and torture against local Patriot sympathizers during his administration at Augusta.

While Williamson threatened Brown at Augusta, Pickens gathered troops and operated in the region between Ninety-Six and Augusta, attempting to prevent British forces at Ninety-Six from reinforcing Brown. On May 8, however, Pickens informed Greene that he was leaving for Augusta to assist in the attack there.[7] By May 12, Pickens was in the Augusta area and wrote Greene again with a positive report about Patriot operations. "Situation of this Country; almost unanimous in our favor," he wrote, but he worried that with Rawdon now in retreat from Camden, "Cruger will endeavour to quit Ninety Six in the Same Manner" and will march "this Way" to relieve Brown, then the two would retreat to Savannah. If Cruger were to make such an attempt, Pickens reported, he would be forced to "move out of his Way."[8]

Under the command of Cruger, and directed by Loyalist engineer Henry Haldane, Ninety-Six's defenses were significantly improved by the spring of 1781.[9] A major addition was the "Star Fort" on the east side of Ninety-Six, adjacent to the Charleston Road. Built of earthen walls about 14 feet high, the fort featured an eight-point "star" design that allowed cannon and rifle fire in all directions. In his memoir, Henry Lee recalled the Star Fort "consisted of sixteen salient and re-entering angles, with a ditch, fraise, and abatis: it was judiciously designed and well executed ... blockhouses were erected, traverses made, and covered communications between different works established." The Star Fort was so expertly made that remnants of the earthen mounds are still on display at the Ninety-Six National Historic Site, a jewel of the

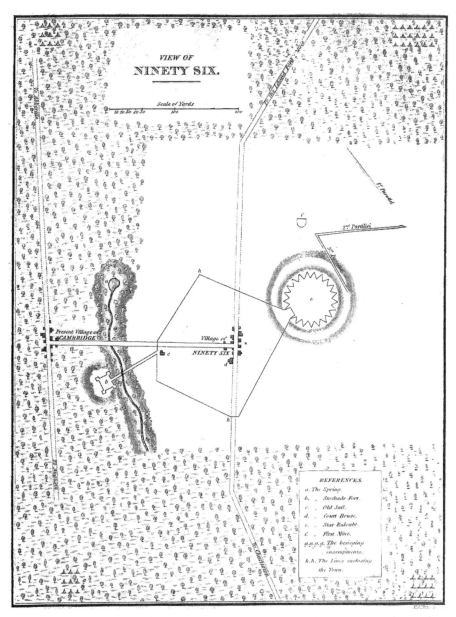

A map depicting the siege of Ninety-Six, May–June, 1781. The Star Fort is depicted on the right, showing the angled siege trenches. The fortified village is in the center, with the small stockade guarding the water supply on the far left. (Johnson, William. *Sketches of the Life and Correspondence of Nathanael Greene, Major General of the Armies of the United States, in the War of the Revolution.* Volume Two. Charleston, SC: A. E. Miller, 1822)

National Park Service. One of the "covered communications" was a long trench that connected the Star Fort to the fortified village. On the west side of the village was another small stockade that guarded the village's water supply, a rivulet fed by a nearby spring, which was also connected to Ninety-Six by a covered trench.[10]

Although Ninety-Six remained a model of British order and engineering excellence, the rest of the South Carolina countryside was awash in chaos and disarray. In his retreat from Camden, Rawdon took with him not "only the militia who had been with us at Camden, but also the well-affected neighbours on our route, together with the wives, children, negroes, and baggage of almost all of them."[11] It was upon this disarray that Sumter had capitalized in his raid toward Monck's Corner, and in fact the Gamecock had been so successful in disrupting Loyalist activity throughout the Wateree-Santee basin that, according to McCrady, "not a single person of any sort whatever, whether with intelligence or on any other account, came near the army," as he retreated south. Nor could Rawdon's spies gain reliable intelligence. Though they reported to him Greene was pushing toward Orangeburg, it was in fact Sumter's militia and State Troops, having captured Orangeburg and now raiding toward Monck's Corner, upon whom they were reporting.[12]

With this false intelligence on Greene, Rawdon believed Charleston was in jeopardy, and to protect the city, he marched toward Monck's Corner, about 40 miles north. By May 16, Greene had reliable intelligence of Rawdon's move toward Charleston,[13] leaving Augusta and Ninety-Six vulnerable to attack. This suited Greene's strategy. He believed he needed to capture or force the evacuation of these two posts before beginning his final push toward Charleston; leaving them active would expose his rear to attack.

Ironically, Rawdon had ordered both Ninety-Six and Augusta abandoned, as Pickens had predicted. Though he sent "several messengers by different routes" and "applied to Colonel Balfour to send others from Charles town ... to abandon that place [Ninety-Six, my note], and to remove ... as speedily as possible," so completely did the Patriots now control the countryside, that such dispatches were either intercepted or didn't reach Cruger until he was already surrounded by Greene.[14] It is a footnote to the history of the Southern Campaign that had Cruger evacuated Ninety-Six and Augusta, Greene could have taken the posts without the sieges to come, though Rawdon would've been considerably reinforced.

Nevertheless, with Ninety-Six and Augusta both still defended by their British and Loyalist garrisons, Greene moved forward with his plans to attack them. His strategy to take Augusta hinged on cooperation with Andrew Pickens, invested there since May 12. For the Augusta operation Greene would also play his trusted ace: Light Horse Harry Lee.

"You will march immediately for Augusta as the advance of the Army will move by the way of Ninety Six and demand the Surrender of these posts," Greene ordered Lee on May 16.[15] "Lt. Col. Lee will be with you in about five days and will bring with him a field piece," he informed Pickens that same day.[16] While Pickens and Lee attacked Augusta, Greene would head to Ninety-Six with the remainder of the Continental Army.

May 16 was the same day Sumter wrote to Greene resigning his commission over the surrender of Fort Granby. To pacify Sumter, and perhaps create some much needed separation between himself and his temperamental partisans, Greene ordered Sumter to monitor the enemy south of Fort Granby and "direct General Marian to take such a position, & employ him in such manner as may most effectually anoy the enemy."[17] With Sumter and Marion now dispatched to points south and east, Greene started his march northwest to Ninety-Six.

Moving ahead of Greene with his mobile Legion, Lee arrived at the outskirts of Augusta on the evening of May 21 and united with the militia forces under Andrew Pickens and the Georgia partisan leader Elijah Clarke. He found the town defended by two forts: the "judiciously constructed, well finished" Fort Cornwallis in the center of Augusta, and an inferior structure called Fort Grierson, named for the militia leader who commanded it, located on the outskirts of the settlement.[18]

With Colonel Grierson in his fort were about 80 militia and two artillery pieces. Burnfoot Brown was lodged inside the superior Fort Cornwallis with 320 Provincial soldiers and about two hundred African-American slaves, not armed but relieving the Provincials and attending to the fortifications. Pickens, Lee, and Clarke decided to attack Grierson, hoping to draw Brown out of Fort Cornwallis to Grierson's defense. Launching their attack on May 23, the plan worked to some degree—Fort Grierson was overwhelmed. Attempting to retreat to Fort Cornwallis, Grierson and all of his men were either killed, wounded, or captured by Clarke and his Georgia militia. Brown did send out a portion of his command in a brief attempt to support Grierson but quickly ordered their withdrawal.

Lee, Pickens, and Clarke set up for a siege of Fort Cornwallis. After two weeks of fighting that resulted in the death of about 52 Provincials and Loyalist militia, along with 16 of the Patriot forces, Brown finally surrendered the outpost on June 5 on the condition that he and his officers would be paroled safely to Savannah. According to historian Edward McCrady, the Patriots did not demand Brown's surrender on June 4, "because, as the 4th of June was the king's birthday, it was supposed that as a point of honor Browne [sic], as a king's officer, would be less inclined to surrender on that day than any other. And so it proved to be. For on the morning of the 5th Browne himself opened negotiations which resulted in the surrender of the fort." Local hatred of Brown was so intense that a special guard had to be assigned to guarantee his safe passage. Historian David Ramsay wrote: "Though he had lately hanged thirteen American prisoners, and delivered to the Indians some of the citizens of the country, who suffered from them all the tortures which savage barbarity has contrived to add poignancy to the pain of death, yet his conquerors, no less generous than brave, saved him from the fate he had so much reason to expect."[19]

Meanwhile, Greene arrived at Ninety-Six on May 22. "We arrived before this place [Ninety-Six] this morning, and find this place much better fortified and garrison much stronger in regular troops than was expected," he admitted to Lee.[20] Inside the impressive defensive works, Lt. Col. John Harris Cruger commanded approximately 350 Provincial troops and two hundred Loyalist militia. Inside also were a considerable number of slaves, who, like at Augusta, were not armed but available to provide labor and support.

To face Cruger, Greene had only about 850 regular army troops, the remaining body of Maryland and Delaware Continentals who had served with him so ably throughout the Southern Campaign along with some Virginia Continentals, and about two hundred militia, more than twice Cruger's numbers but still not enough to overwhelm Ninety-Six's formidable defenses. His only option was to siege the defensive works, which he commenced immediately.[21]

Greene was a self-taught soldier and natural administrator, no classically trained officer, and knew little about siege warfare. Therefore, he entrusted its administration to Thaddeus Kosciuszko, the Polish officer serving as Greene's chief engineer. Though Kosciuszko's engineering skills had provided important service in the defenses of Ticonderoga and West Point earlier in the war, siege warfare wasn't his expertise either.

Both men made numerous mistakes during the siege, beginning when Kosciuszko ordered the initial trenches dug just 70 yards from the Star Fort. Cruger's artillery soon scattered the Continental diggers. Lee, for one, was critical of Kosciuszko's plan, believing the focus of the siege should have been the outpost's vulnerable water supply, not its strongest defenses.[22]

Greene's supervision of the meticulous siege works, misplaced or not, left him ample time for correspondence. To his friend William Davies, a Continental Army officer in Virginia, not to be confused with William R. Davie, the North Carolinian who now served as Greene's commissary general, he complained of the civil war ravishing the Carolina countryside: "In the Southern States there is a great struggle for empire and the Animosity between Whigs and Tories ... There is not a day passes but there are more or less who fall a sacrifice to this savage disposition. The Whigs seem determined to exterpate the Tories and the Tories the Whigs ... Evil rages with more violence than ever."[23]

From Marion and Sumter, he mostly received word of Rawdon's position. Greene wanted close tabs kept on the British commander in case he moved to support Cruger at Ninety-Six, though even entrenched in an arduous siege, Greene couldn't seem to help dusting up trouble with his partisan allies. Marion wrote on May 20 and May 22, requesting permission to attack the weakened British outpost at Georgetown. Eager to avoid the tantrums of less than two weeks before, Greene responded that as long as Rawdon was still ensconced at Monck's Corner, such an attack was alright by him, but first he needed to check with Sumter.[24]

To Sumter he wrote very explicitly, explaining that he authorized Marion's attack on Georgetown only if Sumter approved. He also pre-apologized to Sumter for an incident involving the South Carolina militia: Greene had ordered Colonel Thomas Brandon of the nearby Fairforest militia to raise his troops and support him at Ninety-Six. When Brandon explained he had already received orders to join with the Gamecock, Greene became eager to fend off any offense. "I am sorry to break in upon your arrangement," Greene explained to Sumter, "but I flatter myself you will be persuaded it is for the good of the service at large tho' it may be a little inconvenient to you for a time."[25]

Acting on his own volition, and without awaiting authorization from Sumter, Marion launched his attack on Georgetown on May 28. But the small British force manning the defensive works inside the town had no appetite for battle against Marion's superior numbers, and in fact had been ordered by British Lieutenant Colonel Nisbet Balfour to evacuate if attacked. They slipped out of town to British ships awaiting them in the harbor, allowing Marion and his men to march into Georgetown triumphantly. Sumter was furious at the Swamp Fox's insubordination, but at least his ire was directed at Marion, not Greene. On this occasion, at least, Greene was able to successfully avoid his partisan's games.[26]

While Greene wrote, his men dug. By June 3 Kosciuszko's parallels reached the point where the first trench had been attempted. Kosciuszko constructed a 40-foot-high Maham Tower about 30 yards from the Star Fort, but Cruger countered by piling sandbags on the walls and constructing a 16-foot-high traverse within the fort, providing cover for his men as they moved inside from the snipers on the tower.

Greene considered his position now favorable enough to demand Cruger's surrender, sending Colonel Otho Williams toward the fort under a flag of truce. When Cruger refused, Greene tried to burn the fort with flaming arrows aimed at its wooden buildings, but this tactic failed when Cruger's men tore off their roofs. Though exhausted and suffering in the intense summer heat, Cruger's men proved resilient.[27]

As the siege continued, Greene tried to control Patriot marauding in the countryside. When a settler named John Lark arrived at the Continental camp to complain about the marauding of Patriot commander Le Roy Hammond, Greene did his best to put a stop to it, complaining to Andrew

Pickens, "The party [Hammond's militia] plunders without mercy and murders the defenceless people just on private peak [pique] prejudice or personal resentments shall dictate. Such enormities will soon make the Inhabitants think they are in a more wretched situation than they have been heretofore. Principles of humanity as well as good policy require that proper Measures should be immediately taken to restrain these abuses."[28] Despite Greene's pleas, the plundering continued.

On June 8, Lee arrived at Ninety-Six after the successful capture of Augusta; the next day Pickens arrived with his militia, significantly expanding Greene's forces. No fan of Kosciuszko's plan, Lee immediately requested permission to take the spring on the west side of the defensive works. Greene agreed, and Lee and his Legion began digging approaches toward the stockade defending it. Lee's snipers soon made access to the spring life-threatening. Cruger responded by sending his slaves to procure water under cover of darkness, but the water supply inside the garrison was drastically reduced, the men inside now suffering from intense thirst along with the blistering summer heat.[29]

Had Greene been allowed to conduct the siege to its conclusion, he would have taken Ninety-Six, probably one of his greatest achievements of the war. But this kind of victory was not his lot—not in this war, not ever. By June 10 he had received troublesome reports of British reinforcements. "By a Charles Town Paper of the 2d, I find a Fleet has lately arrived at that place; and it is said with a large reinforcement," Greene wrote to Sumter. That the inveterate spymaster Sumter had not informed him of such importance intelligence, that he only learned of it from a published newspaper report, clearly troubled Greene. "As you do not mention anything of it in your Letter I imagine you have not received an account of it. Please to make particular enquiry into the matter."[30]

The newspaper was correct. On June 3, a fleet carrying several regiments of British reinforcements landed in Charleston harbor. Lieutenant Colonel Nisbet Balfour, commanding at Charleston, and Rawdon agreed that a portion of these regiments would join with Rawdon's men at Monck's Corner and march to relieve Cruger. Now reinforced with these fresh troops, Rawdon set out for Ninety-Six on June 7 with a force of two thousand men.[31]

Believing his position at Ninety-Six threatened by this news of British reinforcements, as would eventually be proved correct, Greene ordered Sumter to his assistance. "Should the Enemy move out in force with a view of raising the Seige of this place, you will give them all the opposition in your power, that their march may be delayed as long as possible and retire before them so as to form a junction with us, as it is my intention to collect our force and give them battle."[32]

Again Sumter's mood shifted dramatically. His letters of early June prior to receiving Greene's orders were full of industry and activity. His letters after receiving Greene's instructions were now dour, his old injury suddenly troubling him once more. "I am unfortunate enough to find that My Indisposition in Creases So fast as Not to have any hopes, from the Nature of it, to be able to Remain with the Troops Many days longer; I Shall in deavour to hold out until you are So Disengage as to take Measure in consequence of My withdrawing."[33]

Greene surely found the Gamecock's grievances both upsetting and uncomfortably familiar. "I am distressed at the increasing pains in your wound," he responded dutifully. "I cannot think of your leaving the service without the greatest pain[.] Few people in any Count[r]y know how to command and fewer in this than is common. It will be of importance to the public good that you continue to command if you are unable to perform active service ... Your name will give confidence to our own people and strike terror into the enemy."[34]

Greene's predicament worsened when a Loyalist rider slipped through his lines on June 12, bringing news of Rawdon's approaching reinforcements, strengthening the resolve of Cruger and his men. Lee states that Greene's plan was to first meet Rawdon, then return to Ninety-Six to finish the siege. "The American general was disposed to imitate Caesar at Alesia; first to beat the relieving army, and then to take the besieged town. But his regular force did but little exceed half of that under Rawdon, which, added to his militia ... still left him numerically inferior to the British general."[35]

To implement his plan, Greene would first have to get his temperamental militia commanders to answer his pleas for assistance—no small task. Over the next few days Greene wrote a flurry of letters to Sumter,

Marion, and Pickens requesting their assistance in delaying Rawdon's approach. Most were answered with excuses and grumbling. Rawdon was now at Orangeburg, about two days' march from Ninety-Six, and Greene was desperate for Sumter to impede his progress.

Though he wrote to Greene on June 14 saying he was "Marching to fall in the 96 Road ahead of the enemy," Sumter in fact remained at Fort Granby until June 15, guarding his headquarters and supply depots, allowing Rawdon to pass out of Orangeburg to Ninety-Six. He might have believed an erroneous report that only a small detachment of Loyalists were at Orangeburg.

As for Marion, "I Do Not Know Gen. Marions Strength," Sumter wrote in this same letter. "I Rather think him but Weak & badly armd and Very little ammunition."[36] In fact, Sumter's orders to Marion "fluctuated between the insistent and the indecisive" at this time, according to Marion's biographer Hugh Rankin. On June 13 Sumter ordered Marion to move to Ninety-Six to support Greene, but on June 14—the same day he was assuring Greene he would fall in ahead of Rawdon on the "96 Road"—he ordered Marion to halt, awaiting more definite indications of the British plans. On June 15 he ordered Marion to move toward Ninety-Six once again, and on June 16 Sumter reported to Greene that Marion was coming up "but at a great distance."[37]

Whether these delays were due to genuine confusion about Rawdon's objectives or Sumter's deliberate machinations, there is no evidence. However, as at Hobkirk's Hill, a pattern of behavior was established: when Greene needed Sumter's support against the British Army, Sumter couldn't, or wouldn't, oblige.

In this case, Greene's expectations of Sumter and Marion may have been unrealistic. Sumter successfully fought British regulars once before, at the Blackstocks, where he operated from a superior defensive position against Banastre Tarleton's much smaller force. For Greene to expect Sumter and Marion to maneuver in front of Rawdon's army of two thousand, somehow delaying it, probably through an open field action, was an expectation never before achieved by the South Carolina militia, not without significant Continental Army support, as at Cowpens. Perhaps Greene's expectations were spoiled by the militia actions at Cowpens and Guilford Courthouse, where they had fought, for the most part, successfully on the battlefield. And though it is true Greene dispatched William Washington's cavalry to support Sumter's efforts to block Rawdon, Washington was no Daniel Morgan. He was an able officer, but not necessarily an inspiring or brilliant one. According to Henry Lee, Washington did not choose to "bestow much time or application" to the "cultivation" of the "mind."[38]

Whatever the case, whether through Sumter's circumventions or Greene's strategic miscalculations, Rawdon now marched toward Ninety-Six unimpeded, leaving Greene in dire straits. Without Sumter's support, his plan to turn and face Rawdon first was no longer sound—he didn't have enough troops to split his force. Greene was left with few options other than to abandon the siege or launch an assault, hoping to capture Ninety-Six before Rawdon's arrival.

He chose attack, determining to simultaneously assault the Star Fort on the east side of Ninety-Six and the smaller fort on the west side guarding the water supply. Two assault forces were formed. Attacking the smaller fort would be a force made up of Lee's Legion infantry and the North Carolina and Delaware Continentals led by Major Michael Rudolph. Attacking the Star Fort would be Colonel Richard Campbell with a party of Virginia and Maryland Continentals. This force was further divided into two groups. An axe party formed the first group, charged with cutting a gap through the abatis. The second party would charge through the gap carrying long poles with iron hooks. Once they reached the fort's inner walls, they would pull down the sandbags with their hooks, allowing fire from the Maham Tower to rake the defenders from the wall.

It was a desperate plan. Not surprisingly then, the two assault groups were grimly nicknamed the "Forlorn Hopes." Greene ordered the attack on June 18, opening up with an artillery barrage. After about an hour of intense fighting, Rudolph and his contingent of Continentals successfully stormed the western fort, holding it while Campbell's "Forlorn Hopes" attacked Star Fort. Under covering fire by Greene's artillery, his infantry manning the siege trenches, and riflemen atop the Maham Tower, the axe party successfully cut its way through the outer abatis, creating a gap for the hook party to storm. As they successfully pulled sandbags from the parapet, rifle fire from the Maham Tower drove the British defenders from the walls.

But seeing their position threatened, the British inside the fort sent a bayonet party into the outer ditches. Lee describes the ensuing events colorfully: "Entering into the ditch through a sally-port in the rear of the star, they [the British bayonet party] took opposite directions, and soon came in contact" with the Continentals. "Here ensued a desperate conflict. The Americans, not only fighting with the enemy in front, but with the enemy overhead, sustained gallantly the unequal contest." Yet the opposition was too strong, and the Continental attackers soon retreated.

"The adverse fortune experienced by our left column made the mind of Greene return to his cardinal policy, the preservation of adequate force to keep the field," recalled Lee, in explaining Greene's decision to abandon the assault. As always, Greene would live to fight another day, but the desperate attack on Ninety-Six was yet another defeat. Greene's losses were approximately 127 killed and wounded, with 20 missing. Of Cruger's force, about 27 were killed and 58 wounded.[39]

The Continental Army was despondent after the loss. "During the proceeding night, gloom and silence pervaded the American camp: every one disappointed—every one mortified," recalled Lee. "Greene alone preserved his equanimity; and, highly pleased by the unshaken courage displayed in the assault, announced his grateful sense of the conduct of the troops."[40]

Greene may have been sanguine on the outside, but inside he seethed. Toward Sumter and Marion he directed the bulk of his ire, as evidenced by the recollections of Andrew Pickens. In a letter written in 1811, Pickens recalled a discussion with Greene about the actions of Sumter and Marion. "The night the siege was raised at Ninety Six, I asked Gen'l Greene if he knew the cause of their not harassing the enemy, or their not joining the army. He was much irritated, and expressed himself in a manner I had not heard him before or after."[41]

To Francis Marion he expressed his frustrations in a more reserved, though still disgruntled, manner. "It was my wish to have fought Lord Rawden before he got to 96 and could I have collected your force and those of Generals Sumter and Pickens I would have done it; and I am perswaded we should have defeated him," he wrote to the Swamp Fox.

"But being left alone I was obligd to retire. I am surprisd the people should be so averse to joining in some general plan of operation. It will be impossible to carry on the war to advantage or even attempt to hold the Country unless our force can be directed to a point."[42]

But such complaints were useless now. With Rawdon's superior force approaching, Greene was forced to pack up his army and leave the field of battle a loser once more. On June 19, he ordered his army to retreat from Ninety-Six.

CHAPTER 10

The Dog Days Expedition

Francis, Lord Rawdon, arrived at Ninety-Six with his army of two thousand on June 21, two days after Greene evacuated his siege there. Rawdon's men had been on the march 14 days from Monck's Corner. Most of this force had recently arrived from Ireland and were unaccustomed to South Carolina's grueling summer heat—after first arriving in Charleston, the officers of the 19th Regiment marched with silk umbrellas to shade them from the sun. In their heavy wool uniforms, their legs still wobbly from the long sea voyage, Rawdon's soldiers arrived at Ninety-Six exhausted.[1]

Rawdon was in poor shape himself; recurring bouts of malaria mixed with exhaustion were taking a toll on his already fragile constitution. Writing to Cornwallis on June 7, the same day he left for Ninety-Six, Rawdon admitted, "I am now, my dear Lord, with great pain to tell you that I ... could not outlive the summer in this climate. I am by no means now in a state of health fit to undertake the business upon which I am going, but as my knowledge of the country and my acquaintance with the inhabitants make me think that I can effect it better than any person here, I am determined to attempt it."[2]

Despite Rawdon's exhaustion, he pursued the retreating Greene, who briefly paused his troops on the Bush River, in the fork between the Saluda and Broad rivers, while he attempted to rally his partisan commanders for a stand. Writing to Sumter on June 20, he asked the Gamecock to join him in order "to give the enemy the most effectual opposition."[3] Sumter was not the only partisan commander to receive such requests. Greene wrote far and wide, pleading for reinforcements. None answered his call.

Meanwhile, Greene's retreat ignited a new round of civil war in the backcountry, Loyalists extracting payback on their Patriot neighbors in the wake of its fleeing army. "Our present situation is truly distressing," Greene wrote to Samuel Huntington, president of the Continental Congress. "In the district of Ninety Six I verily believe there are five for one against us. The Tories swarm around us … We contend with the Enemy upon such an unequal footing that I have nothing less to expect than disgrace and ruin."[4]

But the transgressions were by no means limited to the Loyalist side. Just a few days before he wrote Huntington, Greene had been forced to write the Georgia Patriot commander Elijah Clarke, pleading with him to use his influence to "restrain two very capital evils … I mean private murders and plundering," including the "carrying away" of "Negroes and committing other enormities that want checking. Let me entreat you to exert your self as much as possible to stop the progress of this business."[5] On the same day Greene was writing Clarke, Sumter informed Greene his men had captured "A Number of Negroes."[6]

Rawdon, for his part, had no intention of letting Greene slip from his grasp, nor allow his reunion with Sumter and Marion. Replacing his most grievously sick and wounded troops with fresher ones from the Ninety-Six garrison, he marched out of Ninety-Six in pursuit of Greene on June 23.[7]

Without reinforcements, Greene couldn't face Rawdon and ordered a retreat, moving to the northeast, eluding Rawdon's pursuit by passing with his men over the Broad River to safety. But Rawdon "advanced no farther than the Enoree, as we rendered their subsistence difficult by dismantling the Mills as we retired," recounted Greene.[8] Rawdon's "troops were so spent with fatigue, and overcome by the heat, that it was impossible to do more," adds Tarleton.[9]

Rawdon returned to Ninety-Six, but with Camden abandoned following Hobkirk's Hill and Augusta surrendered on June 5, the outpost was now isolated. "The British commander [Rawdon] found it necessary to abandon the post of Ninety Six," departing with the bulk of his army, approximately 850 men, toward Orangeburg, though leaving behind

Cruger and some of his troops to guard the escape of Loyalists wishing to evacuate the area.[10]

Meanwhile, Greene set up camp near Winnsboro, South Carolina. A detachment of about two hundred North Carolina Continentals under Major John Armstrong, anticipated for weeks, finally reached Greene there, bolstering his spirits, and he still anticipated the arrival of about a thousand militia under the command of Colonel Francis Lock from the area around Salisbury, North Carolina.[11]

With the British finally evacuating the backcountry, and reinforcements arrived or on their way, it was a perfect time for Greene to give his South Carolina partisans exactly what they wanted—liberty to pursue their own objectives. Back on June 14, Sumter had written Greene informing him of his intention to "March Downwards with my whole force ... I beg you will not be apprehensive that I May be out of place by this movement."[12] Indeed Greene had been apprehensive, writing to Sumter several times since with instructions to either retard Rawdon's progress toward Ninety-Six or join with Greene.

But 11 days later, with Greene no longer invested at Ninety-Six, Sumter still wanted to make an expedition toward the British forces at Monck's Corner. Anxious to rouse Patriot sentiment in that region of South Carolina, Greene was inclined to let him do it. "I wish you to file off towards the Congaree," Greene wrote to Sumter on June 25, just six days after evacuating Ninety-Six. "No time is to be lost and you will endeavor to spirit up the people as much as you can."[13] To Governor Thomas Burke of North Carolina, Greene explained his motives: "I thought it most adviseable to detach General Sumter to attack the Enemies outposts near Charles Town, and if possible, force their whole body down into the lower country for the protection of those posts."[14]

To Henry Lee he expressed his sentiments more candidly: "It is next to impossible to draw the Militia to the Country from the different parts of the State to which they belong. Marion is below ... and Sumter wants to make a tour of Moncks Corner; and all I can say to either is insufficient to induce them to join us."[15]

Despite the troubled relationship between Sumter and Francis Marion, and Greene's frustrations with both of them, Greene once more ordered Marion to cooperate with Sumter for the expedition toward Monck's

Corner: "General Sumter is preparing for a manoeuver down into the lower parts of the State, and he requires your aid to carry it into effect. You will therefore call out all the force you can and operate with him in any manner he may direct."[16]

Almost as if genetically predisposed not to follow Greene's orders, even when they authorized him to do exactly as he wished, Sumter didn't "file off towards the Congaree," as Greene had commanded. Instead he decided "to take a Turn through the upper Regiments," traveling north to his headquarters in the Catawba basin, successfully recruiting militia for his planned expedition against the lower posts, but less successfully procuring arms for them. He hired several artificers but reported that "Material for Making of Swords are extreamly Scarce."[17]

Once again, Sumter's disobedience vexed Greene's plans, for in the meantime, Greene learned a British force under Lieutenant Colonel Alexander Stewart sent to reinforce Rawdon had mistakenly returned to Dorchester, South Carolina,[18] leaving Rawdon vulnerable to attack. On July 2, Rawdon was reported by both Lee and William Washington to be at Fort Granby guarding Friday's Ferry, the strategically important crossing on the Congaree River now abandoned by Sumter. Hoping to seize an advantage and prevent the British from "reestablishing themselves at ... the Congarees," Greene ordered Sumter toward Friday's Ferry. "If our force ... is collected we can oblige the Enemy to keep theirs collected; and that will prevent their establishing their posts again ... Having given you a state of matters, I beg you will form a junction with us as soon as possible."[19]

Sumter would do no such thing, for unbeknownst to Greene, he was over 70 miles away, back in the Waxhaws, far from where Greene expected him to be. Greene received news of Sumter's unanticipated diversion on July 3. Nevertheless, he made plans to press his attack against Rawdon at Granby, ordering Francis Marion and Andrew Pickens to join him at Friday's Ferry. Lee and Washington were ordered to harass the British reinforcements of Colonel Alexander Stewart to delay his junction with Rawdon.[20]

Even as Greene was ordering his men to leave their baggage at Winnsboro, in anticipation of an imminent attack, Rawdon received intelligence of Greene's plans and ordered Fort Granby evacuated.[21] Greene's army arrived at Friday's Ferry near Fort Granby on July 6 only to find Rawdon vanished. Though Andrew Pickens united with him there with three hundred men, Pickens's horses were "much worn down from the long march," his men exhausted and "intiarly unfit to perform the service of discovering the enemys movement or even to gett out of their way should they prove too powerfull for us."[22] Marion, for his part, performed as commanded, joining with Lee and Washington, but not in time to prevent Rawdon's junction with Stewart on July 7. According to one source, 50 of Rawdon's men died from heat exhaustion along the way. Stewart's reinforcements were in no better shape.[23] Nevertheless, Rawdon and Stewart's combined force set up a strong defensive position at Orangeburg.

Only Sumter remained absent, writing from Camden on July 6 to explain he intended to set out for Greene's camp "this Morning" but because of the "Movements of the enemy" would await "further orders."[24]

Greene still hoped for a decisive strike at Orangeburg after receiving word from Marion that Rawdon's troops were "so fatigued they cannot possibly move."[25] For once, Sumter performed as Greene desired, marching down from Camden, joining with the forces of Lee, Marion, and Washington outside Orangeburg on July 9.[26]

His partisans and light troops now combined, Greene left his own army camped at a place called Beaver Creek and rode down with a cavalry guard to meet with his commanders outside Orangeburg on July 10. "General Greene ... put himself at the head of his cavalry, commanded by Washington and Lee, accompanied by his principal officers, for the purpose of examining the enemy's position, with a view of forcing it if possible," recalled Lee. "The reconnaissance was made with great attention, and close to the enemy; for being comparatively destitute of cavalry, Rawdon had no means to interrupt it. After spending several hours in examining the British position, General Greene decided against hazarding an assault."

Although Greene's army now numbered approximately two thousand, compared with Rawdon's 1,600, fewer than a thousand were trained Continentals, the rest militia. The British position at Orangeburg was stronger than anticipated, and according to Lee's recollections, Rawdon "had secured his retreat across the Edisto" to his rear, making even a successful assault on Orangeburg little more than a pyrrhic victory.[27]

According to Lee, another reason for Greene's hesitation was the extreme deprivation faced by his troops. Greene's army rarely had adequate supply during the Southern Campaign, but due in part to the intense summer heat, the situation outside Orangeburg was particularly dire. Lee recalled memorably:

> Of meat we had literally none ... Frogs abounded in some neighboring ponds, and on them chiefly did the light troops subsist. They became in great demand from their nutritiousness; and, after conquering the existing prejudice, were diligently sought after. Even the alligator was used by a few; and, very probably, had the army been much longer detained upon that ground, might have rivalled the frog in the estimation of our epicures.[28]

Greene delayed outside Orangeburg for three days, hoping Rawdon would be provoked to launch an attack on him, as at Hobkirk's Hill. But three days of frog and alligator were enough, and the ailing Rawdon had no intention of leaving his defensive position. On July 13, Greene ordered the Patriot position at Orangeburg evacuated and embarked to the more moderate environs of the High Hills of the Santee—a long, narrow, hilly region located north of the Santee and east of the Wateree rivers in present-day Sumter County, South Carolina. Rising about 200 feet, the hills at least gave an impression of relief from the surrounding lowland heat, thanks to a prevalent breeze. There he planned to wait out the summer heat.[29]

★　　★　　★

With his militia now finally gathered and eager for action, Sumter wanted to reinstitute his plan to move into the "lower country" against the British posts protecting Charleston. Lee also wanted to remain in the field, and Marion again was ordered to support their combined operations.

Greene seemed sanguine about letting his partisans and light troops campaign while he bivouacked the main part of his army in the High Hills. "No time is to be lost, therefore push your operations night and day," an enthusiastic Greene advised Sumter, writing on July 14. "Keep

Col. Lee and General Marian advisd of all matters from above and tell Col. Lee to thunder even at the gates of Charleston. I have high expectations from your force and enterprise."[30] Explaining the purpose of the mission to Thomas McKean, president of the Continental Congress, Greene wrote, "we were in hopes to force the Enemy at Orangeburg to retire into the lower Country for the protection of those posts [Monck's Corner and Dorchester]."[31]

Sumter's ambitious plan involved dividing his force of between one thousand and 1,100 men—consisting of mounted militia and Continental cavalry with one fieldpiece—into several different detachments that would attack smaller objectives before converging on the British position at Monck's Corner, now the main British outpost defending Charleston from an interior, land-based attack. At Monck's Corner were six hundred British regulars under the command of Colonel James Coates and about 150 mounted troops from the South Carolina Rangers, a Loyalist division. The British had set up their outpost at Monck's Corner within Biggin's Church, the local parish. The church occupied an elevation at an important intersection of roads that led southeast to the Cooper River and on to Charleston. The British had constructed an abatis surrounding the 60-foot-long church, which itself was sturdily made of 3-foot-thick brick walls.[32]

Sumter's raid against the lower posts has come to be known as the "Dog Days Expedition," thanks to a popular fictionalized account called *The Forayers, or the Raid of the Dogdays* by the writer William Gilmore Simms. Published in 1855, the novel glorified the endurance and bravery of the South Carolina partisans. The "dog days" are the period from July 3 to August 11 that precede the rising of the dog star Sirius, and also happen to frequently be the most brutally hot days of summer.[33]

Though Greene later criticized Sumter's plan for its logistical complexities, Sumter's detachments found initial success. Marion and his mounted men went ahead to guard the approaches to Monck's Corner. Lee raided the British position at Dorchester, South Carolina, taking a convoy of horses and wagons that were headed to Orangeburg to supply Rawdon. Colonel Wade Hampton, leading Sumter's cavalry of State Troops, raided successfully on the very outskirts of Charleston, capturing 50 prisoners and several horses. It was the first time Charleston had been threatened militarily since the British captured it back in May 1780, creating a general state of alarm and fear inside the city. According to historian Edward McCrady, "The news of this inroad as it reached town created the greatest alarm and confusion. The bells were rung, the alarm guns were fired, and the whole city was under arms."[34]

With his detachments wreaking havoc throughout the countryside, Sumter approached Biggin's Church with the main body of his militia on July 16. A battalion of light dragoons under Hezekiah Maham, a loyal subordinate of Francis Marion (also the architect of the Maham Tower) now promoted to lieutenant colonel and given his own command, was fighting with Sumter. This mounted unit would become known as "Maham's Legion." To Maham and his Legion was assigned the strategically important mission of destroying Wadboo Bridge on one of the main routes leading back toward Charleston from Biggin's Church in Coates's rear. Maham was reinforced by a detachment under Colonel Peter Horry, another loyal Marion officer, giving Horry command of the whole.

As Maham and Horry passed the British position at Biggin's Church, Coates sent out some mounted troops to engage them, though this force was quickly driven back by the passing Patriots. However, Sumter mistakenly believed this detachment indicated the British were preparing to attack in force, and ordered his men into a defensive position outside the British position as evening approached. Meanwhile, the party under Horry and Maham reached the Wadboo Bridge. Though Horry ordered a party to commence its destruction, it is thought Horry and Maham's force spent most of their time destroying and looting two schooners found at anchor there.[35]

Under cover of night, while Sumter awaited reinforcements from Lee, Marion, and Hampton, Coates ordered Biggin's Church evacuated. "I Arrived here this morning four O'Clock: & found this post Avacuated [evacuated]," Sumter reported to Greene on the morning of July 17. "Have not been able as yet to ascertain, or even gain the least knowledge of their [the British] rout [route]."[36] Part of Sumter's confusion was because he not only thought the Wadboo Bridge destroyed, but also mistakenly believed Maham and Horry were still in possession of it. In fact, as the British retreated in force toward the bridge, Horry ordered off his men before they had completed its destruction. Coates's men were able to repair the bridge and pass over it safely.

Nevertheless, the Patriots soon discovered Coates's route; the cavalry of Lee and Hampton pursued, eventually joined by Maham's Legion. The cavalry stormed toward Quinby Bridge on the Public Road leading to Charleston, "as it was well known the stream there, the eastern branch of Cooper River, was only passable at the bridge, which it was certain Coates would destroy as soon as he crossed."[37]

Lee's troops overtook Coates's baggage train after an 18-mile chase, easily capturing the baggage and Coates's rear guard, which according to Henry Lee were raw recruits from Ireland. Advance troops under the command of Captain John Armstrong then pressed forward and came upon Coates, "who, having passed the bridge was carelessly reposing, expecting his rear-guard—having determined to destroy the bridge as soon as his rear and baggage should have passed it. With this view the planks were mostly raised from the sleepers, lying on them loosely, ready to be thrown into the stream when the rear should get over."

According to Lee, writing colorfully in his memoirs, Armstrong sent to Lee for instructions, but neglected to inform his commander that Coates had already crossed the bridge, which was now guarded by a howitzer—a cross between a cannon and a mortar. Believing that Coates was still in open ground, Lee "warmly" reminded Armstrong, "the order of the day, which was to fall upon the foe without respect to consequences."

Lee's memoir provides a dramatic description of Armstrong's attack:

> The brave Armstrong put spur to horse at the head of his section, and threw himself over the bridge upon the guard stationed there with a howitzer. So sudden was his charge that he drove all before him—the soldiers abandoning their piece. Some of the loose planks were dashed off by Armstrong's section, which, forming a chasm in the bridge, presented a dangerous obstacle. Nevertheless the second section ... took the leap and closed with Armstrong, then engaged in personal combat with Lieutenant-Colonel Coates, who ... effectually parried the many sabre strokes, aimed

at his head. Most of his soldiers, appalled at the sudden and daring attack, had abandoned their colonel, and were running through the field ... to take shelter in the farm-house.[38]

David John Bell, a British soldier in Coates's command, reported "a party of Rebells galloped over the Bridge in the face of our Field Piece, rode through the Regiment, & wounded two Men: it was the most daring thing I ever heard of: one of them made a stroke at the Colonel which he turned off ... Three of the five paid for their temerity." Neither Sumter nor Greene reported the attack with Lee's dramatic flourishes, suggesting some literary license on Lee's part, yet Bell's account clearly suggests Armstrong and his men acted with dramatic bravery in the skirmish before being chased away by Coates's infantry.[39]

Operating without his cavalry, which he had sent on a separate route, Coates and his infantry now set up a defensive position at the nearby Shubrick's Plantation. Marion came up with his men and the Legion infantry around three in the afternoon on July 17. Together, he and Lee forded the creek upstream of the bridge to survey Coates's position. The British were formed in a hollow square, their front supported by the howitzer, their flanks protected by plantation outbuildings and a rail fence, behind which Coates had posted men. Sumter arrived with his infantry around five o'clock. "Their position was the most Advantageous that cou'd have fallen in their way," Sumter later reported to Greene. "Lodged in a long line of Houses on an Emminence."[40]

Sumter's fieldpiece was still on the way, following far behind in the day's long chase; Lee and Marion deemed the position too strong to attack without artillery, but Sumter commanded an attack. He formed his battle line in a half moon around the front of the British position, with Horry's brigade on the far right and Marion's brigade on the far left. Lee and Hampton's mounted troops were held in reserve, as there was little they could do against Coates's defensive position. In the center, where there were some small slave quarters for cover, Sumter posted his own men.

A little after five, Sumter ordered Thomas Taylor's militia regiment of 45 men forward in a charge to gain the rail fence, commencing the attack. The British counterattacked with a bayonet charge, sending Taylor reeling back. Marion ordered his men up to cover Taylor's retreat. "I marched my men to a fence about fifty yards of the Enimy under a very heavy fire," Marion reported to Greene.

Under Marion's fire, the British broke their formation and most fell back into the plantation's mansion house. "We soon made them take shelter in and behind the houses," Marion continued in his report, "but was fired on from the stoop of the Houses & through the doors, windows & Corners."[41]

After an intense 40-minute firefight, both Sumter's and Marion's men were almost out of ammunition. "Our Ammunition being Intirely Expended I was obliged to retire," Marion continued. "I cannot give any perticulars of Gen. Sumters Brigade as they was too great a distance from me with fences & Corn fields which Interupted the sight."[42]

Sumter retreated 3 miles, "With a Design of Renewing the attack in the Morning," once his fieldpiece arrived.[43] But a renewed attack was not to be. Marion's casualties were eight killed and 19 wounded. Sumter reported 13 killed and 23 wounded. Marion's men were furious with Sumter. They viewed the position of Sumter's men, fighting with cover from the slave quarters, as superior to the open, coverless position where Sumter ordered them. If only Sumter had waited for his fieldpiece, they fumed, their comrades would not have been needlessly slaughtered.

In an account collected by the 19th-century researcher Lyman Draper from Thomas Taylor's son, Taylor was furious with the Gamecock after the battle, feeling that he and his men had been needlessly sacrificed. Taylor "found Gen. Sumter sitting coolly under the shade of a tree—& said: 'Sir, I don't know why you sent me forward on a forlorn hope, promising to sustain me, & failed to do so, unless you designed to sacrifice me. I will never more serve under you' & then retired from Sumter's command."[44]

Marion and Lee drew off in the night, Marion struggling to keep his furious troops from outright mutiny. Neither bothered to inform Sumter of their departure, both clearly disgruntled. Sumter ordered his retreat the following day, worried about news of a British reinforcement and suddenly without Marion and Lee for support.

The disastrous attack at Shubrick's Plantation marked a turning point for the Gamecock. Until now, both Marion and Lee had managed to keep their frustrations with him contained, at least in terms of respecting his command; Shubrick's was the first time they expressed their disdain through direct insubordination. This disdain was also evident within Sumter's own ranks, in a way not seen since the end to the disastrous Sumter's Rounds expedition back in March 1781. A year before, Sumter's unimaginative battle plans were accepted by his troops, partly because he found some limited success with his straight-ahead attacks, partly because the Gamecock's personal magnetism neutralized any criticism. But after a year of fighting, exacerbated by his serious wound at the Blackstocks, his subordinates and colleagues no longer tolerated the Gamecock's tactical shortcomings.

Francis Marion. The Swamp Fox shown in a flattering depiction. His biographers describe him as "dark-visaged" and "small," with knees and ankles deformed at birth. The portrait here neglects to include the hook nose and narrow face that made him "homely." (Library of Congress)

"It cannot, however, escape the observation of even a panegyrist of the great leader that it was the misfortune of Sumter to incur in succession the hostility of Morgan, Greene, and Lee, as well as the want of cordiality upon the part of Marion," admits the 19th-century historian Edward McCrady.[45]

Anne King Gregorie tried to put a positive spin on the "Dog Days" expedition, noting that it resulted in the destruction of the post at Biggin's Church and the capture and/or destruction of considerable British stores. In his report to Congress, Greene listed the toll as "near one Hundred and forty Prisoners ten of which were Officers, between one and two hundred Horses, several Waggons, one loaded with Ammunition, and all the Baggage of the 19th Regiment." Among the captured items was a regimental paymaster's chest containing 720 gold guineas, which Sumter ordered distributed to his men.[46]

Greene's report attempted to frame the expedition positively, perhaps because he had not participated in it, congratulating Sumter on his success: "Tho our advantages are not as great as our prospects once promised, they nevertheless will have their advantages, and reflect honor upon your command." Yet in his private correspondence, Greene continued to express frustrations with the Gamecock, writing to Daniel Morgan, "had you been with me a few weeks past, you would have had it in your power to give the world the pleasure of reading a second Cowpen affair. General Sumter had the command; but the event did not answer my expectations."[47] To the Marquis de Lafayette he complained similarly: "Our late movements below did not fully answer my expectations. Never was a better opportunity afforded an officer than General Sumter had; but he had detached his force so much and was so deceived by the enemies false appearance of an attack as to suffer the Garrison at Biggens Church to escape him."[48]

But Greene's sour grapes serve him poorly here, revealing his limitations as a personnel manager. Sumter was no savant as a battlefield commander, of that we have already established. Clearly, Marion's and Lee's insubordination here signals some fundamental fracture in the authority of his command. The Gamecock was at his best when sweeping the countryside, his intelligence network employed to the utmost, the manic spirit of industry he exuded at these times infectious to his troops. This is the Sumter Gates employed at Camden, and the Sumter whose raids following Hobkirk's Hill and here now in the Dog Days created such terror and confusion in the Loyalist population. If Marion was the master of guerilla warfare tactics, then Sumter was the master of guerilla warfare propaganda, his innate understanding of backcountry psychology his most potent weapon. True, the American Revolution was a time when military success was still defined by battlefield glory, a time long before the IRA, Al-Qaeda, or ISIL. In a more cynical age, Greene might have employed the Gamecock more effectively, recognizing his penchant for psychological operations. Still, from our modern perspective, we can acknowledge Greene never sufficiently recognized the Gamecock's expertise, preferring to denigrate him for his shortcomings on the battlefield rather than celebrate him as a propagandist extraordinaire.

Indeed, the most important consequence of the Dog Days expedition was the psychological toll taken on Charleston, now largely inhabited by Loyalist refugees, who suddenly found the city threatened by Patriot forces. In a letter to Sir Henry Clinton, British Colonel Nisbet Balfour, commanding at Charleston, admitted that Sumter's expedition, together with the American superiority in cavalry and a "general Revolt of the Province," would "much circumscribe any future Position" the British could take in South Carolina.[49]

The Southern Campaign was entering its final phase, with Sumter's power and influence diminishing. Yet it was not the style of the Gamecock to go quietly into that good night. Though he no longer held the respect of Marion, Lee, Greene, and others among the Patriot officer corps, his status among the rank and file of the South Carolina backcountry remained strong.

CHAPTER II

Eutaw Springs

"Governor Rutledge is arrived, and I hope will take measures for regulating Militia upon a proper footing, & also for raising Continental and State Troops for a longer time than those are engaged for serving with you," Nathanael Greene wrote Thomas Sumter on August 1, 1781. For Greene, the news of Rutledge's return must have brought some measure of satisfaction. The governor's departure for Philadelphia in March, where he tried to gain support among Congress for his occupied colony, had left Sumter a force unto himself. Previously answerable only to Rutledge, he was answerable to no one in the governor's absence. In this vacuum Greene had few options for managing the temperamental Gamecock, aside from his sometimes pedantic and frequently ignored "requests."

But with Rutledge's return, the political landscape shifted, and Greene seemed determined to press his advantage. "You will please to have a return made of your whole State Troops; and of all the Horse that are public property. As I am going to make a report to Congress of the State of the War, and the force of the respective States in this department, You will be very particular in this matter."[1]

Greene's motives for this request were complex. With his army enjoying a much-deserved respite at the High Hills of Santee, Greene contemplated a complicated strategic landscape. "With his small means, to sustain Virginia, to restore North Carolina, and continue to face the British force in South Carolina and Georgia, to Charleston and Savannah, called for unceasing efforts of mind and body," recounted Lee. "He [Greene] gave both without reserve; and finally determined, first to liberate North

Carolina, by carrying the garrison at Wilmington; then to pass into the enemy's country south of the Congaree, and compel him to give it up; afterward to hasten to Virginia with the *elite* of his force, uniting to it the army of La Fayette, and once more to face Cornwallis."[2]

Greene seemed to enjoy such complex deliberations, especially in moments of repose, and spent the early part of August putting the necessary elements in place. Yet again, he would need Sumter's support if he hoped to execute his plan, State Troops perhaps offering the most dependable support for the proposed expedition, even if hard experience suggested such need would go unmet. "I wish it was practicable to get the State troops to join the Army," Greene admitted in a letter to Henry Lee on July 29, "but be assured it would prove so fully my opinion of a certain person to give such an order, as not only to prevent farther exertions, but even opposition; and it is uncertain how far disappointed ambition may lead a man."[3]

There can be little doubt this wink–wink, nudge–nudge to his trusted subordinate was aimed at the Gamecock. Still, his request for an accounting of the State Troops suggests Greene believed Rutledge's return might effect some change in Sumter's attitude.

But there were other reasons for Greene's renewed interest in Sumter's State Troops. Rutledge arrived determined to quell the civil war ravishing the South Carolina countryside. In his absence, the governor had received numerous complaints about the plundering and bloodshed, including those of influential Whigs blaming Sumter's Law for the problem. Rutledge's first official act on his return to South Carolina was a proclamation against plundering; it was widely rumored Sumter's Law would soon be abandoned.[4]

If Greene hoped to improve his own strength by somehow wresting authority over the State Troops from Sumter, he was also very much embroiled in the effort to staunch the partisan bloodshed staining the countryside. Just a few days before, Colonel Wade Hampton, now one of Sumter's most trusted subordinates, wrote to Greene with deep concerns from Friday's Ferry, where the majority of Sumter's militia now reposed: "The Situation in which I found this Neighbourhood ... is truely to be lamented. Almost every person that remain'd in this Settlement after the army marched, seems to have been comin'd in committing Robberies the most base & inhuman that ever disgraced man kind."[5]

Greene's reply to Hampton clearly laid blame on Sumter's Law:

> What you write … respecting the plundering parties renders the affair truly alarming, and I have always dreaded this evil more than any other, and I foresee a dispute will arise between the Militia and State Troops. To lay a foundation to check the evil effectually no person must be allowed to take property, of any kind particularly horses unless he has written instructions for the purpose and that no officer short of a General officer presume to give them … A strict watch over your State troops will be necessary if you mean to render them useful.[6]

No doubt, the Sumter polemicist could note Greene expressed no such angst back in March, when the terms of Sumter's Law were first presented to him. Then, Greene had approved the practice of confiscating horses, slaves, and personal goods as payment, recognizing then, as now, longer enlistments were required to give the state militia some degree of stability. And again, following Sumter's attempted resignation at Fort Granby, Greene had endorsed Sumter's Law. So let us not suggest Greene was a man of impregnable morals, nor that his opinions were immune to shifting tides and circumstance. In his renewed focus on Sumter's Law, Greene clearly sensed some political advantage. Yet South Carolina's civil war also had clearly reached new heights, with plunder, attack, and violent reprisal sweeping almost every corner of the state, and evidence was mounting that Sumter's Law exacerbated it.

With his vast and complex intelligence network, his almost preternatural ability to hear every whisper of gossip, Sumter also sensed the political influences collecting against him. In response, he did what he tended to do when Greene tried to impose on him some will contrary to his own: he made himself scarce. Sometime during the first week of August, shortly after receiving Greene's letter, Sumter traveled into North Carolina, where he would remain for the next several weeks.

The reasons for Sumter's departure were many. Marion's biographer Hugh Rankin suggests he considered Rutledge's proclamation against plundering a personal rebuke. To his State Troops he was in arrears with payment, and they were becoming disgruntled.[7] Perhaps he still felt some resentment over Marion's and Lee's blunt departure following the disastrous assault on Shubrick's Plantation. In correspondence dated July 18, 1781, with Major Ichabod Burnet, Greene's aide de camp, Sumter comments vaguely, "I don't march with the troops, having some necessary matters of business to attend." He also complains, "Indisposition also interfering rather too much," referencing his ongoing health issues.[8]

According to Anne King Gregorie, Sumter moved through central North Carolina, stopping in Charlotte on August 6, collecting provision and paying debts.[9] One reason for the trip was the procurement of swords and clothing. On August 21 he was in the Moravian settlement of Salem, North Carolina, apparently accompanied by two attendants. An entry from the "Diary of the Congregation of Salem" dated August 21–22 reads:

> A Quartermaster and a Treasurer arrived today, with a message from General Sumter. They wished lodging for themselves, a house for all sorts of stores, another house for four artisans, and a smith with five or six fire-places. They made their request courteously, accepted the apologies of the Committee [of the town], looked over the town for themselves and saw the impossibility of securing what they wished.[10]

He then moved to Salisbury on August 23, where conditions for procuring the armaments and provisions he wanted were also unsuitable. In his next correspondence to Greene, dated September 10 from "Catawba River, N.C.," he claimed to be gathering supplies and material to outfit his troops, but admitted that "By Sickness and Moving have Not had Much done."[11]

Whatever the true reason for this mysterious business trip, Sumter furloughed a large segment of his brigade and gave temporary command over the State Troops to Lieutenant Colonel William Henderson, the former commandant of the 6th South Carolina Continentals, before he essentially vanished into North Carolina.

Henderson was from the Ninety-Six district and began his military career fighting the Cherokee in 1776. During the first siege of Charleston, his militia unit was annexed into the Continental Army, like Marion's and Sumter's, earning him a promotion to lieutenant colonel of the newly formed 6th. Captured by the British in the second siege of Charleston in May 1780, he was released in a prisoner exchange later that year and joined Sumter's militia brigade in time to participate at the Blackstocks in November 1780. During Sumter's convalescence after that battle, he briefly commanded Sumter's militia.[12]

Henderson and Greene enjoyed a cordial correspondence in which, unlike Sumter, Henderson solicited the Quaker General's counsel. After taking command of Sumter's State Troops, a dismayed Henderson wrote to Greene, "With expectations of Seeing at least four or five hundred men fit for the field ... I find Gen. Sumter has played the *old Soldier* with me, for I have not been able to Collect quite Two hundred fit for action, and they in a most Shatter'd condition."

Later that same day, Henderson wrote Greene again, after discovering a memorandum left for him by Sumter ordering his horses sent into the swamp, protected from additional service by a militia guard, and his troops to be furloughed until the first of October. Henderson was furious: "That I Should Cum here for no other purpose but to furlow a parsel of Troops: & that When the Enemy is at Our Very Doors: & there horses To be Guarded by militia; No Readier a way To Dismount the men Could be Devisd; Should be much Oblig[ed] To you for your Opinion on Evry Subject."[13]

Writing to Governor Rutledge on the same day, Henderson wrote of the men and officers he inherited from Sumter: "The thirst after plunder that seems to prevail among the soldiery, makes the command almost intolerable."[14]

Upon receiving Henderson's letter, Greene became furious with the Gamecock:

> I receivd your favor of the 14th inclosing General Sumters order for disbanding his brigade for I can consider it in no other light. What can be his reasons for such an extraordinary measure I cannot imagine, nor can I conceive how he could think of taking such a step without consulting me ... If he supposes himself at liberty to employ those troops independent of the Continental Army, it is time he should be convinced of the contrary ... I can by no means give my consent to it, and therefore you will not furlough a man or officer unless for some particular reasons.[15]

Despite Sumter's orders, most of his men remained in the field, though this was not enough to salvage Sumter's reputation among his fellow officers. "General Sumpter is become almost universally odious, as far as I can discover," Lee wrote to Greene. "I lament that a man of his turn was ever useful, or being once deservingly great should want the wisdom necessary to continue useful & to preserve his reputation."[16]

But Greene and his officers had little opportunity to ruminate over the Gamecock's betrayals, for by the end of August, the American war strategy was shifting up and down the east coast, and Greene was determined to play a role in its execution. On August 19, George Washington began his march to Virginia, where he hoped to set a trap for Lord Cornwallis at Yorktown. Unaware that a French fleet under Admiral the Comte de Grasse was headed his way, Cornwallis had set up camp on the Chesapeake peninsula, where he awaited orders from Clinton for a possible reinforcement of New York. To deceive Clinton, Washington left a force in front of New York, then marched south, planning to block the route of Cornwallis's retreat by land. The plan worked perfectly; Cornwallis would be trapped at Yorktown; and after a lengthy siege, forced to surrender on October 19, 1781.

Greene had learned of Comte de Grasse's anticipated arrival off the Virginia coast from Governor Rutledge, who apparently obtained the information during his sojourn in Philadelphia. Again, Lee provides a summary of Greene's strategic considerations:

> In consequence of this information [the French fleet heading for the Chesapeake coast], General Greene changed his plan, believing it most eligible to devote his means toward the accomplishment of the immediate liberation of South Carolina and Georgia ... This change in measures, too, was extremely agreeable to Governor Rutledge ... delighted with the prospect of seeing his State completely freed ... and desirous that the force of Greene should be held for that end primarily.[17]

So Greene turned his focus once more to the British force now under command of Lieutenant Colonel Alexander Stewart, for Rawdon was now returned to England. Born in 1741 and first entering the British Army as an ensign in 1755, Stewart was a seasoned and experienced officer, arriving in Charleston back in June with the reinforcements from Ireland that had marched to save Ninety-Six.

Finding his position at Orangeburg difficult to provision due to the sniping and plundering of the local Patriot militia, Stewart moved his force of approximately 1,400 men to a position just south of the confluence of the Congaree and Wateree rivers, where these rivers merge to become the Santee River. Though he was now only 15 miles from Greene's camp at the High Hills of Santee, Stewart was on the other side of the river, protecting his position from attack.

On August 22 Greene called in all of his detachments except those under Marion and Colonel William Harden, who commanded the militia in the southernmost part of South Carolina, and Hezekiah Maham's Legion. Finding the rivers swollen by recent rains, Greene was forced to march north with his army to Camden before he could find a suitable Wateree crossing, then turned south for a rendezvous on August 28 with Andrew Pickens and William Henderson, commanding Sumter's State Troops, at Howell's Ferry on the Congaree River, just south of modern-day Columbia.[18]

Hearing of Greene's movement toward him, Stewart again moved his camp to Eutaw Springs, a location "where I might have the opportunity of receiving my supplies, and disencumber myself from the sick, without risking my escorts, or suffer myself to be attacked at a disadvantage," Stewart later recounted to Cornwallis. Eutaw Springs was actually the above-ground appearance of an underground river, the same spot that had captivated the young Thomas Sumter when he first traveled through the interior of South Carolina. As the water came to the surface, it formed a creek feeding the nearby Santee River. A small settlement there was located on the main road to Charleston, improving Stewart's supply routes. Today the site is located on the shores of the modern-day Lake Marion, just east of where Interstate 95 crosses the lake, about halfway between Columbia and Charleston.

After his rendezvous with Pickens and Henderson, Greene now had under him his most formidable body of troops since the battle at Guilford's Courthouse back in March 1781. In addition to his 1,300 Continentals, including Washington's and Lee's mounted legions, Greene's force included Pickens's militia and approximately two hundred State Troops under Henderson, along with the remnants of Sumter's militia. Marion and an additional 250 were on the way. He also had with him a battalion of North Carolina militia under Lieutenant Colonel William Polk, whose cousin James K. Polk would go on to become the 11th president of the United States. Estimates vary, but altogether Greene's fighting force would eventually number approximately two thousand to 2,400 men.[19]

Greene now marched leisurely toward Stewart's position at Eutaw Springs, sending Lee in advance to scout out the British position. "Greene continued to pursue his march with unvarying attention to the ease and comfort of his troops," Lee wrote, "preserving unimpaired their strength by withholding them from the midday sun, which continued to be keen and morbid." According to Lee, this was a strategy by Greene to announce his approach to Stewart, hoping the British would retreat toward Charleston rather than face his superior force: "Greene … was disposed to stimulate further retreat [by the British]; his sole object being the recovery of the country, which, though determined to effect, he preferred doing without further waste of blood. Lee was accordingly instructed to announce rather than conceal the advance of the American army, in order that Stewart might, if he chose, fall back a second time."[20]

As magnanimous as Lee's account makes Greene seem, it is apparently an instance of his memory failing him, or an attempt to embellish his own narrative. In Greene's official account of the battle at Eutaw Springs to Thomas McKean, President of the Continental Congress, Greene reported: "We moved by slow and easy marches; as well as to disguise our real intention, as to give General Marion a chance to join us."[21]

Greene's 19th-century biographer William Johnson says Greene delayed his approach after learning from Lee, writing to Greene on September 1, that Stewart had been reinforced with six hundred troops from Fair Lawn, a British garrison near Monck's Corner, under the command of Major Archibald McArthur. Up until that point, Greene had been determined to fight Stewart as soon as possible, but after learning of these reinforcements, delayed his approach to wait for a junction with Francis Marion.[22]

Whatever the reason for his slow pace, Greene finally joined with Marion on September 7 on the outskirts of Eutaw Springs. He ordered his army to march at 4 a.m. the next day to "Attack the Enemy."[23] Aware of Greene's steady approach, Stewart nevertheless had no idea an attack was imminent. "Notwithstanding every exertion being made to gain intelligence of the enemy's situation, they rendered it impossible, by way-laying the bye paths and passes through the different swamps;

and even detained different flags of truce which I had sent on public business," Stewart recounted to Cornwallis in his account of the battle.[24]

Stewart had set up his camp in an open field on both sides of a main road. In his rear was a large, two-story brick house. From the house to the banks of Eutaw Creek extended a garden enclosed in a wall of palisades. Behind the sturdy house were various wood outbuildings, including a barn of some size. In his camp Stewart now had between 1,800 and two thousand men, almost all British Army regulars or trained Provincials. His artillery consisted of two 6-pounders, one 4-pounder, one 3-pounder, and a swivel gun.[25]

Provisions were so low in Stewart's camp that he sent out foraging parties each morning at dawn to dig for the local sweet potatoes until it became too hot. So oblivious was Stewart to Greene's approach that he sent out one of these "rooting" parties unarmed. A little later that morning, two deserters from Greene's army appeared in Stewart's camp to warn of the impending attack. Though skeptical, Stewart sent out a scouting party of 140 infantry and 50 cavalry under a Major Coffin to investigate the deserters' claims.[26]

Around 8 a.m. Coffin's scouting party encountered an advance guard of Lee's Legion cavalry under Captain James Armstrong about 4 miles west of the British camp. Coffin ordered an attack, charging directly into an ambush. Four of Coffin's infantry were killed; Coffin himself and 40 of his men were captured. The British rooting party, now in the rear of Lee's Legion, heard the shooting and rushed to Coffin's aid, only to be slaughtered by the Americans, losing 60 men either killed, wounded, or captured.[27]

When Greene heard the shooting between Coffin and Lee's Legion he paused to organize his order of battle, forming his lines in a version of the now-familiar "Cowpens" formation: in the front line he placed the militia of North and South Carolina, including the seasoned militia of Marion and Pickens. On the second line were his trained and dependable Continentals. William Washington's Legion and Delaware Continentals under Robert Kirkwood formed the reserve.

Stewart formed his main line about a hundred yards in front of his encampment, straddling the main road. On the right side of his line Stewart placed in a dense thicket along the banks of Eutaw Creek three hundred light infantry and grenadiers under the command of Major John Marjoribanks. Major Henry Sheridan was ordered to occupy the brick house at the rear of the camp, guarding a possible line of retreat. Major Coffin was ordered to remain in reserve with about a hundred infantry and 50 mounted cavalry.[28]

The action began a little past 9 a.m., with Marion's militia driving Stewart's skirmishers back toward the British camp but struggling to maintain their battle formation. As the Americans approached the main line of the British, Lee, on the far-right of the American attack, attempted to flank the British left, but was driven back by British artillery. Marion, meanwhile, led the initial attack on the American right.

In his report on the battle, Greene spoke highly of his militia's conduct:

> The militia were ordered to keep advancing as they fired. The Enemies advanced parties were soon driven in, and a most tremendous fire began on both sides from right to left … General Marion, Col. Malmady [Colonel Marquis Francis de Malmedy, a French officer commanding a body of North Carolina dragoons] and General Pickens conducted the Troops with great spirit and firmness that reflects the highest honor upon this class of Soldiers. But the Enemies fire being greatly superior to ours, and continuing to advance the Militia began to give ground.[29]

Stewart had ordered his men to stand firm against the militia attack, but against his orders, the troops on the British left advanced, pushing back the militia, who were almost out of ammunition. Against this counter-attack, the militia finally broke; Marion's militia, in particular, retreated in good order. Greene now called up Jethro Sumner's North Carolina Continentals to plug the gap left by the departing militia. Though they were not seasoned troops, the North Carolinians fought well, pushing the British counterattack back to their original position.

Stewart ordered up his reserves under Coffin, breaking the North Carolina Continentals. Meanwhile, heavy fighting continued on both flanks, the left faltering briefly when William Henderson was wounded, but Lieutenant Colonel Wade Hampton quickly assumed command, steadying the line. Greene now ordered up the Delaware and Virginia Continentals, his most experienced troops. They moved forward, firing at 40 yards then falling into a bayonet charge. At the same time the Legion infantry turned the British left flank. Stewart's left and center were routed and retreated in confusion through their tents.[30]

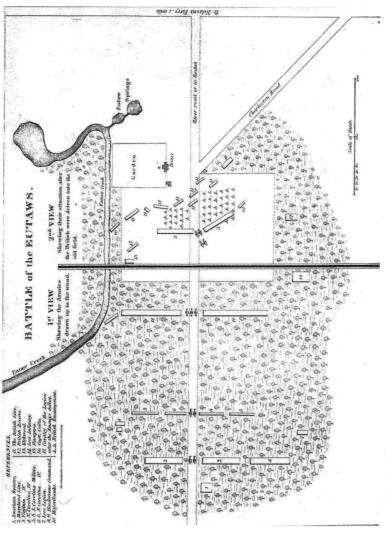

This map of the Battle of Eutaw Springs depicts the British position on the right and the alignment of the American attack on the left. The house and walled garden that played an important role during the battle are depicted just left of the springs. (McCrady, Edward. *The History of South Carolina in the Revolution, 1780–1783.* New York: The Macmillan Company, 1902)

Victory was seemingly at hand, but once again battlefield fortune turned against Greene. As the American militia and Continentals chased the retreating British Army through their camp, they paused to loot the British tents, gorging themselves on British food and swilling captured liquor. The delay allowed Stewart to order some of his retreating men back to the safety of the house and palisaded garden. Meanwhile, Marjoribanks's flank battalion held fast against Washington's cavalry from the defensive cover of the blackjack thicket. Washington was eventually wounded and captured. Although Wade Hampton once again stepped in to continue the attack, the Americans could not take Marjoribanks's position.

With the assistance of two swivel guns mounted at second-story windows, the British poured a deadly fire from the house. Greene ordered up four 6-pounders to bombard the house, including two captured from the British. But fire from the swivel guns shot down the American artillerymen. With the Americans in disarray, Marjoribanks counterattacked, pinning Hampton's cavalry between his infantry and the British inside the house. Caught in a devastating crossfire, a third of Hampton's men were either killed or wounded, the rest scattered. Marjoribanks now attacked Greene's infantry, capturing the 6-pounders, but receiving a serious wound in the process.

At this point the battle had been fought for over three hours. "Finding our Infantry galled by the fire of the Enemy, and our Ammunition mostly consumed, tho' both Officers and Men continued to exhibit uncommon acts of heroism, I thought it proper to retire out of the fire of the House and draw up the Troops at a little distance in the Woods, not thinking it adviseable to push our advantages farther," Greene recalled.[31]

The Battle of Eutaw Springs was the last major military engagement of Greene's Southern Campaign. It was also the bloodiest. The official American casualty figures published by Congress were 139 killed, 375 wounded, and eight missing. Estimates agree roughly a quarter of Greene's army was either killed or wounded. Greene's officer corps was decimated. Of the six Continental officers commanding regiments at Eutaw Springs, only Henry Lee and Otho Holland Williams escaped unscathed. Both Andrew Pickens and William Henderson were wounded, though Marion was not hit.

Though he retained the field at the end of the battle, Stewart's command was devastated. According to his official report, he lost 85 killed and 351 wounded, as well as 257 missing. Stewart surely underreported his missing: Greene reported taking five hundred British prisoners. Stewart lost approximately a third of his command at Eutaw Springs. According to historian Mark Boatner, "the British suffered the highest percentage of losses sustained by any force during the war" at Eutaw Springs.[32]

Greene planned to renew the battle on the following day, but Stewart was in no mood for another fight. After the battle, he retreated to Monck's Corner, burning his stores, leaving his dead unburied, and abandoning 70 wounded men. Both Greene and Stewart claimed victory. "With particular satisfaction I have the honour to inform your lordship, that on the 8th instant I was attacked by the rebel General Greene, with all the force he could collect in this province and North Carolina, and after an obstinate engagement, which lasted near two hours, I totally defeated him, and took two six-pounders," Stewart reported to Cornwallis.[33]

In his report to Governor John Rutledge, Greene put a similarly sanguine spin on the day's bloodbath: "We have had a most Obstinate and Bloody action. Victory was ours. We drove the Enemy, more than four Miles. We took between three and four hundred prisoners, and had it not been for the large Brick Building, at the Eutaw Springs, and the peculiar kind of Brush that surrounds it, we should have taken the whole Army prisoners."[34]

The debate over who won Eutaw Springs still rages today, though most historians give Stewart the edge. But as he'd done at Guilford Courthouse, Hobkirk's Hill, and Ninety-Six before, Greene lost the battle while winning the war. The British would never again challenge Greene's Continental Army in battle in South Carolina. After briefly pursuing Stewart's retreat, Greene paused to rest his troops, allowing Stewart to slip away. After the battle, Greene ordered his army to return to the High Hills of Santee, where Greene would "give the troops time to refresh after their Glorious Expedition in which they behaved with such Extraordinary fortitude and bravery."[35]

Could it be a coincidence that immediately following the Battle of Eutaw Springs, as Greene was considering a respite for his battered army,

Thomas Sumter finally emerged from his mysterious sojourn in North Carolina? With Sumter's vast and complex intelligence network there was little the British or Continental Army either did or contemplated of which Sumter was not aware. As with both Hobkirk's Hill and Ninety-Six, where circumstances prevented Sumter from serving under Greene during battle, but somewhat miraculously reversed themselves immediately thereafter, Sumter was now available for action. Writing on September 10, two days after the battle, from a location in North Carolina on the Catawba River, not far from his home territory, Sumter reported, "I am far from being harty, but Riding aGrees Very well with me [and] together with the air and water Might prove Rather an advantage to me in health … I am D[ear] Sir with the Greatest Respect your Most obdt [obedient] Hble [humble] servant."[36]

Bitter Ends

From his camp at the High Hills of the Santee, where he'd taken his battered army to rest and recuperate following the bloodbath at Eutaw Springs, General Nathanael Greene was scheming again. The French fleet had arrived off Yorktown, threatening Cornwallis's position there. Greene believed Cornwallis would attempt a retreat to Charleston, and once more he called on his militia troops to help him face the British lord.

With the Gamecock now returned from his mysterious business trip, Greene wrote him on September 16, requesting once more that he collect his State Troops and as much of the militia "as can be brought out" in order to cut off Cornwallis's possible retreat.[1]

One can only imagine what reaction Greene believed this request would engender in Sumter, who had shown himself averse to such requests time and time again. But Greene seemed to have another trick up his sleeve. Writing to Sumter a day later, Governor John Rutledge delivered Greene's bombshell: Sumter's militia were ordered to travel to Greene's camp on foot, without their horses, to do duty as infantry in the coming campaign against Cornwallis.

The Southern militia's practice of always traveling by horse had always been a thorn in the side of the regular army officer during the Revolutionary War, both American and British. Back in 1780, after first evaluating his South Carolina Loyalist troops, Cornwallis had written, "this militia can be of little use for distant military operations, as they will not stir without a horse."[2]

Aside from the fact that the regular army officers believed the best horses should be reserved for their own mounted troops, the main problem was that militia horses were voracious eaters, devouring the countryside's precious grain and forage, a problem the Continental Army had been dealing with since the start of the campaign. "We have to feed such a number of horses that the most plentiful country must soon be exhausted," Morgan had complained to Greene back in January. "Could the militia be persuaded to change their fatal mode of going to war, such provision might be saved, but the custom has taken such deep root that it cannot be abolished."[3] Greene had written frequently and vehemently on the subject, complaining in January that "their [the militia's] mode of going to war is so destructive, as well as uncertain, that it is the greatest folly in the world."[4]

This opinion hadn't changed in the intervening months, especially when his own army was in such desperate need of dependable mounts. Back in May, his frequent requests to Marion for horses had become so irritating to the Swamp Fox that he had offered his resignation, adding petulantly at the end of his resignation letter, "I send ... horse for yourself. He is very tender foot, & must be shod before he can be of use."[5]

But there was something new in Rutledge's command, a Greene power play Sumter sensed instinctively. "The order to dismount the South Carolina militia, therefore, although transmitted through Rutledge, was Greene's declaration of independence of the militia," writes Anne King Gregorie.[6]

But this was not winter 1780, nor spring 1781, and Sumter found his stature much reduced in fall 1781. Indicative of his diminished state, Sumter replied only with familiar tropes: "I have it to lament that My present indisposition, renders me incapable of carrying the whole of your requisitions into Execution, being Scarce able to Sign My Name," he responded to Greene's request for troops on September 19, 1781, "but rest assured that every thing in My Power shall be done to promote your designs."[7]

At this point, Greene could have hardly found the Gamecock's equivocal response unusual, yet still he pressed Sumter for support, writing him again on September 28 and yet again on October 3, "reminding" Sumter of Rutledge's orders to embody one-third of his militia and march them to Greene's headquarters for a three-month term.[8]

After a brief sojourn to Charlotte around October 11, where Greene expected to meet one thousand militia under the command of Isaac Shelby and Colonel John Sevier for his effort to drive the remaining British troops into Charleston, Greene returned to his headquarters at the High Hills of the Santee not only without Shelby and Sevier or their army of a thousand, but also to find that neither Sumter nor his militia had arrived pursuant to his orders. Greene seems nonplussed in a letter to Marion, in which he explains he had "urged General Sumter to collect his militia & State Troops as soon as possible, but I am afraid it will be some time before ... Genl. Sumter will be ready to Join us in the attempt."[9]

The hinge of history was swinging in favor of the American cause, with or without Sumter's acquiescence. On October 19, 1781, Cornwallis surrendered his army of seven thousand at Yorktown. Of Thomas Sumter's great notoriety among the British and their allies, Gregorie notes that though the Gamecock was not at Yorktown, a German mercenary serving with Cornwallis wrote in his diary that he was, and "showed great kindness to our men."[10]

"The news of the surrender of Lord Cornwallis reached us the 27th in the evening," Greene reported to Washington on November 2, "and it came so well warranted that we had a feu de joy upon it the 28th... Nothing can equal the joy that it gives to this Country; and I contemplate the consequences with infinite pleasure."[11]

Though Greene was clearly elated, the news came bittersweet. In September, Greene had proposed a consolidated attack against Charleston with the French fleet once Cornwallis's anticipated surrender was complete. Only a few days earlier, Greene received word from Washington such an operation would not be possible. "It gives me great pain to find that what ever may be our success in Virginia, the circumstances of our Ally will not permit them to cooperate with us in an attempt on Charles Town," Greene had lamented to Washington in a letter dated October 25, 1781.[12]

Nevertheless, a celebration was warranted, and even Sumter could not resist, arriving in Greene's camp unexpectedly as the Patriots reveled. Sumter's appearance caused some consternation for Greene and Rutledge: though he no longer commanded the respect of his fellow officers, he

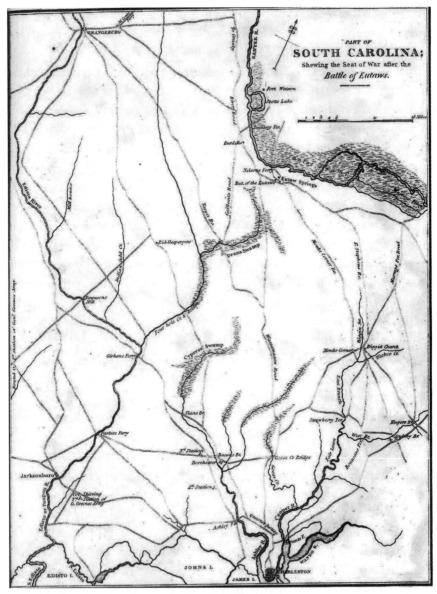

South Carolina Showing the Seat of the War After the Battle of Eutaw Springs. Several sites from Thomas Sumter's "Dog Days Expedition" are shown on this map of lower South Carolina, including Monck's Corner, Biggin's Church, and Quinby Bridge, on the lower right. (Johnson, William. *Sketches of the Life and Correspondence of Nathanael Greene, Major General of the Armies of the United States, in the War of the Revolution*. Volume Two. Charleston, SC: A. E. Miller, 1822)

was still revered by the South Carolina militia. But now that Sumter was in camp, what was to be done with him? "I find from the reports of several people the Tories are getting troublesome and insolent in the neighbourhood of Orangeburgh, in the Forks of the Edisto, and even as high as the ridge towards Ninety Six," Greene wrote to Sumter on November 2. "To check their insolence and prevent supplies from going to Charles Town ... I wish to know what force you can collect to take post there of the State Troops and Militia, including such of General Pickens brigade."[13]

Orangeburg remained a trouble spot in the South Carolina interior, in part because of the area's large population of German settlers. For the most part, South Carolina's German population had tried to remain neutral during the war, though their sympathies tended to lie with King George III, whose German heritage they appreciated. This was especially true in Orangeburg, where Loyalist sympathies ran so deep the area mostly avoided the bloody civil war plaguing other parts of South Carolina. Thanks to this relative tranquility, and the strong Loyalist sentiment there, Orangeburg became a refuge for many of the Loyalists who fled the Ninety-Six area following its evacuation in June.[14]

But this tranquility was disrupted after the return of Governor John Rutledge in fall 1781. Upon his return, Rutledge offered pardons to South Carolinians who had fought for or with the British, or adhered to the British cause, under the condition those who accepted the pardon serve in the Patriot militia for a six-month term. To those Loyalists who would not accept the pardon, Rutledge commanded them "to abandon their properties in this State forever and go with their wives and children whither, for what purpose, on whom to depend, or how to submit they know not, most probably to experience in some strange and distant land all the miseries and horrors of beggary, sickness and despair."[15] As with the conditions of British general Henry Clinton's similar pardon offer to South Carolina Patriots a year before, this offer caused sharp divisions between those who tacitly accepted it, believing the Loyalist cause lost, or perhaps not caring much one way or the other as long as their families and property remained safe, and those who vowed never to fight for the enemy cause despite Rutledge's threats.

The latter situation was true in Orangeburg, where fighting between Loyalist and Patriot now flared. Surprisingly, Sumter obeyed Greene's command. Perhaps his unexpected appearance in Greene's camp left him unable to claim the "indisposition" from lingering ailments he had claimed so many times before. Perhaps he found independent command in Orangeburg preferable to Greene's direct supervision. Whatever the case, Sumter now traveled to Orangeburg, though he clearly found the post distasteful. "The Militia I have are Trifeling Consisting of the Worst men and arms in the Brigade," he complained to Greene in a letter dated November 14. "Neither is the State Troops equal to What I expected."[16]

With a force of just over four hundred, plagued by "Considerable desertion," Sumter tried to maintain control over a region now wracked by civil war. In mid-November, one of his regiments skirmished with a large Loyalist force under the command of Major William Cunningham, who would go on to everlasting infamy in South Carolina as the notorious "Bloody Bill" Cunningham. A disgruntled Loyalist whose crippled brother was murdered by Patriot marauders earlier in the war, Cunningham left Charleston in early November 1781 with a recruited force of three hundred Loyalist militia on a mission of vengeance and terror to the South Carolina backcountry. At this point, Cunningham was only passing through Orangeburg, headed to present-day Laurens and Spartanburg County, but Cunningham's "Bloody Scout" would go on to kill almost a hundred men, including the murder of several dozen in cold blood.[17]

Sumter's reduced force could not detain Cunningham, leaving Sumter to subdue local Loyalist partisans, many of whom had escaped into the nearby swamps. "I had a party out yesterday which took a few prisoners," Sumter reported to Greene in his letter of November 24, 1781. "The officers that was out informs me that they think there is Not less than fifteen hundred persons of one Kind or an other … all Lying in deep swamps Close upon the banks of the river which they pass in an Instant either upon logs or by Swimming, from one side to the other as occasion May Require." Both Loyalist and Patriot were hiding there, finding the murky waters more secure than sleeping at home, where they were easy targets for assassination in South Carolina's brutal civil war. "We are every day in the swamps," Sumter informed Greene, noting that some Loyalists surrender, but "they go at large and are Very much threatened by their Brethren ... out lying parties through this Country are Numerous and Troublesome."[18]

No doubt the Gamecock, once in command of the entire state, found this garrison duty drudgery, beneath his station. Perhaps that was the point. But for the most part he bore the indignity in silence, at least in his correspondence with Greene. Still, Sumter's innate industry had not failed him. He proposed to Greene an action against the British garrison at Monck's Corner, which he deemed "exposed" and that a "large body of horse properly disposed of" might do "considerable Damage."[19]

However, with his own force insufficient for the attack, Sumter needed Marion's cooperation for the raid on Monck's Corner. "If you think you can give the Enemy a deadly blow by General Marions joining you with part or all of his party, please inform him therof and desire you to second him in an attack," Greene counselled Sumter.[20]

Sumter sent an envoy to Marion, proposing the attack, but it never materialized because of Greene's larger designs. As Sumter trudged through the swamps around Orangeburg, Greene was finally reinforced by militia under the command of Colonels John Sevier and Isaac Shelby from the Overmountain settlements in present-day western North Carolina and eastern Tennessee, putting him in position for an attempt to drive the enemy into Charleston.

Though Greene had contemplated a move against the forces outside of Charleston throughout the fall of 1781, this particular scheme was precipitated by Governor John Rutledge's call for general elections issued in late November, the first statewide legislative elections in South Carolina since November 1778. Since February 1780, prior to the British capture of Charleston, Rutledge had governed the state under extraordinary powers granted to him by the last South Carolina legislature. With Greene reinforced and the majority of the state under Patriot control, Rutledge was now anxious to restore a representative government and restore civil government.[21] Part of Greene's objective was to sweep the last of the Loyalist and British forces from the countryside prior to the elections to insure their safe and orderly administration. And, as usual, low on provisions and stores, he also hoped to capture the rice fields between the Edisto and Ashley rivers outside Charleston to feed his army for the winter.[22]

Preparing for this push, Greene moved his army from the High Hills of the Santee on November 19 downward by way of McCord's Ferry on the Santee River to camp near Four Holes Swamp in the Orangeburg District. From there, Greene appropriated Sumter's cavalry under Wade Hampton as escort for a scouting trip toward Charleston. Meanwhile, Sumter's State Troops and wagons were kept busy supporting the nearby army, preventing his planned attack on Monck's Corner.[23]

The degradation of Sumter's command continued in early December, as Greene moved his army further south from Four Holes to the Round O, an important crossroads about 20 miles west of Charleston. Though surrounded by swamps, Round O was on high ground, had potable water and readily defensible approaches. The location gave Greene access to British positions in both Charleston and coastal Georgia.

Rutledge meanwhile announced the upcoming General Assembly would be held in Jacksonborough, South Carolina, a small town on the Edisto River about 30 miles from British-occupied Charleston and less than 20 miles south of Round O. These twin moves were designed to demonstrate the Patriots' firm control over the state, improving Greene's access to provisions in the fertile low country region but also quelling Loyalist dissent by demonstrating total control over the South Carolina interior, compared to the British Army's increasingly isolated position inside Charleston. But the move also left Sumter behind the front lines, the state's onetime supreme commander now little more than the commandant of a backwater post.

In a letter written December 2 ordering Sumter to guard the strategically important Four Holes Bridge, Greene again chastised Sumter about his mounted militia. "As the Enemy have no longer the command of the Country it is our interest to change the plan of the war and as subsisting a great body of horse is expensive as well as distressing the sooner they can be lessened the better."[24]

In this letter, and a subsequent letter written on December 15, Greene ordered Sumter to reorganize his State Troops into two regiments, one of cavalry and one of infantry. The cavalry unit of 128 men, under the command of Wade Hampton, was dispatched to service in Georgia.[25] Ordered to abandon their mounts, many of the remaining infantry instead chose to desert, irking Sumter: "With Respect to Reducing and Dismounting the battalions of State Troops, it is by No means the trouble or difficulty that may attend the undertaking that is Requarded [i.e. required?], but the equity and policy of the Measure ... I therefore beg leave to observe that the State Troops Was Raised as light dragoons, of Course Mounted, and Shoud have been equiped as such," Sumter wrote to Greene on December 22.

His troops abandoning him, Sumter's frustrations seethe in this letter, the matter of the horses even more irksome because he'd learned Marion's men were allowed to keep theirs:

> The Militia of My Brigade also think themselves Much injured by being obliged to perform a Two month & ten days tour of duty of foot, Not even Suffered to Ride from home & Send their horseback [i.e. horse back]. When at the Same Time they are Told that Governor Rutledge Suffers other divisions of Militia to do duty as horse or Mounted Infantry & Remain but one month in the field before Relieved ... It is evident that the Brigades I Command has been Neglected With design ... and has been Ludicrously treated insomuch that he Who would any longer Submit to it Might Justly be Charged with Meanness & Pusillanimity.[26]

By now inured to Sumter's histrionics, Greene responded to Sumter's accusations of "Meanness & Pusillanimity" with his now customary detachment:

> I do not know of any partia(lity) in the matter, but General Marion being ne(ar) the enemies lines I suppose led to the indu(lgence) if any was granted. You know the nature of service must always govern the mode of equi(pp) ing troops. At the time you raised your State Troops the circumstances of this country was widely different from what it is at present; and to have more Men Mounted than is essential to service is distressing both to the inhabitants and the rest of the Cavalry ... It is for these reasons that I wish your Moun(ted) infantry to be dismounted.

Greene's habit of slipping into sanctimony now reappears at the closing of this letter: "Let me beg of you not to suffer any little incidents or even neglects or partialities whether real or imaginary to divert you from the same line of conduct you have been pursuing."[27]

At this point Greene clearly hoped the upcoming General Assembly would put to rest his difficulties with Sumter. The issue of Sumter's Law continued to plague the Gamecock. General Isaac Huger was but one prominent South Carolina Whig who had suffered retaliation for Sumter's measure, and it was widely presumed there would be some reckoning of the practice at the General Assembly, for which Sumter had been nominated as a delegate.[28]

"(Do y)ou intend to get into the General Assembly, and have the appropriation of the house upon the measure taken to raise State Troops?" Greene prodded Sumter in his letter of December 12, 1781. "Nothing like the time present when the gratitude is warm, and danger not past, to get business of this sort approved?"[29]

Greene's insincerity nearly bleeds through the page in his following letter of December 15, in which the General Assembly's address of Sumter's Law is not mentioned but clearly implied:

> Never mind little difficulties[;] we have gone through greater and I persuade my self we shall triumph at last, and your Country if they have any justice and gratitude will not fail to bless and reward you for your exertions made in the darkest hours they ever felt. I shall always bear testimony to your services and dont fail to tell the people how much you did when many others hid their head.[30]

Picking up on the subtext of Greene's platitudes, Sumter responded in his letter of December 22:

> You asked if I did Not intend to get into the General Assembly. It is probable I May Serve if elected, but as I Never have Solicited any publick appointment I Cant think of doing it Now. NotwithStanding I have the Matter you have Mentioned Very much at heart ... I Shall be prepared to Make a True & fair Representation of Matter to the house, perhaps the Result may prove favourable. I have Nothing to urge upon my own account, more than to enable me to Comply With the promises Made to the Troops. If they are paid, & I am Sensured, my expectations will not be disappointed.[31]

As Greene anticipated, Sumter was elected to the state senate in the December elections. Writing on January 2, 1782, and again on January 4, Sumter requested permission from Greene to leave his command at Orangeburg to prepare for the General Assembly, the last letter containing an unusual request not to be called on for military service again until the issue of Sumter's Law was addressed. "In my last I took the liberty to Request permission to Withdraw from this place ... to Prepare to Attend the Assembly. I hope to be Indulged, and Beg Not to be honour again With any of your Commands Untill a proper inquiry Can be Made Whether I am Worth[y] of them."[32]

The letter must have been received with mixed emotion by Greene. Clearly, he understood Sumter's value as a leader of the South Carolina partisans, yet just as clearly the relationship had frayed, with Greene ever more frequently expressing his frustrations about the Gamecock in correspondence with Lee and others. Sumter had been relegated to guard duty at Orangeburg, his horses and State Troops stripped from him, and was staring in the eye official censure, or worse, over Sumter's Law.

If Greene accepted the letter in triumph, as we imagine some part of him must have felt, it was surely a bittersweet one. Ever the reconciler, the pacifier, at least in his official correspondence, Greene replied to Sumter on January 8:

> I do not comprehend you fully in that part of your letter where you desire not to be honored with any further commands from me until a proper enquiry can be made ... If there are complaints of a civil nature errors in these matters is no absolute disqualification for Military command. I hope and doubt not you will find matters and things more to your mind upon investigation ... and I hope you will meet in the Senate and Assembly in perfect good humour and that harmony and concord will prevail among you. You have my full consent to attend the house of Assembly.[33]

This letter is the last known correspondence between Greene and Sumter. As he'd indicated to Greene, Sumter attended the Jacksonborough Assembly in January 1782, where the issue of Sumter's Law was addressed. There, a House committee determined that the terms upon which the State Troops had been enlisted should be honored, recommending that the governor be empowered to deliver not more than four hundred negroes to General Sumter, who would be responsible for their distribution to his enlisted men. But the issue was far from settled, and would continue to plague Sumter for the next few years.

Elected at the General Assembly was new governor John Mathews, to whom Sumter submitted resignation of his brigadier general commission following the adjournment of the assembly on February 26, 1782. Turning now to political and business interests, Sumter took no further active part in the war.[34]

Indeed, the war was essentially over, although the British would not evacuate Charleston until December 14, 1782. Greene continued to command the Continental Army, preferring to isolate Charleston rather than launch what would surely be a long, bloody, and meaningless siege on the city. But as he continued to squeeze the city, the condition of his troops deteriorated, resulting in an unfortunate decision by Greene to privately finance his army's provision. Thomas Sumter would attempt some measure of revenge against Greene for this decision many years down the line; for now, both men were content to let the war wind down, their attention focused on other pressing matters, not one another.

Contemporary assessments of Sumter's performance as a brigadier general almost always start with the following observance: in the summer of 1780, following the British capture of Charleston, he was the first and most prominent military officer to form an organized resistance in the southern colonies. Through initiative and sheer force of will, he forged a partisan resistance to British subjugation, becoming an important symbol to a temporarily defeated people. His successful attack on the Tory garrison at Hanging Rock on August 6, 1780, was the first significant Patriot victory following the British occupation, demonstrating to both the British and the people of South Carolina that the colony's Patriots would not quietly submit to British rule. And you can add to that legacy his victory over Tarleton on November 20, 1781, at the Blackstocks, an action whose broader implications, particularly in regard to Morgan's victory at Cowpens less than two months later, are still little understood or appreciated by history.

To be fair to Sumter's legacy, it should be noted that the period covered in this book, beginning roughly when Nathanael Greene arrived in Charlotte to take command of the Continental Army on December 2, 1780, to the convening of the Jacksonborough General Assembly in January 1782, was far from Thomas Sumter's best. The wounds he suffered at Blackstocks were serious and painful, perhaps taking a psychological toll on the Gamecock along with a physical one. In convalescence when Greene took command, Sumter struggled with issues of resentment and pride, perhaps never earning the respect of Greene and his Continental officers to the extent he felt due. A healthy Sumter may have been in position to be a more magnanimous and cooperative one. I like to think of this period as Sumter's *Empire Strikes Back*—the second, downcast installment of a trilogy that would surely see the Gamecock emerge triumphant in Act Three.

In an account of the Southern Campaign prior to Greene's arrival, taken from the summer and fall of 1780, a more noble, less querulous portrait of Sumter would emerge. Of the Sumter of that period, no less an expert than Banastre Tarleton, his frequent foil, wrote: "This active partisan was thoroughly sensible, that the minds of men are influenced by enterprise and that to keep undisciplined people together, it is necessary to employ them." Employ them he did, with zest and zeal, and his men loved him for it, despite his frequent battlefield losses. "His reputation for activity and courage was fully established by his late enterprising conduct," Tarleton wrote of Sumter's attack on Hanging Rock. This enterprising, courageous Sumter presents a more sympathetic portrait of the man than the one we see following Blackstocks.[35]

But let us not completely discount the Thomas Sumter of 1781, nor his overall contributions to the Revolutionary War. Like his fellow populist demagogues before and since, Sumter's obvious charisma, combined with his keen understanding of backcountry psychology, clearly galvanized his constituents in a way in which Greene was incapable, and the armchair historians of the American Revolution can debate endlessly whether there would have been a Marion or Pickens or Maham or Wade Hampton if there had not first been a Thomas Sumter. Those men were great leaders, but they were no match for the appeal and kinetic energy of the Gamecock. As Anne King Gregorie writes: "Sumter obtained and held his leadership because he was one with his followers and understood them; and he should be measured not by the standards of Cornwallis or of Greene but by those of the men who chose him as their leader."[36]

Nor should we forget Sumter's role as the Southern Campaign's most relentless and industrious spymaster, maintaining a vast and wildly successful network of both intelligence and counterintelligence operations, almost in his spare time. Again and again in their correspondence, Greene's deep reliance on Sumter's intelligence is obvious, both within the enemy ranks and in the surrounding countryside. A book on Sumter's role as one of the American Revolution's greatest spies is yet to be written.

And if Sumter was all too prone to the human conditions of pride, jealousy, and resentment, he at least demonstrated the common sense to keep his opinions on such matters to himself. Unlike Greene, whose frank criticisms and complaints about Sumter all too frequently appeared in his correspondence and recorded conversations, with consequences that, as we shall soon see, plagued him and his family long after his death, Sumter had the good sense to keep his innermost thoughts, no matter how dark and disparaging, to himself, a practice only a true leader understands, often through painful experience.

As we have so often, we will leave it to Henry Lee to summarize Sumter's strength and devoted patriotism:

> His aspect was manly and stern, denoting insuperable firmness and lofty courage. He was not over scrupulous as a soldier in his use of means, and apt to make considerable allowances for a state of war. Believing it warranted by the necessity of the case, he did not occupy his mind with critical examinations of the equity of his measures, or of their bearings on individuals; but indiscriminately pushed forward to his end—the destruction of his enemy and liberation of his country. In his military character he resembled Ajax; relying more upon the fierceness of his courage than upon the results of unrelaxing vigilance and nicely adjusted combination. Determined to deserve success, he risked his own life and the lives of his associates without reserve. Enchanted with the splendor of victory, he would wade in torrents of blood to attain it.[37]

Yes, Sumter was a bad field commander, often needlessly putting his men's lives at risk. His go-to strategy was the straight-ahead attack. Yes, he was lousy at camp discipline and security. And yes, despite his military training and service in the Continental Army, Sumter too often led by instinct, not procedure and tactics. But by any measure he was a hero of the American Revolution, and thus a bona fide American hero.

CHAPTER 13

The People Versus Nathanael Greene

In his own time, even before the war officially ended, Nathanael Greene was a branded hero for his service in the Southern Campaign. In late 1781 Greene was a leading candidate for the newly created position of Secretary of War. But weary of public service, and with an eye toward establishing a family fortune, he withdrew his name from consideration for the job, knowing full well from his days as quartermaster general that accumulating wealth would be difficult, if not impossible, as a government administrator.[1]

Along with Henry Lee and Daniel Morgan, Greene was one of only seven Americans awarded a congressional gold medal for his service in the Revolutionary War, the highest American military honor of its time. With it he also joined Horatio Gates, Anthony Wayne, John Paul Jones, and George Washington in the pantheon of American heroes to earn the accolade.[2]

The southern colonies he'd helped liberate from British control were especially eager to express their gratitude. On January 27, 1781, the South Carolina House of Representatives (not including Sumter, who was serving in the Senate) adopted a resolution of thanks to Nathanael Greene reading, in part: "We shou'd betray a great degree of insensibility and be wanting in Justice to his merit shou'd we omit the occasion of acknowledging with the Warmest gratitude our Obligations to the Great and Gallant General Greene, his achievements in this State while they rank him with the greatest Commanders of Antient or Modern date, will engrave his Name in indelible Characters on the Heart of every Friend to this Country."

At the same session, both houses approved ten thousand guineas to purchase an estate for Greene in thanks and acknowledgment for his service to the state. This money would eventually be used to purchase a 6,600-acre estate on the Edisto River called Boone's Barony. The North Carolina and Georgia assemblies would soon follow suit, gifting to Greene estates of 25,000 and 2,000 acres respectively.[3]

For Greene, these accolades must have been both gratifying and surreal, since he was technically still fighting the war. His battered, destitute army was in no position to attack the strong British defenses in Charleston, though after Cornwallis's surrender at Yorktown there wasn't a need. Both sides would play a waiting game around Charleston until the British finally evacuated it on December 14, 1782, almost a full year after the Jacksonborough General Assembly. But even then, the war was not technically over, and Greene did not dismiss his men until June 21, 1783, departing Charleston on August 11 for a tour of the north, before he returned to occupy Mulberry Grove, his Georgia estate, in October 1785.

During the long two years following the Battle of Eutaw Springs, the condition of Greene's army continued to deteriorate, despite his constant pleas to Congress and the colonial governments for support. On March 11, 1782, he wrote to John Hanson, President of the Continental Congress:

> You must also readily conceive how disagreeable the situation of the Army must be, employed for the defense of such a Country ... Add to this the deplorable situation of our troops ... Your officers are in distress, having drained every private resource for support. Your soldiers are complaining for want of pay and clothing ... We have three hundred men without Arms, and more than a thousand men are so naked, for want of cloathing, they can only be put on duty in cases of a desparate Nature.[4]

In an effort to help Greene, Secretary of War Benjamin Lincoln authorized him to negotiate local contracts for supplies and provisions, but the Continental government's credit was so bad, few local merchants would accept it. A contract bid to supply Greene's Continental Army in spring 1783 was accepted by only one creditor, a merchant named John Banks with the Virginia firm of Hunter, Banks, and Co., who concocted a complicated scheme to use tobacco imported from the British West Indies as collateral for durable goods sold to the Continental Army. With no other options, Greene eventually agreed to award Banks the contract. But the scheme collapsed, and Banks's credit became worthless. With his army destitute and near mutiny, Greene signed a personal bond of 30,000 pounds sterling to cover debts to merchants who had sold goods through Banks.[5]

Such agreements were not unusual in the Revolutionary War. As Greene alluded to in his letter to Hanson, officers frequently undertook debt to provision their soldiers during the war, assuming the debts would be acknowledged and paid by the government after the war. In assuming responsibility for Banks's debt, Greene was probably influenced by the action of the Marquis de Lafayette, who made a similar gesture to clothe his troops in 1781. But Lafayette was a French aristocrat with a substantial fortune. Greene descended from middle-class merchant stock.

The decision proved a disastrous one. Following the war, as Greene attempted to settle into life as a gentleman farmer, with the estates in Georgia and South Carolina as the basis of his agricultural enterprises (the land in North Carolina was sold), Banks evaded his creditors, who increasingly pressured Greene, the guarantor of Banks's debts, for payment. "I have made use of every argument in my power to induce Mr. Banks to settle and pay you," Greene pleaded with one particularly tenacious creditor, "& have told him that he & I would not live long in the same World if he brought me into difficulties in the matter, and I will follow him to the Ends of the Earth for Satisfaction."[6]

True to his word, Greene set sail from Newport, Rhode Island, to Charleston in July 1784 to track down Banks. Find him he did, in Washington, North Carolina, dead and buried two days before Greene arrived there.

In many ways, Greene's postwar life was marked by this kind of bad fortune. As if he'd exhausted his supply of luck with the success of his unlikely strategies during the Southern Campaign, every move he made once returned to civilian life turned sour. Caty Greene lost one infant child and miscarried another; his rice crops were ruined by bad weather and pilfered by untrustworthy employees; his debts became insurmountable, bringing Greene to the point of despair. "I tremble at my own situation when I think of the enormous sums I owe and the great difficulty of obtaining money," he lamented. "I seem to be doomed to a life of slavery and anxiety."[7]

But Greene failed to equate the state of slavery he abhorred with the condition of the enslaved men and women he employed on his Southern farms. Eager to make a go of the plantation business, Greene purchased slaves valued at over four thousand pounds sterling for Boone's Barony, his South Carolina estate, in the winter and spring of 1783. Ironically, these slaves were confiscated from South Carolina Loyalists, just as Sumter had confiscated Loyalist slaves for the terms of Sumter's Law.[8] In embracing the slavery system, Greene ignored the Quaker principles of his youth, which condemned the slave trade, even if his papers suggest he tried to have his slaves treated humanely. "Don't fail to find and cloth the Negroes well," he instructed one of his farm managers,[9] though this type of conditional moralizing hardly justifies his advocacy for human bondage from our modern perspective. We have already established that Greene was no paragon of moral virtue. At heart, he was both a pragmatist and a man of his times, and in his slave ownership he joined other renowned leaders of the American cause: Washington, Jefferson, and Madison, to name but a few. Still, this turn toward plantation "master" late in life sours his historic legacy.

On June 13, 1786, Nathanael and Caty Greene stopped at the plantation of William Gibbons Jr. while returning to Mulberry Grove after a short visit to Savannah, where Greene had refinanced some debt. While Caty Greene rested inside the house, Nathanael toured Gibbons's plantation in the hot sun. After they departed Gibbons's plantation, Greene began to complain of headaches. His condition continued to deteriorate after they arrived at Mulberry Grove. Diagnosed with heat stroke, Greene died in his bed on the morning of June 19. He was only 44 years old.[10]

In contrast, Thomas Sumter's fortunes were restored after the war, though he, too, was dogged by the obligations he had incurred under Sumter's Law. At the General Assembly of 1782, the same one in which Greene was awarded the money for his South Carolina estate, a motion to ratify the terms of Sumter's Law, proposing that over four hundred slaves be confiscated from known Tories and turned over to Sumter for distribution among his troops, was approved by his loyal subordinates in the House of Representatives. But when the General Assembly adjourned without taking action on the House's motion, Sumter considered it a personal insult.[11]

When the General Assembly convened again in 1783, Sumter requested a committee inquire into his conduct and disposal of Tory property. When his supporters moved to award him a medal for his service, a controversial debate arose over his conduct and methods. Only when a motion to bestow similar honors on Pickens and Continental General Isaac Huger was adopted did the motion to honor Sumter pass.[12]

Though Sumter considered the medal a vindication for his conduct during the war, it wasn't until the General Assembly session of 1784, with bitterness over the Revolution finally subsiding, that he was finally exonerated for Sumter's Law. In this session, the Assembly passed a law exempting all officers who had seized private property for public use from liabilities of civil suit. Although Sumter happily accepted the exemption, for which he had vigorously lobbied, Marion angrily refused it, stating, "If, in a single instance, in the course of my command, I have done that which I cannot fully justify, justice requires that I should suffer for it." But now free of Sumter's Law legal repercussions, Sumter was still saddled with its administration. In the same session, he was appointed head of a commission to arbitrate the demands of the State Troops, and it wasn't until 1794 that he finally settled all of the claims.[13] By then, even Sumter might admit the disposition of Sumter's Law was more trouble than it was ever worth. Instead of the five regiments he intended to raise under its terms, he only ever raised three, and those undersized, many of their soldiers of dubious character.

With memories of the war beginning to fade, the people of South Carolina were inclined to remember Sumter for his leadership, not punish him for his shortcomings. He remained wildly popular with his backcountry constituents, and retained the support of many, if not most, of the militia commanders who served under him, Francis Marion a notable exception. Sumter was elected as a representative to the first

Congress of the United States in 1789, at a time when the state General Assembly elected both congressmen and senators to the national body. Though never one of the most vocal members of Congress, he became known as a fierce defender of states' rights and went on to become a stalwart of the South Carolina congressional delegation, losing an election in 1793 but regaining his seat in the election of 1795.

In 1801, Thomas Sumter became a United States senator, winning an election in the South Carolina General Assembly over his old benefactor and sometimes-adversary John Rutledge. He served in the United States Senate until 1810, when he resigned at the age of 76. Yet he continued to live an active life at his plantation in Stateburg, South Carolina, dying on June 1, 1832, at the age of 97, the last surviving general of the American Revolutionary War.[14]

As a congressman and senator, Sumter leveraged his popular appeal to champion a new brand of democratic populism focused on states' incipient right to control their own laws regarding a broad range of issues including finance, commerce, military power, and slavery. In contrast stood the Federalists, men who believed the states needed a strong and united central government. According to one of his biographers, his chief principles as a congressman were justice to claims of veterans and widows of veterans, economy in government, and limitation of federal powers.[15]

Today, Sumter's legacy is confined mostly to his home state, where he is revered as a symbol of the American Revolution and the state's defiant character, his reputation treated delicately by South Carolina historians, who don't ignore the moral implications of Sumter's Law or his recalcitrance to Greene, but prefer instead to focus on his leadership in the wake of Charleston's surrender and his postwar career as a politician.

In popular culture, his most important contribution may be as the namesake mascot for the University of South Carolina—the "Fighting Gamecocks." According to the university's website, the nickname was adopted in 1903 by Columbia's *The State* newspaper in their reporting on the school's athletic teams; the University of South Carolina has shared an association with the historical "Gamecock" ever since. And even if it seems unlikely the thousands of garnet-and-black-clothed fans chanting the Gamecock's nickname on football game days are celebrating the folly of Sumter's Rounds, or the bloodbath of Shubrick's Plantation, they definitely understand the nature of his defiant temperament—his revolutionary character and penchant for straight-ahead attack.

In South Carolina, Sumter County is named in his honor along with its county seat, the town of Sumter. Sumter National Forest, comprising over 370,000 acres in three different ranger districts across a broad swath of the state's northwest corner, also honors him. However, Sumter is most prominently associated with his namesake fort in Charleston Harbor, site of the Civil War's commencement, when it was attacked by the nascent Confederate Army on April 12, 1861. Fort Sumter was initiated in 1829 as part of the federal government's coastal defense system, but not completed until 1860. For its role in the Civil War, Fort Sumter became an enduring symbol of the states' rights populism Sumter endorsed as a politician, as well as South Carolina's complicated legacy of slavery, even though Sumter himself was long since dead and buried before ground was broken on the site. Today Fort Sumter is run by the National Park Service and visited by close to one million people every year, making it one of the state's most popular tourist destinations, indoctrinating thousands each day into the Sumter legacy.

★   ★   ★

During the second session of Congress, in January 1792, a petition from Catherine Greene came to the floor. Her husband now dead for five long years, Caty had worked tirelessly to relieve his wartime debts, enlisting in the effort many of her husband's former colleagues—ranging from Secretary of the Treasury Alexander Hamilton to Secretary of War Henry Knox to President George Washington himself. All were sympathetic. Yet none could provide her relief without an official act of Congress.

Unfortunately for Caty, there was no paper trail acknowledging the federal government's authorization for Greene's wartime debt. Though Secretary of War Henry Knox had authorized Greene to negotiate local contracts on the army's behalf, Greene had failed to obtain written permission from Congress for his contract with Banks, an omission that now haunted his widow. Caty Greene spent two long years obtaining affidavits, documents, and eyewitness accounts in support of her argument while staving off her husband's creditors, relying on private loans from her admirers for living expenses after she had long since liquidated her personal items, including her carriage and all the furniture in her house.

When the petition finally came to the House floor, Representative Thomas Sumter rose in opposition. Though he rarely made public speeches, Sumter could not now resist the urge to bear his long-simmering grievances with Nathanael Greene, exacerbated by the British writer and minister William Gordon's four-volume *History of the Rise, Progress, and Establishment of the United States of America* published in 1788. Gordon had befriended Greene during the early 1780s, and used some of Greene's correspondence as source material. Included in Gordon's book was one of Greene's indiscrete observations on Sumter, written to his friend Joseph Reed: "Generals Marion and Sumter have a few people who adhere to them, perhaps, more from a desire and opportunity of plundering, than from any inclination to promote the independence of the United States."[16]

Upon reading those words, Sumter had been so rankled that he issued a circular to his constituents in August 1789 with the above quote, followed by the admonition: "View this and suppress your indignation if you can."[17] Now, with Caty Greene's petition on the House floor, the usually taciturn Sumter rose and launched into an attack on his former colleague, arguing that Greene's connections with Banks had been foolish and unwise, and noting that Greene had already been sufficiently awarded for his service with the gifts of land and estate from North Carolina, South Carolina, and Georgia. He ended his tirade by quoting the letter to Joseph Reed. "The reflections are gross calumnies on, and misrepresentations of, the character of the people," Sumter fumed, "which are invalidated by facts that then took place, and by the general tenor of the conduct of South Carolina throughout the whole course of the war."[18]

Though Sumter and several of his colleagues voted against Caty Greene's petition, the motion passed by nine votes and was subsequently passed by the Senate. On April 27, 1792, George Washington signed the act; Secretary of the Treasury Alexander Hamilton signed a government check for $23,500 and a promissory note for another $23,500 payable by Congress within three years. On June 1, 1796, Congress passed another provision for the payment of 11,297 pounds to Greene's creditor Harris & Blachford, finally indemnifying Greene for the debts he incurred on behalf of his army.[19]

Though such relief was cold comfort for Nathanael Greene, now dead and buried, it was surely a warm one for Caty Greene. According to 18th-century law, a widow would lose claim to her dead husband's benefits if she remarried. Finally free from her husband's creditors, she was wed in 1796 to Phineas Miller, who had been in her employ for several years, first as a tutor to her children, then as the overseer of her estates.

Congressional relief did not solve all of Caty Greene's financial woes. Prior to his death, Nathanael Greene had received 11,000 acres on Georgia's Cumberland Island in exchange for a debt. Greene had planned to move his family to the island, but these plans were ruined by his untimely death. To escape her other debts, Caty was forced to sell the Mulberry Grove plantation and moved her family to the Cumberland Island property, where she built a four-story mansion she called "Dungeness" in 1803, the same year Phineas Miller died. Caty continued to live at Dungeness until she died in 1814 at the age of 59.

Four years after Caty's death, Nathanael Greene's old companion Henry Lee was en route to Virginia from the West Indies, where he had moved to escape his own creditors. Like his esteemed general, Lee had been as spectacular a failure as a businessman as he was a success as a military commander. In 1812 he had been beaten severely in a political riot and never fully recovered. Now the end was in sight for the 62-year-old Lee. His health failing, he asked to be put ashore at Cumberland Island. After a month's convalescence at Dungeness, he died there on March 25, 1818.

★   ★   ★

As commander of the Southern Army, Nathanael Greene commanded in four major military actions. At Guilford Courthouse on March 15, 1781, Lord Cornwallis's seasoned but outmanned army pushed Greene back after a bloody slugfest. At Hobkirk's Hill on April 25, 1781, Lord Rawdon achieved similar results, as did British Lieutenant Colonel

Alexander Stewart at Eutaw Springs on September 8. At Ninety-Six in May and June of 1781, Greene's poorly conceived strategy of sieging the main British defensive works, rather than seizing their water supply, along with the imminent arrival of British reinforcements, forced the Continentals into a desperate, failed attempt to storm the fortified outpost. Four battles, four losses.

Such is hardly the stuff of military glory. Another general, under other circumstances, might have suffered such a battlefield record with a legacy of failure, both in his own time and history everlasting. Yet Greene was not such a general.

"It is true, that untoward occurrences had deprived us of two victories, and lost us Ninety-Six," admitted Henry Lee, describing the failure at Ninety-Six. He continued:

> But it is no less true, that the comprehensive views of the general, with his inflexible perseverance, and unvarying activity, had repaired these mortifying disappointments, and had closed the campaign with the successful execution of his object. Defeat had been changed by consequence into victory, and our repulse had been followed by accession of territory. The conquered States were regained, and our exiled countrymen were restored to their deserted homes—sweet rewards of toil and peril.[20]

"Inflexible perseverance" and "unvarying activity" are, perhaps, phrases as accurate as any to summarize the curious nature of Greene's success, but that hasn't stopped contemporary historians from adding their own. The esteemed Southern Campaign historian John Buchanan cites Greene's mental toughness and endurance, his capacity for foresight and careful planning, as the key attributes endowing Greene with "the strategic vision of a master soldier."

In summarizing Greene's idiosyncratic military prowess, Buchanan quotes Abner Nash, the governor of North Carolina, in noting Greene was master of the "peculiar Art of making your Enemies run away from their Victories leaving you master of their Wounded and of all the fertile part of the Country."[21]

No less an expert than Dennis M. Conrad, one of the primary editors of the monumental, 13-volume series *The Papers of Nathanael Greene*, identifies Greene's primary genius as his ability to succeed by adapting to circumstances. Clearly, Greene's preternatural abilities in logistics and planning were another. Yet among the many secondary geniuses Conrad identifies in Greene, his ability to recognize the importance of public opinion and "willingness to work well with militia and politicians" were also critical.[22]

It is this latter skill, his relationships with the Southern Campaign's partisan commanders, primarily Thomas Sumter, that has been the focus of this book. Greene was no rookie general, no patsy, when he arrived in Charlotte in December 1780. For six long years, he had served as a major general in the Continental Army under difficult circumstances. And though he had experienced his share of professional setbacks and disappointments during that time, he was accustomed to the respect and capitulation of his subordinates. As an officer, he had served with honor during the war, but some innate insecurity too often exposed itself when this service veered into the political realm. Again and again he overreacted—behaved boorishly—when his military aspirations were frustrated by congressional oversight, to the point of damaging his reputation and probably, if his fortune had not turned with the command of the Southern Department, his military career. Prior to his arrival in the South, to call Greene a political genius would have been an attempt at ironic humor, not an attempt to summarize his historic legacy.

But far away from Congress, far away from the steadying influence of George Washington, and far away from the New England society to which he was born and bred, Nathanael Greene found some inner reservoir of empathy for his rivals. From the very beginning of their relationship, Greene understood Thomas Sumter's need for status, his craving for deference and respect.

One could argue he had no choice in the matter. Greene commanded a small army of not much more than two thousand men. The Gamecock commanded all of South Carolina, at least for a time. Even the most ardent Greene zealot must admit Greene needed Sumter, just as he needed the cooperation of Marion, Pickens, and the other militia commanders. Yet Greene could have reacted differently, asserting his military rank and authoritarian control over Thomas Sumter and the rest. Other, less intuitive generals have tried as much.

But in seeking Sumter's cooperation, not his obedience, Greene improvised his way into the history books as one of America's greatest generals. Certainly, it was no easy journey. Sumter's independent nature, his recalcitrance, frustrated Greene again and again. And to his discredit, and his family's misfortune, Greene all too readily expressed these frustrations in his correspondence, and in indiscrete conversations with his officers. Nathanael Greene was a man, not a superman, plagued by human flaws just as he was blessed with a certain type of genius. And in the end, it is this duality that intrigues us about both the Quaker and the Gamecock.

Endnotes

Introduction

1 Dennis M. Conrad. "General Nathanael Greene: An Appraisal." Published in *General Nathanael Greene and the American Revolution in the South*, edited by Gregory D. Massey and Jim Piecuch (Columbia, SC: The University of South Carolina Press, 2012), 7.

2 John M. Moseley and Robert M. Calhoun. "Nathanael Greene and Republican Ethics," in Gregory D. Massey and Jim Piecuch (eds), *General Nathanael Greene and the American Revolution in the South*, 158–164.

3 "Nathanael Greene (hereafter NG) to Alexander Hamilton, January 10, 1781," in Richard K. Showman and Dennis Conrad (eds.), *The Papers of Nathanael Greene* (Chapel Hill: University of North Carolina Press, 1976–2006), vol. 7, 88. Hereafter cited as *NG* with appropriate volume and page numbers, e.g. 7:88. Spelling grammar, punctuation, and capitalization are presented as in the original. Author's notes in brackets for clarification.

4 "Benjamin Lincoln to George Washington, December 19, 1778," Jared Sparks, ed., *Correspondence of the American Revolution*, 4 vols. (Boston: Little, Brown, 1853), 2:241.

5 Conrad, "General Nathanael Greene: An Appraisal." *General Nathanael Greene and the American Revolution in the South*, 17.

6 "NG to Thomas Sumter," February 3, 1781, *NG*, 7:245.

7 Walter Edgar, *Partisans & Redcoats: The Southern Conflict That Turned the Tide of the American Revolution* (New York: HarperCollins Publishers, 2001), 20–25.

8 Showman and Conrad (eds.), *NG*, 6:563, Note 1.

9 William R. Davie, *The Revolutionary War Sketches of William R. Davie* (Raleigh, NC: North Carolina Department of Cultural Resources, 1976), 44.

Prologue

1   "Nathanael Greene (hereafter NG) to Thomas Sumter (hereafter TS), April 19, 1781," in Richard K. Showman and Dennis Conrad (eds.), *The Papers of Nathanael Greene* (hereafter *NG*), 8:119.

2   "NG to TS, April 23, 1781," *NG*, 8:135–136.

3   Davie, *The Revolutionary War Sketches of William R. Davie*, 45.

4   "NG to TS, April 23, 1781," *NG*, 8:135.

5   Samuel Mathis, "A Letter on the Battle of Hobkirk's Hill, written in 1819," edited by Millard H. Osborne and Charles Baxley, SouthernCampaign.org, accessed on June 24, 2018, http://southerncampaign.org/hobkirk/ps.html. Samuel Mathis wrote this account of the Battle of Hobkirk's Hill in a letter to General William Richardson Davie dated 1819. Mathis was born in Camden. He was captured at the fall of Charleston in May 1780 and paroled to his native Camden during the Battle of Hobkirk's Hill.

6   "NG to Samuel Huntington, April 27, 1781," *NG*, 8:155.

7   John S. Pancake, *This Destructive War: The British Campaign in the Carolinas, 1780–1782* (Tuscaloosa, AL: University of Alabama Press, 2003), 196.

8   "General Greene's Orders, April 24, 1781," *NG*, 8:142.

9   Pancake, *This Destructive War*, 196.

Chapter 1

1   Anne King Gregorie, *Thomas Sumter* (Columbia, SC: The R.L. Bryan Company, 1931), 105.

2   Robert D. Bass, *Gamecock: The Life and Campaigns of General Thomas Sumter* (Orangeburg, SC: Sandlapper Publishing Co., 1961), 6.

3   Edward McCrady, *The History of South Carolina in the Revolution, 1775–1780* (New York: The Macmillan Company, 1901), 564.

4   Bass, *Gamecock*, 5.

5   Gregorie, *Thomas Sumter*, 5.

6   Bass, *Gamecock*, 6.

7   Mark M. Boatner, *Encyclopedia of the American Revolution* (Mechanicsburg, PA: Stackpole Press edition, 1994), 220.

8   Gregorie, *Thomas Sumter*, 13.

9   Bass, *Gamecock*, 15.

10 Gregorie, *Thomas Sumter*, 21–22.

11 *Ibid*, 23.

12 Walter Edgar, *Partisans & Redcoats* (New York: HarperCollins Publishers, 2001), 1–2.

13 *Ibid*.

14 Walter Edgar, *South Carolina: A History* (Columbia, SC: University of South Carolina Press, 1998), 56.

15 John Buchanan, *The Road to Guilford Courthouse: The American Revolution in the Carolinas* (New York: John Wiley & Sons, Inc., 1997), 87.

16 Edgar, *Partisans & Redcoats*, 2.

17 *Ibid*, 15–17.

18 Bass, *Gamecock*, 22.

19 Gregorie, *Thomas Sumter*, 34.

20 *Ibid*, 36–44.

21 *Ibid*, 47.

22 Bass, *Gamecock*, 46.

23 Gregorie, *Thomas Sumter*, 70.

24 Boatner, *Encyclopedia of the American Revolution*, 1087.

25 *Ibid*, 1174.

26 Edgar, *Partisans & Redcoats*, 55–57.

27 Gregorie, *Thomas Sumter*, 75.

28 Lyman C. Draper, *King's Mountain and Its Heroes* (Cincinnati, OH: Peter G. Thomson, Publisher, 1881), 239–242.

29 Oscar E. Gilbert and Catherine R. Gilbert, *True for the Cause of Liberty: The Second Spartan Regiment in the American Revolution* (Havertown, PA: Casemate Publishers, 2015), 48.

30 Buchanan, *The Road to Guilford Courthouse*, 121.

31 Gregorie, *Thomas Sumter*, 80. According to Gregorie's sources, the assembled militia elected Sumter to the rank of "Brigadier General." This distinction is probably related to Sumter's later conflict with James Williams, who was alleged to have been commissioned brigadier general by Governor James Rutledge in September 1780, creating a dispute between those loyal to Sumter and those loyal to Williams. In arguing for Sumter's primacy in rank, Gregorie observes: "It is interesting to note that Cornwallis in his letters at once accorded him that title, while Rutledge and other South Carolinians punctiliously kept to the old title of colonel until after Rutledge issued a brigadier's commission [to Sumter] four months later."

32 Edgar, *Partisans & Redcoats*, 60–65.

33 Patrick O'Kelley, *Nothing But Blood and Slaughter: The Revolutionary War in the Carolinas* (Blue House Tavern Press, 2004), 2:211–214.

34 Buchanan, *The Road to Guilford Courthouse*, 134–135.

35 "Letter from Thomas Sumter to Thomas Pinckney, August 9, 1780," http://docsouth.unc.edu/csr/index.php/document/csr14-0437.

36 Gregorie, *Thomas Sumter*, 99.

37 Buchanan, *The Road to Guilford Courthouse*, 174–175.

38 "Earl Cornwallis to Sir Henry Clinton, December 3, 1780," *Correspondence of Charles, First Marquis Cornwallis* (London: John Murray, 1859), 1:498.

39 Boatner, *Encyclopedia of the American Revolution*, 367–368.
40 Buchanan, *The Road to Guilford Courthouse*, 251–259.

Chapter 2

1   "General George Weedon to Nathanael Green (hereafter NG), October 17, 1780," in Richard K. Showman and Dennis Conrad (eds.), *The Papers of Nathanael Greene* (hereafter *NG*), 6:408; this letter mistakenly identifies Sumter as the commander of Patriot militia at the Battle of King's Mountain. Also "Col. Charles S. Myddelton to NG, November 20, 1780," *NG*, 6:498; in this letter Myddelton, a militia colonel, informed Greene of Sumter's victory and wound at the Battle of Blackstock's Farm. Also *NG*, Note 9, 6:259; a letter from Thomas Sumter to Horatio Gates dated August 15, 1780, detailing Sumter's operations on the Wateree in support of Gates's attack on Camden was published by Congress after the battle. Greene makes reference to this material in a letter to Governor William Greene of Rhode Island in a letter dated September 5, 1780.

2   "NG to Nathaniel Peabody, September 6, 1780," *NG*, 6:266.

3   "NG to Governor William Greene of Rhode Island, September 5, 1780," *NG*, 6:258.

4   "NG to Thomas Jefferson, November 20, 1780," *NG*, 6:492.

5   John M. Moseley and Robert M. Calhoun. "Nathanael Greene and Republican Ethics." Published in *General Nathanael Greene and the American Revolution in the South*, edited by Gregory D. Massey and Jim Piecuch (Columbia, SC: The University of South Carolina Press, 2012), 151, 158–164.

6   Terry Golway, *Washington's General: Nathanael Greene and the Triumph of the American Revolution* (New York: Henry Holt and Company, 2006), 13–14.

7   *NG*, Note 2, 1:4.

8   Golway, *Washington's General*, 14.

9   Buchanan, *The Road to Guilford Courthouse*, 262.

10 *NG*, Note 2, 1:69–70.

11 "NG to Samuel Ward, October 9, 1772," *NG*, 1:47–48.

12 *NG*, Note 3, 1:28–31.

13 *NG*, Note 1, 1:65–66.

14 "NG to Colonel James M. Varnum, October 31, 1774," *NG*, 1:75–76.

15 "Introduction to Volume I," *NG*, 1:xviii.

16 Golway, *Washington's General*, 67.

17 Boatner, *Encyclopedia of the American Revolution*, 388.

18 Buchanan, *The Road to Guilford Courthouse*, 268–269.

19 Boatner, *Encyclopedia of the American Revolution*, 454.

20 Gerald M. Carbone, *Nathanael Greene: A Biography of the American Revolution* (New York: Palgrave Macmillan, 2008), 70.

21 Ron Chernow, *Alexander Hamilton* (New York: The Penguin Press, 2004), 284.

22 "Petition to the Rhode Island General Assembly, October 27, 1769," *NG*, 1:7.

23 Buchanan, *The Road to Guilford Courthouse*, 272.

24 Carbone, *Nathanael Greene*, 109–111.

25 Golway, *Washington's General*, 158.

26 *Ibid*, 196.

27 *Ibid*, 171–172, 203. Quoted letter appears in *NG*, 3:403.

28 *Ibid*, 199.

29 *Ibid*, 225–226.

30 Boatner, *Encyclopedia of the American Revolution*, 455.

31 "George Washington to NG, October 14, 1780," *NG*, 6:384–385. The editors of Greene's papers note this is one of the few letters from Washington's military service written in his own hand.

32 "NG to George Washington, October 16, 1780," *NG*, 6:396.

33 Buchanan, *The Road to Guilford Courthouse*, 398.

34 Henry Lee, *The Revolutionary War Memoirs of General Henry Lee* (New York: De Capo Press edition, 1998), 220–221.

Chapter 3

1 Buchanan, *The Road to Guilford Courthouse*, 257.

2 *Ibid*, 257.

3 O'Kelley, *Nothing But Blood and Slaughter*, 2:372. Draper is quoted directly in this passage.

4 Buchanan, *The Road to Guilford Courthouse*, 257.

5 Gregorie, *Thomas Sumter*, 123. This account appears in several secondary sources and is attributed to a letter from William Cain to Lyman Draper dated May 27, 1875, in Draper's *Sumter Papers* 5VV57.

6 Bass, *Gamecock*, 108. This account also appears in Buchanan and seems to come from Draper, though neither reference it to him. Bass rarely references his sources.

7 Gregorie, *Thomas Sumter*, 124; Bass, *Gamecock*, 108.

8 Buchanan, *The Road to Guilford Courthouse*, 259.

9 Banastre Tarleton, *History of the Campaigns of 1780 and 1781, in the Southern Provinces of North Carolina* (London, 1787), 179.

10 Cornwallis, *Correspondence of Charles, First Marquis Cornwallis*, 70.

11 William Read, "Reminiscences of Dr. William Read, Arranged From His Notes and Papers," R.W. Gibbes, editor, *Documentary History of the American Revolution, 1776–1782* (New York: D. Appleton & Co., 1857), 281.

12 Dennis M. Conrad and Richard K. Showman, eds., *The Papers of Nathanael Greene* (hereafter *NG*), Note 2, 6:564.

13 Bass, *Gamecock*, 113.

14 Otho Holland Williams, "A Narrative of the Campaign of 1780," taken from *Sketches of the Life and Correspondence of Nathanael Greene, Major General of the United States* by William Johnson (Charleston: A.E. Miller, 1822), Volume 1, Exhibit B, 510.

15 *NG*, Note 2, 6:562.

16 "NG to TS, December 12, 1780," *NG*, 6:563–564.

17 *NG*, Note 1, 6:539.

18 Boatner, *Encyclopedia of the American Revolution*, 735–736.

19 "NG to George Washington, December 7, 1781," *NG*, 6:543–544.

20 David Ramsay, *The History of the Revolution of South Carolina, from a British Province to an Independent State* (Trenton, NJ: Isaac Collins, 1785), 2:199.

21 "NG to Samuel Huntington, November 2, 1780," *NG*, 6:459.

22 "NG to TS, December 15, 1781," *NG*, 6:581. Sumter's notes to John Rutledge have not been found, according to a note in *NG* accompanying this letter.

23 "William Davidson to N.C. Board of War, November 27, 1780," State Records of North Carolina, Walter Clark, ed. (Winston, NC: M.I. and J.C. Stewart), 14:759–760. Quoted from William Lee Anderson, *Camp New Providence: Large Encampment of Southern Continental Army and militia on Providence Road at Six Mile Creek, October–December 1780*, https://elehistory.com/amrev/MecklenburgDuringAmericanRevolution.pdf

24 "NG to Daniel Morgan, December 16, 1781," *NG*, 6:589.

25 Bass, *Gamecock*, 116.

26 Henry Clinton, *The American Rebellion: Sir Henry Clinton's Narrative of His Campaigns, 1775–1782* (New Haven: Yale University Press edition, 1954), 245.

27 Christopher Ward, *The War of the Revolution*, (New York: Skyhorse Publishing, 2011), 751

28 "NG to Daniel Morgan, December 16, 1781," *NG*, 6:589.

29 Gregorie, *Thomas Sumter*, 128–129. Bass, *Gamecock*, 117. The meeting between Morgan and Sumter never took place.

30 Edward McCrady, *The History of South Carolina in the Revolution, 1780–1783* (New York: The Macmillan Company, 1902), 69. This letter is dated only "Sunday night, nine o'clock," but evidence suggests it was written on Sunday, December 21, 1780.

31 "NG to TS, January 8, 1781," *NG*, 7:74–75.

32 McCrady, *The History of South Carolina in the Revolution, 1780–1783*, 59.

33 "NG to Daniel Morgan, January 8, 1781," *NG*, 7:73.

34 "Daniel Morgan to NG, January 15, 1781," *NG*, 7:127.

35 "NG to Daniel Morgan, January 19, 1781," *NG*, 7:146.

36 "NG to TS, January 19, 1781," *NG*, 7:149.

37 "TS to NG, January 29, 1781," *NG*, 7:216–217.

38 Gregorie, *Thomas Sumter*, 134.

39 *Ibid.*

40 "NG to TS, January 30, 1781," *NG*, 7:221.

Chapter 4

1 Gregorie, *Thomas Sumter*, 136; Robert Gray, "Col. Robert Gray's Observations on the War in Carolina," *South Carolina Historical and Genealogical Magazine*, XI (July 1910), https://archive.org/details/Col.RobertGraysObservationsOnThe WarInCarolina1782

2 "Nathanael Green (hereafter NG) to Thomas Sumter (hereafter TS), January 8, 1781," in Richard K. Showman and Dennis Conrad (eds.), *The Papers of Nathanael Greene* (hereafter *NG*), 7:74.

3 "NG to TS, January 29, 1781," *NG*, 7:217.

4 *NG*, Note 4, 7:240. The note excerpts a letter from Thomas Sumter to Isaac Huger from February 6, 1781.

5 "Marquis de Malmédy to NG, March 10, 1781," *NG*, 7:424–425.

6 "NG to TS, February 3, 1781," *NG*, 7:245–246.

7 *Ibid.*

8 *Ibid.*

9 "Revolutionary War Pension Application of Hamilton Brown," September 22, 1832, transcribed by Will Graves; "Revolutionary War Pension Application of Hicks Chappel," March 13, 1833, transcribed by C. Leon Harris; "Revolutionary War Pension Application of Zachary Kitchens," January 7, 1833, transcribed by C. Leon Harris; all located online at Southern Campaigns Revolutionary War Pension Statements & Rosters, http://www.revwarapps.org.

10 Boatner, *Encyclopedia of the American Revolution*, 79.

11 O'Kelley, *Nothing But Blood and Slaughter*, 3:114; Date from Gregorie, *Thomas Sumter*, 136.

12 The naming of South Carolina's river system can be confusing; the Broad River flows south out of North Carolina into South Carolina and becomes the Congaree River at the confluence with the Saluda River near present-day Columbia, then becomes the Santee River at the confluence with the Wateree River at present-day Lake Marion. Despite the different names, this campaign occurred primarily along this main Congaree–Santee river channel.

13 Robert B. Roberts, *Encyclopedia of Historic Forts: The Military, Pioneer, and Trading Posts of the United States* (New York: McMillan, 1988), 713–714.

14 Boatner, *Encyclopedia of the American Revolution*, 377.

15 O'Kelley, *Nothing But Blood and Slaughter*, 3:89.

16 Lee, *Revolutionary War Memoirs*, 332.

17 "General Sumter to the Honourable General Marion, February 20, 1781," from Robert W. Gibbes, *Documentary History of the American Revolution* (Columbia, SC: Banner Steam-Power Press, 1853), 3:22.

18 "Thomas Sumter to Francis Marion, March 4, 1781," from Gibbes, *Documentary History of the American Revolution*, 3:27–28.

19 O'Kelley, *Nothing But Blood and Slaughter*, 3:90.

20 McCrady, *The History of South Carolina in the Revolution, 1780–1783*, 107.

21 "Revolutionary War Pension Application of James Gill," September 22, 1832, transcribed by Will Graves, Southern Campaigns Revolutionary War Pension Statements & Rosters, http://www.revwarapps.org; O'Kelley, *Nothing But Blood and Slaughter*, 3:93.

22 *NG*, Note 2, 7:465.

23 "Revolutionary War Pension Application of James Gill," September 22, 1832, transcribed by Will Graves; "Revolutionary War Pension Application of Zachary Kitchens," Southern Campaigns Revolutionary War Pension Statements & Rosters, http://www.revwarapps.org.

24 Gregorie, *Thomas Sumter*, 140.

25 Bass, *Gamecock*, 350.

26 McCrady, *The History of South Carolina in the Revolution, 1780–1783*, 109.

27 Gregorie, *Thomas Sumter*, 141.

28 "General Sumter to General Marion, March 4, 1781," from Gibbes, *Documentary History of the American Revolution*, 3:27–28.

29 Bass, *Gamecock: The Life and Campaigns of General Thomas Sumter*, 133.

30 McCrady, *The History of South Carolina in the Revolution, 1780–1783*, 110.

31 "Col. Watson to General Marion, March 15, 1781," from Gibbes, *Documentary History of the American Revolution*, 3:39–40.

32 Gregorie, *Thomas Sumter*, 142–143.

33 "Lord Rawdon to Lieut. Col. Watson, March 7, 1781 (Intercepted Letter)," from Gibbes, *Documentary History of the American Revolution*, 3:31–32.

34 Gray, "Col. Robert Gray's Observations on the War in Carolina," 152.

35 Pancake, *This Destructive War*, 207.

Chapter 5

1 Edgar, *South Carolina: A History*, 215.

2 Edgar, *Partisans & Redcoats*, 22.

3 William T. Graves, *Backcountry Revolutionary* (Lugoff, SC: Woodward Corporation, 2012), 26–35.

4 Edgar, *Partisans & Redcoats*, 39–40.

5 Edgar, *South Carolina: A History*, 142, 151.

6 Edgar, *Partisans & Redcoats*, xi.

7 Graves, *Backcountry Revolutionary*, 14.

8 Edgar, *Partisans & Redcoats*, 40.

9 M. Foster Farley, "The South Carolina Negro in the American Revolution, 1775–1783," *The South Carolina Historical Magazine*, Vol. 79, No. 2 (April, 1978), 75–86.

10 *Ibid.*

11   Douglas R. Egerton, *Death or Liberty: African Americans and Revolutionary America* (New York: Oxford University Press, 2009), 84–85.

12   Farley, "The South Carolina Negro in the American Revolution, 1775–1783," 75–86.

13   Ramsay, *The History of the Revolution of South Carolina*, 2:375–376.

14   Robert Olwell, *Masters, Slaves, and Subjects: The Culture of Power in the South Carolina Low Country* (Ithaca, NY: Cornell University Press, 1998), 269–270.

15   "Nathanael Greene (hereafter NG) to Samuel Huntington, December 28, 1780," in Richard K. Showman and Dennis Conrad (eds.), *The Papers of Nathanael Greene* (hereafter *NG*), 7:9.

16   "NG to General Robert Howe, December 29, 1780," *NG*, 7:17.

17   "NG to Catherine Greene, January 25, 1780," *NG*, 7:193.

18   "Francis Marion to NG, January 20, 1781," *NG*, 7:165.

19   "Rawdon to Cornwallis, December 5, 1780," *The Cornwallis Papers* (East Sussex, England: The Naval and Military Press, 2010), arranged and edited by Ian Saberton, vol. 6, 196. Hereafter cited as *CP* with appropriate volume and page numbers, i.e. *CP*, 6:196. The identity of Major Harrison is not provided though he appears to be an officer in the provincial corps.

20   Davie, *The Revolutionary War Sketches of William R. Davie*, 23.

21   "Cornwallis to Cruger, January 16, 1781," *CP*, 3:292.

22   "Cornwallis to Gen. Henry Clinton, December 3, 1780," *CP*, 3:25.

23   "NG to Thomas Sumter, February 21, 1781," *NG*, 7:328.

24   McCrady, *The History of South Carolina in the Revolution, 1780–1783*, 142.

25   "Gov. John Rutledge to General Francis Marion, March 8, 1781," from Robert W. Gibbes, *Documentary History of the American Revolution* (Columbia, SC: Banner Steam-Power Press, 1853), 3:32–33. Hereafter cited as *Gibbes* with appropriate volume and page number.

26   "Gen. Sumter to Gen. Marion, March 28, 1781," from *Gibbes*, 3:44–45.

27   "Col. Richard Hampton to Maj. John Hampton, April 2, 1781," from *Gibbes*, 3:47–48. A slave under 10 or over 40 was considered a "half"; Sumter's plan valued a "full" slave at $400.

28   "Gen. Sumter to Gen. Marion, April 30, 1781," from *Gibbes*, 3:64–65.

29   "NG to TS, April 15, 1781," *NG*, 8:101.

30   *NG*, 8:67–68, note 2.

Chapter 6

1   "Nathanael Greene (hereafter NG) to George Washington, March 29, 1781," in Richard K. Showman and Dennis Conrad (eds.), *The Papers of Nathanael Greene* (hereafter *NG*), 7:481.

2   "NG to Colonel James Emmet, April 3, 1781," *NG*, 8:33.

3   Golway, *Washington's General*, 264.

4   Lee, *Revolutionary War Memoirs*, 326.

5   Pancake, *This Destructive War: The British Campaign in the Carolina, 1780–1782* (Tuscaloosa, AL: The University of Alabama Press, 2003), 189–191.

6   Lee, *Revolutionary War Memoirs*, 326.

7   John Ferling, *Almost a Miracle: The American Victory in the War of Independence* (New York, Oxford University Press, 2007), 509.

8   "NG to George Washington, March 29, 1781," NG, 7:481.

9   "NG to TS, March 30, 1781," NG, 8:12.

10   "NG to TS, January 8, 1781," NG, 7:74–75.

11   "TS to NG, April 7, 1781," NG, 8:65–67.

12   "NG to TS, February 3, 1781," NG, 7:245.

13   "TS to NG, April 7, 1781," NG, 8:67.

14   "TS to NG, April 13, 1781," NG, 8:91.

15   "NG to TS, April 14, 1781," NG, 8:94.

16   "NG to Governor Thomas Jefferson, March 23, 1781," NG, 7:466.

17   "NG to Governor Thomas Jefferson, March 27, 1781," NG, 7:471.

18   "NG to Governor Abner Nash of North Carolina, March 29, 1781," NG, 7:480.

19   "NG to Samuel Huntington, President of the Continental Congress, March 23, 1781," NG, 7:465.

20   Walter Edgar, *Patriots & Redcoats: The Southern Conflict That Turned the Tide of the American Revolution* (New York: William Morrow, 2001), 110–111.

21   Pancake, *This Destructive War*, 100.

22   "NG to Samuel Huntington, April 22, 1781," NG, 8:131.

23   "NG to TS, April 19, 1781," NG, 8:119.

24   Lee, *Revolutionary War Memoirs*, 331.

25   This sketch of Henry Lee is taken primarily from Charles Royster's Introduction to Lee's *Memoirs*. A biographical note in NG, 6:430–431 (Note 1), also proved helpful, as did a sketch in John Buchanan's *The Road To Guilford Courthouse*, 352–354.

26   Lee, *Revolutionary War Memoirs*, 320.

27   Note 4, NG, 7:482.

28   Lee, *Revolutionary War Memoirs*, 325.

29   O'Kelley, *Nothing But Blood and Slaughter*, 3:191.

30   Pancake, *This Destructive War*, 191.

31   NG, Note 1, 8:215.

32   O'Kelley, *Nothing But Blood and Slaughter*, 3:191–192.

33   Buchanan, *The Road to Guilford Courthouse*, 367–368.

34   "Andrew Pickens to NG, April 8, 1781," NG, 8:71.

35   "TS to NG, April 13, 1781," NG, 8:91.

36   "TS to NG, April 25, 1781," NG, 8:149–150.

37   O'Kelley, *Nothing But Blood and Slaughter*, 3:193–194.

38   Boatner, *Encyclopedia of the American Revolution*, 919.

39 John Buchanan, *The Road to Guilford Courthouse: The American Revolution in the Carolinas* (New York: John Wiley & Sons, Inc., 1997), 131.

40 Pancake, *This Destructive War*, 193.

41 "NG to General Thomas Sumter, April 7, 1781," *NG*, 8:64.

42 "NG to TS, April 19, 1781," *NG*, 8:119.

43 "NG to General Thomas Sumter, April 23, 1781," *NG*, 8:135.

44 "NG to General Thomas Sumter, April 14, 1781," *NG*, 8:94; "NG to General Thomas Sumter, April 15, 1781," *NG*, 8:100.

45 "TS to NG, April 25, 1781," *NG*, 8:149–150.

46 "NG to Henry Lee, April 22, 1781," *NG*, 8:133.

47 "NT to Henry Lee, April 24, 1781," *NG*, 8:143.

48 O'Kelley, *Nothing But Blood and Slaughter*, 3:195.

49 Pancake, *This Destructive War*, 195.

50 O'Kelley, *Nothing But Blood and Slaughter*, 3:196.

Chapter 7

1 "Rawdon to Cornwallis, April 26, 1781," *The Cornwallis Papers* (East Sussex, England: The Naval and Military Press, 2010), arranged and edited by Ian Saberton, vol. 4, 180. Hereafter cited as *CP* with appropriate volume and page numbers, i.e. *CP*, 4:180.

2 Patrick O'Kelley, *Nothing But Blood and Slaughter* (Blue House Tavern Press, 2005), 3:205.

3 "Rawdon to Cornwallis, April 26, 1781," *CP*, 4:180.

4 *Ibid.*

5 "Samuel Mathis to Gen. William R. Davie, 1819," online version edited by Rev. Millard B. Osborne, 1969, and Charles B. Baxley, *Southern Campaigns of the American Revolution*, www.southerncampaigns.org.

6 "General Greene's Orders, April 24, 1781," in Richard K. Showman and Dennis Conrad (eds.), *The Papers of Nathanael Greene* (hereafter *NG*), 8:142.

7 O'Kelley, *Nothing But Blood and Slaughter*, 3:202–203.

8 "Colonel Edward Carrington to Nathanael Greene (hereafter NG), April 24, 1781," *NG*, 8:145.

9 Boatner, *Encyclopedia of the American Revolution* (David McKay Company, 1994), 505; O'Kelley, *Nothing But Blood and Slaughter*, 3:205–206.

10 "Samuel Mathis to Gen. William R. Davie, 1819," www.southerncampaigns.org.

11 William Moultrie, *Memoirs of the American Revolution* (New York: David Longworth, 1802), 2:276.

12 "NG to Samuel Huntington, President of the Continental Congress, April 27, 1781," *NG*, 8:155–156.

13 "Samuel Mathis to Gen. William R. Davie, 1819," www.southerncampaigns.org.

14 "Rawdon to Cornwallis, April 26, 1781," *CP*, 4:181.

15 Pancake, *This Destructive War*, 196–198; Lee, *Revolutionary War Memoirs*, 337–338; O'Kelley, *Nothing But Blood and Slaughter*, 3:207–209.

16 William Johnson, *Sketches of the Life and Correspondence of Nathanael Greene* (Charleston, SC: A.E. Miller, 1822), 2:81–82.

17 "Samuel Mathis to Gen. William R. Davie, 1819," www.southerncampaing.org.

18 "NG to Samuel Hunting, April 27, 1781," *NG*, 8:160 (note 7); "Rawdon to Cornwallis, April 26, 1781," *CP*, 4:182–183; O'Kelley, *Nothing But Blood and Slaughter*," 3:199–202.

19 "NG to Samuel Huntington, April 27, 1781," *NG*, 8:156.

20 Pancake, *This Destructive War*, 198.

21 Lee, *Revolutionary War Memoirs*, 340–341.

22 William R. Davie, *The Revolutionary War Sketches of William R. Davie*, 44.

23 Lee, *Revolutionary War Memoirs*, 341.

24 Davie, *Revolutionary War Sketches*, 44.

25 "Thomas Sumter to NG, April 25, 1781," *NG*, 8:149–150.

26 Gregorie, *Thomas Sumter*, 155.

27 "NG to Joseph Reed, President of the Pennsylvania Council, May 4, 1781," *NG*, 8:199–201.

28 "NG to Thomas Sumter, April 30, 1781," *NG*, 8:176.

29 "Thomas Sumter to NG, May 2, 1781," *NG*, 8:193.

30 "Extract of a letter from Lord Rawdon to Earl Cornwallis, dated camp at Monck's corner, May 24, 1781," in Tarleton, *A History of the Campaigns of 1780 and 1781* (London: T. Cadell, 1781), 476. Hereafter "Rawdon to Cornwallis, May 25, 1781."

31 *Ibid.*

32 "NG to Col. Henry Lee, May 4, 1781," *NG*, 8:198.

33 "NG to Gen. Thomas Sumter, May 4, 1781," *NG*, 8:202; "NG to Gen. Thomas Sumter, May 5, 1781," *NG*, 8:208.

34 "NG to Samuel Huntington, President of the Continental Congress, May 5, 1781," *NG*, 206–207.

35 "Rawdon to Cornwallis, May 25, 1781."

36 Davie, 44–45.

37 "Rawdon to Cornwallis, May 25, 1781."

38 Davie, 45–46.

39 "NG to the Chevalier de La Luzerne, April 28, 1781," *NG*, 8:168.

Chapter 8

1 Hugh F. Rankin, *Francis Marion: The Swamp Fox* (New York: Thomas Y. Crowell Company, 1973), 113; quote about "swamps and defiles" from Tarleton, *A History of the Campaigns of 1780 and 1781*, 172.

2   Rankin, *Francis Marion*, Chapters 1 & 2; Gregorie, *Thomas Sumter*, Chapters 1 & 4.

3   Boatner, *Encyclopedia of the American Revolution*, 212. Source of Continental soldiers captured.

4   William Johnson, *Sketches of the Life and Correspondence of Nathanael Greene* (Charleston, SC: A.E. Miller, 1822), 1:488.

5   John Buchanan, *The Road to Guilford Courthouse*, 394–395; Pancake, *This Destructive War*, 110–111. Boatner, Rankin, and Gregorie also informed this comparison of Marion and Sumter.

6   "Thomas Sumter (hereafter TS) to Nathanael Greene (hereafter NG), May 2, 1781," in Richard K. Showman and Dennis Conrad (eds.), *The Papers of Nathanael Greene* (hereafter *NG*), 8:193.

7   "NG to TS, May 4, 1781," *NG*, 8:202.

8   Nat and Sam Hilborn, *South Carolina in the Revolution: Battleground of Freedom* (Columbia, SC: Sandlapper Press, 1970), 190. Also Robert B. Roberts, *Encyclopedia of Historic Forts: The Military, Pioneer, and Trading Posts of the United States* (New York: Macmillan, 10th Printing, 1998), 716.

9   "NG to Francis Marion, May 4, 1781," *NG*, 8:198–199.

10 Rankin, *Francis Marion*, 202.

11 "Gen. Francis Marion to NG, May 6, 1781," *NG*, 8:214–215.

12 "NG to Francis Marion, May 9, 1781," *NG*, 230–231.

13 "TS to NG, second letter of May 6, 1781," *NG*, 8:217.

14 Bass, *Gamecock*, 165.

15 Benson J. Lossing, *The Pictorial Field-Book of the Revolution* (New York: Harper & Brothers, Publishers, 1860), 2:490.

16 O'Kelley, *Nothing But Blood and Slaughter* (Blue House Tavern Press, 2005) 3:232–233.

17 Thomas Young, "The Memoir of Thomas Young," *Orion Magazine* (October & November, 1843).

18 "TS to NG, May 11, 1781," *NG*, 8:244.

19 "TS to NG, May 12, 1781," *NG*, 8:248.

20 Gregorie, *Thomas Sumter*, 159.

21 Lee, *Revolutionary War Memoirs*, 345–349.

22 Rankin, *Francis Marion*, 207–209.

23 "NG to Colonel Henry Lee, Jr., May 13, 1781," *NG*, 8:249.

24 Rankin, *Francis Marion: The Swamp Fox*, 211.

25 Lee, *Revolutionary War Memoirs*, 350–352.

26 "TS to NG, May 14, 1781," *NG*, 8:258–259.

27 Boatner, *Encyclopedia of the American Revolution*, 377.

28 Bass, *Gamecock*, 175.

29 "TS to NG, May 16, 1781," *NG*, 8:274.

30 Davie, *The Revolutionary War Sketches of William R. Davie*, 45.

31 "NG to TS, May 17, 1781," *NG*, 8:277–278.

32 "NG to TS, May 17, 1781, second letter," *NG*, 8:278.

33 Gregorie, *Thomas Sumter*, 161.

34 "NG to Francis Marion, May 17, 1781," *NG*, 8:276–277.

Chapter 9

1   Robert D. Bass, *Ninety Six: The Struggle for the South Carolina Backcountry* (Orangeburg, SC: Sandlapper Publishing Co., 1978), 16–18.

2   Richard K. Showman and Dennis Conrad (eds.), *The Papers of Nathanael Greene* (hereafter *NG*), 8:340, Note 1. Also Boatner, *Encyclopedia of the American Revolution*, 310.

3   Pancake, *This Destructive War*, 209.

4   Boatner, *Encyclopedia of the American Revolution*, 291–296, 866; biographical information about Pickens also compiled from Buchanan, *The Road to Guilford Courthouse*, 299–301; and *NG*, 8:33 (note 3).

5   "NG to Samuel Huntington, President of the Continental Congress, May 14, 1781," *NG*, 8:251.

6   Edward J. Cashin, "Thomas Brown," *New Georgia Encyclopedia*, http://www.georgiaencyclopedia.org/articles/history-archaeology/thomas-brown-1750–1825.

7   "Andrew Pickens to NG, May 8, 1781," *NG*, 8:223–224.

8   "Andrew Pickens to NG, May 12, 1781," *NG*, 8:246–248.

9   Boatner, *Encyclopedia of the American Revolution*, 804.

10 Lee, *Revolutionary War Memoirs*, 358–359.

11 "Extract of a letter from Lord Rawdon to Earl Cornwallis, dated camp at Monk's corner, May 24, 1781," from Tarleton, *A History of the Campaigns of 1780 and 1781*, Appendix, 478.

12 McCrady, *The History of South Carolina in the Revolution, 1780–1783*, 250–251.

13 "Francis Marion to NG, May 16, 1781," and Note 2 to that letter, *NG*, 8:274.

14 "Extract of a letter from Colonel Lord Rawdon to Sir Henry Clinton, dated Charles town, June 6th, 1781," from Tarleton, *A History of the Campaigns of 1780 and 1781*, Appendix, 484.

15 "NG to Col. Henry Lee, May 16, 1781," *NG*, 8:272.

16 "NG to Andrew Pickens, May 16, 1781," *NG*, 8:272.

17 "NG to Thomas Sumter (hereafter TS), May 17, 1781," *NG*, 8:278.

18 Lee, *Revolutionary War Memoirs*, 356.

19 McCrady, *The History of South Carolina in the Revolution, 1780–1783*, 268–273. Ramsay, *The History of the Revolution of South Carolina*, 2:240.

20 "NG to Col. Henry Lee, May 22, 1781," *NG*, 8:291–292.

21 Pancake, *This Destructive War*, 209–210.

22 Lee, *Revolutionary War Memoirs*, 371.

23 "NG to Colonel William Davies, May 23, 1781," *NG*, 8:298.

24 "NG to Francis Marion, May 26, 1781," *NG*, 8:312–313.
25 "NG to TS, May 26, 1781," *NG*, 8:313–314.
26 Rankin, *Francis Marion: The Swamp Fox*, 213–215.
27 Pancake, *This Destructive War*, 210.
28 "NG to Andrew Pickens, June 5, 1781," *NG*, 8:349–350.
29 Lee, *Revolutionary War Memoirs*, 373–374.
30 "NG to TS, June 10, 1781," *NG*, 8:374–375.
31 *NG*, 8:368–369, Note 5.
32 "NG to TS, June 10, 1781," *NG*, 8:374–375.
33 "TS to NG, June 11, 1781," *NG*, 8:378.
34 "NG to TS, June 13, 1781," *NG*, 8:385.
35 Lee, *Revolutionary War Memoirs*, 375.
36 "TS to NG, June 14, 1781," and Note 1 to this letter, *NG*, 8:390–391.
37 Rankin, *Francis Marion: The Swamp Fox*, 216.
38 *NG*, Note 1, 8:389.
39 Lee, *Revolutionary War Memoirs*, 375–377; also O'Kelley, *Nothing But Blood and Slaughter*, 245–247; and Pancake, *This Destructive War*, 213–214.
40 Lee, *Revolutionary War Memoirs*, 378.
41 *NG*, Note 2, 8:423.
42 "NG to Francis Marion, June 25, 1781," *NG*, 8:457–458.

Chapter 10

1 O'Kelley, *Nothing But Blood and Slaughter*, 3:257.
2 "Rawdon to Cornwallis, June 7, 1781," *The Cornwallis Papers*, edited by Ian Saberton (East Sussex, England: The Naval & Military Press Ltd., 2010), 5:293.
3 "Nathanael Green (hereafter NG) to Thomas Sumter (hereafter TS), June 20, 1780" and "NG to TS, Second Letter, June 20, 1780," in Richard K. Showman and Dennis Conrad (eds.), *The Papers of Nathanael Greene* (hereafter *NG*), 8:426–427.
4 "NG to Samuel Huntington, June 20, 1781," *NG*, 8:422.
5 "NG to Elijah Clarke, June 7, 1781," *NG*, 8:356.
6 "TS to NG, June 7, 1781," *NG*, 8:360.
7 Tarleton, *A History of the Campaigns of 1780 and 1781*, 498.
8 "NG to Thomas McKean, President of the Continental Congress, July 17, 1781," *NG*, 9:28.
9 Tarleton, *A History of the Campaigns of 1780 and 1781*, 498.
10 *Ibid*, 502–503.
11 "NG to Henry Lee, June 25, 1781, Second Letter," *NG*, 8:456–457; also Note 6, *NG*, 8:457.
12 "TS to NG, June 14, 1781," *NG*, 8:390.
13 "NG to TS, June 25, 1781," *NG*, 8:458.

14 "NG to North Carolina Governor Thomas Burke, July 16, 1781," *NG*, 9:20.

15 "NG to Henry Lee, June 24, 1781," *NG*, 8:452.

16 "NG to Francis Marion, June 25, 1781," *NG*, 8:458.

17 "TS to NG, July 2, 1781," *NG*, 8:482–483.

18 "Rawdon to Cornwallis, August 2, 1781," referenced in *NG*, 8:487, Note 1.

19 "NG to TS, July 3, 1781," *NG*, 8:484.

20 "NG to Co. William Washington, July 3, 1781," *NG*, 8:486.

21 "Rawdon to Cornwallis, August 2, 1781," referenced in *NG*, 8:487, Note 4.

22 "Andrew Pickens to NG, July 6, 1781," *NG*, 8:502.

23 *NG*, 8:505, Note 1.

24 "TS to NG, July 6, 1781," *NG*, 8:503.

25 "Francis Marion to NG, July 7, 1781," *NG*, 8:505.

26 "TS to NG, July 8, 1781," *NG*, 8:511, also Note 1 to this letter.

27 Lee, *Revolutionary War Memoirs*, 384–386.

28 Lee, *Revolutionary War Memoirs*, 386.

29 "General Greene's Orders, July 12, 1781," *NG*, 9:3.

30 "NG to TS, July 14, 1781," *NG*, 9:8.

31 "NG to Thomas McKean, President of the Continental Congress, July 17, 1781," *NG*, 9:29

32 Gregorie, *Thomas Sumter*, 173.

33 "Headnote on the Dog Days Expedition," *NG*, 9:13.

34 McCrady, *The History of South Carolina in the Revolution, 1780–1783*, 329.

35 "Headnote on the Dog Days Expedition," *NG*, 9:14.

36 "TS to NG, July 17–19, 1781," *NG*, 9:50–51.

37 McCrady, *The History of South Carolina in the Revolution, 1780–1783*, 333.

38 Lee, *Revolutionary War Memoirs*, 390.

39 "David Charles Bell to Charles (no last name given), August 11, 1781," Papers of the Continental Congress, Intercepted British Letters, Item 51, 1:659–661. This letter is misattributed in "Headnote on the Dog Days Expedition," *NG*, 9:14–16, as having been written by "D. John Brailsford." The author wishes to express his sincere thanks to Dog N. Hagist at *Journal of the American Revolution* for the correct attribution and sharing the original source material.

40 "TS to NG, July 17–19, 1781," *NG*, 9:52.

41 "Francis Marion to NG, July 19, 1781," *NG*, 9:47–48.

42 *Ibid.*

43 "TS to NG, July 25, 1781," *NG*, 9:81.

44 Gregorie, *Thomas Sumter*, Footnote 83, 179.

45 McCrady, *The History of South Carolina in the Revolution, 1780–1783*, 324.

46 "NG to Thomas McKean, President of the Continental Congress, July 26, 1781," *NG*, 9:85. Also Gregorie, *Thomas Sumter*, 178–180.

47 *Ibid.*

48 "NG to Marquis de Lafayette, July 24, 1781," *NG*, 9:72.

49 "Headnote on the Dog Days Expedition," *NG*, 9:16–17.

Chapter 11

1   "Nathanael Greene (hereafter NG) to Thomas Sumter (hereafter TS), August 1, 1781," in Richard K. Showman and Dennis Conrad (eds.), *The Papers of Nathanael Greene* (hereafter *NG*), 9:121–122.

2   Lee, *Revolutionary War Memoirs*, 446.

3   "NG to Colonel Henry Lee, July 29, 1781," *NG*, 9:102–103.

4   Gregorie, *Thomas Sumter*, 182.

5   "Col. Wade Hampton to NG, July 29, 1781," *NG*, 9:105.

6   "NG to Col. Wade Hampton, July 30, 1781," *NG*, 9:107.

7   Rankin, *Francis Marion: The Swamp Fox*, 231–232.

8   "TS to Major Ichabod Burnet, July 28, 1781," *NG*, 9:99–100.

9   Gregorie, *Thomas Sumter*, 184.

10 "TS to NG, September 10, 1781," Note 1, *NG*, 9:325.

11 "TS to NG, September 10, 1781," *NG*, 9:325.

12 "Note 1," *NG*, 9:25.

13 "Colonel William Henderson to NG, August 14, 1781, first letter," and "Colonel William Henderson to NG, August 14, 1781, second letter," *NG*, 9:181–182.

14 Gregorie, *Thomas Sumter*, 183–184.

15 "NG to William Henderson, August 16, 1781," *NG*, 9:188.

16 "Henry Lee to NG, August 20, 1781," *NG*, 9:215–216.

17 Lee, *Revolutionary War Memoirs*, 448.

18 "Col. William Henderson to NG, August 25, 1781," Note 1, *NG*, 9:245.

19 Pancake, *This Destructive War*, 217.

20 Lee, *Revolutionary War Memoirs*, 463–464.

21 "NG to Thomas McKean, September 11, 1781," *NG*, 9:328.

22 McCrady, *The History of South Carolina in the Revolution, 1780–1783*, 441; also "Henry Lee to NG, September 1, 1781," *NG*, 9:278, and Note 1 to this letter.

23 "General Greene's Orders, September 7, 1781," *NG*, 9:305.

24 "Stewart to Cornwallis, September 9, 1781," from Tarleton's *Campaigns*, 509.

25 Boatner, *Encyclopedia of the American Revolution*, 351. Also McCrady, *History of South Carolina in the Revolution, 1780–1783*, 449.

26 McCrady, *History of South Carolina in the Revolution, 1780–1783*, 447.

27 O'Kelley, *Nothing But Blood and Slaughter*, 3:347.

28 Boatner, *Encyclopedia of the American Revolution*, 352–353.

29 "NG to Thomas McKean, September 11, 1781," *NG*, 9:329.

30 Boatner, *Encyclopedia of the American Revolution*, 353.

31 "NG to Thomas McKean, September 11, 1781," *NG*, 9:332. Accounts of the battle are primarily from Boatner, O'Kelley, and Pancake as cited above.

32 Boatner, *Encyclopedia of the American Revolution*, 355.

33 "Stewart to Cornwallis, September 9, 1781," from Tarleton's *Campaigns*, 508.

34 "NG to Governor John Rutledge, September 9, 1781," *NG*, 9:308.

35 "General Greene's Orders, September 16, 1781," *NG*, 9:350.

36 "TS to NG, September 10, 1781," *NG*, 9:325.

Chapter 12

1 "Nathanael Greene (hereafter NG) to Thomas Sumter (hereafter TS), September 16, 1781," in Richard K. Showman and Dennis Conrad (eds.), *The Papers of Nathanael Greene* (hereafter *NG*), 9:351–352.

2 Gregorie, *Thomas Sumter*, 186.

3 "Daniel Morgan to NG, January 15, 1781," *NG*, 7:127–128.

4 "NG to General James Varnum, January 24, 1781," *NG*, 7:187–188.

5 "Francis Marion to NG, May 11, 1781," *NG*, 7:242.

6 Gregorie, *Thomas Sumter*, 187.

7 "TS to NG, September 19, 1781," *NG*, 9:378.

8 "NG to TS, September 28, 1781," *NG*, 9:404; and "NG to TS, October 3, 1781," *NG*, 9:423.

9 "NG to Francis Marion, October 16, 1781," *NG*, 9:447.

10 Gregorie, *Thomas Sumter*, 188.

11 "NG to George Washington, November 2, 1781," *NG*, 9:519.

12 "NG to George Washington, October 25, 1781," *NG*, 9:484–485.

13 "NG to TS, November 2, 1781," *NG*, 9:517–518.

14 Gregorie, *Thomas Sumter*, 187.

15 "Footnote 2," *NG*, 9:458.

16 "TS to NG, November 14, 1781," *NG*, 9:575–576.

17 Ramsay, *The History of the Revolution of South Carolina*, 2:272–275.

18 "TS to NG, November 24, 1781," *NG*, 9:623–624.

19 "TS to NG, November 24, 1781," *NG*, 9:623–624; also "TS to NG, November 23, 1781," *NG*, 9:615.

20 "NG to TS, November 17, 1781," *NG*, 9:581.

21 "Note 1 to letter from Francis Marion to NG, December 1, 1781," *NG*, 9:646.

22 "Note 9 to letter from NG to Thomas McKean, November 21, 1781," *NG*, 9:599.

23 Gregorie, *Thomas Sumter*, 191.

24 "NG to TS, December 2, 1781," *NG*, 9:648.

25 "NG to TS, December 15, 1781," *NG*, 9:57–58.

26 "TS to NG, December 22, 1781," *NG*, 10:92.

27 "NG to TS, December 27, 1781," *NG*, 10:120.

28 William Johnson, *Sketches of the Life and Correspondence of Nathanael Greene* (Charleston, SC: A.E. Miller 1822), 2:215.

29 "NG to TS, December 12, 1781," *NG*, 10:40.

30 "NG to TS, December 15, 1781," *NG*, 10:57–58.

31 "TS to NG, December 22, 1781," *NG*, 10:90–93.

32 "TS to NG, January 4, 1782," *NG*, 10:159.

33 "NG to TS, January 8, 1781," *NG*, 10:168.

34 Gregorie, *Thomas Sumter*, 196–197.

35 Tarleton, *A History of the Campaigns of 1780 and 1781*, 94–96.

36 Gregorie, *Thomas Sumter*, 198.

37 *Ibid*, 199.

Chapter 13

1   Golway, *Washington's General*, 291.

2   Gary Shattuck, "Seven Gold Medals of America's Revolutionary Congress," *All Things Liberty: A Journal of the American Revolution*, https://allthingsliberty.com/2015/04/7-gold-medals-of-americas-revolutionary-congress/

3   Notes 1 and 2 from "Hugh Rutledge, Speaker of the House of Representatives, to Nathanael Greene (hereafter NG), February 26, 1781," in Richard K. Showman and Dennis Conrad (eds.), *The Papers of Nathanael Greene* (hereafter *NG*), 10:411–412. Also Gerald M. Carbone, *Nathanael Greene* (New York: Palgrave Macmillan, 2008), 218.

4   "NG to John Hanson, President of the Continental Congress, March 11, 1782," *NG*, 10:481–483.

5   Dennis M. Conrad, "Introduction," *NG*, 12:xvii.

6   "NG to E. John Collett, June 23, 1784," *NG*, 13:333.

7   "NG to Catherine Littlefield Greene, April 14, 1785," *NG*, 13:493.

8   Note 4 to "General Andrew Williamson to NG, December 22, 1782," *NG*, 12:341.

9   "NG to Roger Parker Saunders, January 4, 1784," *NG*, 13:217.

10 Gregory D. Massey, "The Transformation of Nathanael Greene," from *General Nathanael Greene and the American Revolution in the South*, 254–257. This excellent essay served as the primary reference for the depiction of Greene's transaction and subsequent conflict with Banks, including quotes and the account of Greene's tragic death. Also influential for the depiction of Greene's business relationship with John Banks was Dennis M. Conrad's "Introduction" to Volume XII of *The Papers of Nathanael Greene*, xv–xvii.

11 Bass, *Gamecock*, 218–220.

12 Gregorie, *Thomas Sumter*, 202.

13 Bass, *Gamecock*, 222–223.

14 Gregorie, *Thomas Sumter*, 282.

15 Bass, *Gamecock*, 235.

16 *Ibid*, 234. Also Note 1 from "Rev. William Gordon to NG," *NG*, 10:439.

17 William Johnson, *Sketches of the Life and Correspondence of Nathanael Greene*, Note 2, 437.

18 United States Second Congress, *Annals* (Washington, D.C., 1849), 326–327.

19 Johnson, *Sketches of the Life and Correspondence of Nathanael Green*, Note 2, 436–437.

20 Lee, *Revolutionary War Memoirs*, 393–394.

21 Buchanan, *The Road to Guilford Courthouse*, 398–399.

22 Dennis M. Conrad, "General Nathanael Greene: An Appraisal," from *General Nathanael Greene and the American Revolution in the South*, 10, 24.

Bibliography

Primary and Contemporary Sources

Clinton, Henry. *The American Rebellion: Sir Henry Clinton's Narrative of His Campaigns, 1775–1782*. New Haven: Yale University Press edition, 1954.

Cornwallis, Charles, and Charles Ross, ed. *Correspondence of Charles, First Marquis Cornwallis*. London: John Murray, 1859. In three volumes, although only Volume One pertains to the American Revolution.

Cornwallis, Charles, and Ian Saberton, ed., *The Cornwallis Papers: The Campaigns of 1780 and 1781 in The Southern Theatre of the American Revolutionary War*, Vols. 1–5. East Sussex, England: The Naval & Military Press Ltd, 2010.

Davie, William R. *The Revolutionary War Sketches of William R. Davie*. Raleigh, NC: North Carolina Department of Cultural Resources, 1976.

Gibbes, R.W. *Documentary History of the American Revolution, 1776–1782*. New York: D. Appleton & Co., 1857.

Gray, Robert. "Col. Robert Gray's Observations on the War in Carolina." *South Carolina Historical and Genealogical Magazine*, XI (July 1910). https://archive.org/details/Col.RobertGraysObservationsOnTheWarInCarolina1782.

Greene, Nathanael, Richard K. Showman, Margaret Cobb, and Robert E. McCarthy. *The Papers of Nathanael Greene*. Chapel Hill: University of North Carolina Press for Rhode Island Historical Society, 1976. Greene's papers, especially his correspondence with Sumter, are the basis for this book. To the University of North Carolina Press I am indebted, and proud (class of '92). Go Heels!

Lee, Henry. *The Revolutionary War Memoirs of General Henry Lee*. Edited by Robert E. Lee with introduction by Charles Royster. New York: De Capo Press edition, 1998; originally published in 1812.

Mathis, Samuel. "A Letter on the Battle of Hobkirk's Hill, written in 1819." Edited by Millard H. Osborne and Charles Baxley. SouthernCampaign.org. Accessed on June 24, 2018. http://southerncampaign.org/hobkirk/ps.html.

Revolutionary War pension applications were referenced from the Southern Campaigns Revolutionary War Pension Statements & Rosters Website at http://www.revwarapps.org. I am indebted to William Graves, C. Leon Harris, and all who were involved in creating this amazing historical resource.

Tarleton, Banastre. *A History of the Campaigns of 1780 and 1781, in the Southern Provinces of North America.* London: 1787.

Secondary Sources

Bass, Robert D. *Gamecock: The Life and Campaigns of Thomas Sumter.* Orangeburg, SC: Sandlapper Publishing Co., Inc, 1961.

Boatner, Mark M., III. *Encyclopedia of the American Revolution.* Mechanicsburg, PA: Stackpole Books edition, 1994. (Originally published in 1966 by David McKay Company.)

Buchanan, John. *The Road to Guilford Courthouse: The American Revolution in the Carolinas.* New York: John Wiley & Sons, Inc., 1997. Like so many, I am deeply indebted to Buchanan's scholarship and creativity. Anyone who wants to learn more about the Southern Campaign should start here.

Carbone, Gerald M. *Nathanael Greene.* New York: Palgrave MacMillan, 2008.

Chernow, Ron. *Alexander Hamilton.* New York: The Penguin Press, 2004.

Draper, Lyman C. *King Mountain and Its Heroes: History of the Battle of King's Mountain, October 7th, 1780, and the Events Which Led To It.* Cincinnati: Peter G. Thomson, Publisher, 1881.

Edgar, Walter. *Partisans & Redcoats: The Southern Conflict That Turned the Tide of the American Revolution.* New York: HarperCollins, 2001.

Edgar, Walter. *South Carolina: A History.* Columbia, SC: University of South Carolina Press, 1998.

Egerton, Douglas R. *Death or Liberty: African Americans and Revolutionary America.* New York: Oxford University Press, 2009.

Farley, M. Foster. "The South Carolina Negro in the American Revolution," *The South Carolina Historical Magazine*, Vol. 79, No. 2 (April 1978). A wonderful article from which I drew much of the portrait of the South Carolina slave experience in the American Revolution.

Johnson, William. *Sketches of the Life and Correspondence of Nathanael Greene: Major General of the Armies of the United States in the War of the Revolution,* Vol. 1. Charleston, SC: A. E. Miller, 1822.

Gilbert, Oscar E., and Catherine R. Gilbert. *True for the Cause of Liberty: The Second Spartan Regiment in the American Revolution.* Havertown, PA: Casemate Publishers, 2015.

Golway, Terry. *Washington's General: Nathanael Greene and the Triumph of the American Revolution.* New York: Henry Holt and Company, 2006.

Gordon, John W. *South Carolina and the American Revolution: A Battlefield History*. Columbia, SC: University of South Carolina Press, 2003.

Gregorie, Anne King. *Thomas Sumter*. Columbia, SC: The R.L. Bryan Company, 1931. Though both Gregorie and Bass draw heavily from the Lyman Draper manuscript collection for their biographies of Sumter, Gregorie has the good grace to footnote her sources. Therefore, it is from her Thomas Sumter biography I drew most, although sometimes Bass was too juicy to resist.

Massey, Gregory D., and Jim Piecuch. *General Nathanael Greene and the American Revolution in the South*. Columbia, SC: University of South Carolina Press, 2012. Essays on Greene by leading scholars. Essential for a deeper dive into Greene's character.

McCrady, Edward. *The History of South Carolina in the Revolution, 1775–1780*. New York: The Macmillan Company, 1901.

McCrady, Edward. *The History of South Carolina in the Revolution, 1780–1783*. New York: The Macmillan Company, 1902.

O'Kelley, Patrick. *Nothing But Blood and Slaughter: The Revolutionary War in the Carolinas*. Blue House Tavern Press, 2004. In four volumes, one for each year beginning in 1779–1782. A former soldier, O'Kelley is particularly useful for troop strength and casualty figures, which he researches extensively.

Olwell, Robert, *Masters, Slaves, & Subjects: The Culture of Power in the South Carolina Low Country, 1740–1790*. Ithaca, NY: Cornell University Press, 1998.

Pancake, John S. *This Destructive War: The British Campaign in the Carolinas, 1780–1782*. Tuscaloosa, AL: University of Alabama Press, 2003 (originally published 1985).

Ramsay, David. *The History of the Revolution of South-Carolina, from a British Province to an Independent State*, Vol. 2. Trenton, NJ: Isaac Collins, 1785.

Rankin, Hugh. *Francis Marion: The Swamp Fox*. Thomas Y. Crowell Company, 1973.

Robert B. Roberts, *Encyclopedia of Historic Forts: The Military, Pioneer, and Trading Posts of the United States*. New York: McMillan, 1988.

Index